The Escort Carrier in The Second World War

Combustible, Vulnerable, Expendable!

The Escort Carrier in The Second World War

Combustible, Vulnerable, Expendable!

by

DAVID WRAGG

Pen & Sword
MARITIME

First published in Great Britain in 2005 by
Pen & Sword Maritime
an imprint of
Pen & Sword Books Ltd
47 Church Street
Barnsley
South Yorkshire
S70 2AS

ISBN 1 84415 220 0

A CIP catalogue record for this book is
available from the British Library

Typeset in Meridien by
Phoenix Typesetting, Auldgirth, Dumfriesshire

Printed and bound in England by
CPI UK

For a complete list of Pen & Sword titles please contact
PEN & SWORD BOOKS LIMITED
47 Church Street, Barnsley, South Yorkshire, S70 2AS, England
E-mail: enquiries@pen-and-sword.co.uk
Website: www.pen-and-sword.co.uk

CONTENTS

ACKNOWLEDGEMENTS

As always, in writing any book such as this, the author is indebted to those who have made his life so much easier. In particular I am once again very grateful for the help always so willingly provided by Ian Carter and his team at the Photographic Archive and John Stopford-Pickering at the Sound Archive of the Imperial War Museum in London. It is only fair as well to remember those former members of the Fleet Air Arm, including Lord Kilbracken with *Bring Back my Stringbag*, giving the pilot's view of life on MAC-ships and escort carriers, and C.S. 'Bill' Drake with *A Bit of a Tiff*, giving an all too rare maintainer's impression of life aboard an escort carrier: recommended reading, both of them. In addition, both Lord Kilbracken and Bill Drake were kind enough to help with illustrations, as was Mrs Marjorie Schupke, with photographs from the collection of her late brother, Sub Lieutenant (A) Gordon Maynard, RNVR.

David Wragg
Edinburgh
November 2004

INTRODUCTION

To the US Navy, although initially classified as auxiliary carriers, AVCs, they soon became escort carriers or CVEs, sometimes known to their crews as 'Jeep carriers'; to the Royal Navy, they were always auxiliary carriers, nicknamed by the members of the wartime Royal Navy as 'Woolworth carriers'; to the crews of the endangered merchantmen in convoys on the North Atlantic and to Arctic Russia, they were protection; but to the more cynical, they were Combustible, Vulnerable, Expendable.

Their role was unglamorous, but essential. The need for the escort carrier was foreseen by the Admiralty Trade Protection Division before the outbreak of the Second World War and, in their search for additional carriers, at one time even conversion of the giant ocean liners *Queen Mary* and *Queen Elizabeth* was suggested! Traditional seafarers were appalled by the concept and doubted whether such conversions could succeed. Every merchant vessel was needed, and few could be spared for conversion but at the same time, without air cover in mid-Atlantic, merchant shipping losses were increasing, especially in the so-called Atlantic Gap, also known, appropriately enough as the 'Black Gap', beyond the range of land-based aircraft. Grudgingly, a captured German ship was allocated to the Admiralty for conversion, and later work proceeded on the merchant aircraft carriers, MAC-ships, tankers and grain ships with a flight deck and capable of carrying three or four Swordfish for anti-submarine patrols while continuing to deliver most of their precious cargo. While this was going on, even before the United States entered the Second World War, work went ahead on the first American escort carrier, the USS *Long Island*, the prototype of many ships that were to follow.

The choice of ocean liners for conversion may seem strange in

1

retrospect, since clearly a cargo ship or tanker hull would be easier to convert and cheaper. Ocean liners had two advantages however, size and speed, while the Royal Navy's pre-war carrier force already included one ship converted from a liner under construction, the service's second aircraft carrier, HMS *Argus*. In fact, it can fairly be assumed that had either of the two 'Queens' been converted, they would not have become escort carriers but additions to the fleet carrier strength. They would have been larger than any of the other carriers in the Royal Navy, or indeed any other navy at the time, and faster than the Royal Navy's older ships.

Converting lesser merchantmen may have been quick and cheap, but it also brought with it limitations, as the ships were slow and small. The lack of speed didn't matter, as convoy speeds were usually either slow or dead slow, and even then some ships couldn't keep up and were left as stragglers, often falling prey to the U-boats. Size, on the other hand, did matter. Any carrier was better than no carrier at all, but it did mean that often the number of aircraft was very limited, perhaps little more than a dozen, while on some it was as few as six, and high performance fighter operations could be difficult. There was another point as well. In pre-war days, the USS *Ranger* had been transferred from the Pacific to the Atlantic because she was regarded as being too small for operation in the heavy ocean swell of the Pacific. Nevertheless, despite the difficulty of operating from a flight deck that is rolling and pitching, such ships were soon ideal for many operations that would have made operation of a large fleet carrier seem wasteful, and these included not only convoy escort work, but deck landing training, aircraft transport, aircraft maintenance and close air support for forces fighting ashore before airfields could become available.

In an ideal world, of course, the solution would have been to take shipyards not normally used to warship work, and get them to work on a new design of aircraft carrier built to merchant standards, but designed from the keel upwards as a carrier. That is what eventually happened with the British light fleet carriers of the Colossus-class and the slightly more robust Majestic-class, but the first of the Colossus-class ships did not enter service until shortly before the end of the war, and far too late to see action,

2

while the Majestic-class was later still. Even so, one criticism of these ships in later years, as aircraft weights and speeds increased, was that their speed was too low at 24 knots, and one cannot help wonder whether they really would have been popular with naval commanders under harsh wartime conditions, with battleships and cruisers capable of 30 knots or more having to hang back for their carrier.

The desperation felt by the two Allied navies found an echo in the mind of the American president, Franklin Roosevelt, who told the US Navy to convert the Cleveland-class cruisers under construction to aircraft carriers. As with most suggestions made by wartime leaders on both sides, this was not welcomed with the service concerned, as the narrow cruiser hulls restricted the width of the flight deck and the pronounced curve of the bows, a feature of such an attractive ship as a cruiser, created problems in the hangar deck and meant that the forward lift was virtually amidships! There were also questions of stability. In fact, there was no history of cruisers being converted to aircraft carriers as the early warship conversions had all used either battleship or battle-cruiser hulls, which were much larger and far more satisfactory. It could even be argued, with the benefit of hindsight, that the Royal Navy could have used the brief period of frantic rearmament to convert the pride of the fleet, the so-called battlecruiser the 'mighty *Hood*', to an aircraft carrier. As it was, she failed the test and blew up on her first and only big gun engagement.

Although there were a few British-converted CVEs, largely because the Admiralty believed that their riveted hull construction would be better suited to service in Arctic waters, most CVEs were provided by the United States; some converted from merchantmen, others built from scratch, but based on merchant designs for easy conversion once hostilities ceased. Using a small number of standard designs, more than 100 ships were provided by American shipyards to meet the needs of two navies, but there was nothing standard about the work these ships were employed to do. The initial American classification and the British Admiralty designation of 'auxiliary' carrier was correct: In addition to convoy escort duties they became maintenance carriers, aircraft transports and, during the landings at Salerno in Italy, in the south of France and in the Pacific, they carried the aircraft providing air cover and strike support over the beaches. Wherever they appeared, their support was invaluable, but they also established a poor reputation for safety amongst their crews, and this included the naval and USMC aircrew who found operating high performance aircraft from their short decks, sometimes without catapults and with their 'merchantman' speeds, extremely difficult and dangerous.

Augmented by eyewitness accounts by those who served aboard MAC-ships and escort carriers, *The Escort Carrier in The Second World War* covers the history and work of these ships, with appendices giving a complete list of all ships, including technical details and, where applicable, their Merchant Navy, US Navy and Royal Navy names, along with the actions in which they took part and their fates, which included post-war service with the French and Dutch navies.

The terminology was not the only difference between the two main Allied navies. Differences went deeper than whether riveted or welded hulls were better, with British objections to American fuel-handling systems and the number of watertight compartments, while the Americans were furious at the delays brought by British modifications when ships were urgently needed at sea.

I

A SHORTAGE
OF FLIGHT DECKS

As the 1930s drew to a close, naval planners on both sides of the Atlantic were wrestling with a problem, for both the Royal Navy and the US Navy realized that they had insufficient aircraft carriers for what lay ahead. If the problems were the same, the reasons behind them were different. The Royal Navy was well aware that it would need to defend the shipping, on which the British economy was so dependent, from German surface raiders and submarines; the U-boats whose predecessors during the First World War had nearly brought the nation to its knees. On the other hand, the US Navy was not so concerned about Germany or the protection of trade, but was sharing the concern felt by American politicians about Japanese territorial ambitions. To both navies, it was clear that air power would hold the key to eventual victory, and that the air power would have to be based at sea as neither the Pacific nor the Atlantic could provide sufficient bases for land-based aircraft, given the limited range of the aircraft of the day.

Having been criticized for its slowness in introducing a convoy system during the First World War, the Royal Navy was anxious that it should not be seen to make the same mistake again. Despite attempts to hinder German re-armament, it was clear to the Admiralty Trade Division that in any future war, the submarine would be an even greater threat than it had been in the earlier conflict. Unlike the United States, which was largely self-sufficient, the United Kingdom, densely populated and with limited natural resources, especially short of oil and grain, was heavily dependent upon imports from across the North Atlantic and from the vast British Empire, with examples being meat and dairy products from

Australia and New Zealand, rubber from Malaya and tea from India. This situation led Captain (later Rear Admiral) M. S. Slattery, Director of Material for the Fleet Air Arm, to advise the Admiralty that they should fit 'the simplest possible flight deck and landing equipment to suitable merchant ships'. Apart from Slattery at the Admiralty, the idea had also occurred to and been proposed by the Scottish shipowner, Sir Douglas Thomson, a director of the Ben Line, who favoured using both tankers and grain ships. Nevertheless, time passed without any action being taken and more than one naval aviator felt that the provision of air cover for the convoys on the North Atlantic occurred two years later than it should have done, and the crippling losses of 1942 would have been much reduced had this been the case.

While shore-based aircraft were effective, the problem was that these could not be counted upon to provide the constant protection that convoys required. Even without the constraints of range, to keep just one aircraft above a convoy, it meant that another aircraft would be on its way back to base while yet another was heading out to relieve the aircraft on patrol. At the very least one aircraft would be on the ground refuelling and re-arming, while its crew snatched a well-deserved rest. Given the poor reliability (by modern jet-age standards) of the piston engines of the day, and the need for many hours of rest for the aircrew between the long and tedious patrols, in fact for every aircraft in the air, several were likely to be on the ground. By contrast, carrier-borne aircraft were always present with the fleet or the convoy, maximizing the time spent on patrol and eliminating what airlines would call 'positioning flights' altogether. Having their base with them, they could quickly change armaments to meet the perceived threat, with torpedoes for surface raiders and either depth charges or, later, rockets for submarines.

The U-boat menace was not the only threat to merchant shipping. Apart from surface raiders, there was also the threat from the air. Even during the First World War, this had been so much in evidence that in desperation the Royal Navy had even launched Sopwith Camel fighters from lighters towed at speed behind destroyers, usually referred to at the time as 'torpedo boat destroyers'. The move was essential as the seaplanes operating with the fleet lacked the power and speed to be able to outclimb a German Zeppelin dirigible, but it was costly as the aircraft had to ditch in the sea after its one and only sortie, leaving the pilot to be picked up while the aircraft was abandoned. This had been another compelling reason behind the development of the aircraft carrier so that landplanes could be operated successfully at sea.

While the Royal Navy in 1939 lacked high performance fighters, it was clear that once such aircraft were available these would also have to be at sea with the fleet. Fighter aircraft generally have far shorter ranges than those used for maritime-reconnaissance, anti-submarine and anti-shipping operations. Yet, such was the state of British naval aviation in 1939 that its fighter aircraft lacked the performance to take on enemy fighters, or even to attack enemy aircraft such as the Focke-Wulf Fw200 Condor or the Junkers Ju290, used by the Luftwaffe on anti-shipping operations.

The poor performance of the British naval fighter aircraft at the outset of the war was due in part to the Admiralty having lost control of naval aviation to the newly-formed Royal Air Force in 1918, and only having regained full control in 1939. During the years of recession, the Royal Air Force had been hard put to fund its own shore-based equipment needs. Lacking senior officers with first-hand knowledge of naval aviation, many in the Royal Navy also doubted that high performance aircraft could operate from aircraft carriers. The insistence on longer range and a second crew member also meant that even the latest British naval fighters were crippled by the extra weight, and because of this even the famous Rolls Royce Merlin engine produced a far poorer performance in the Royal Navy's Fairey Fulmar than in the Royal Air Force's Supermarine Spitfire.

Biplane fighters were present aboard the British fleet carriers in 1939 and 1940, while the main attack and anti-submarine aircraft was another biplane, the Fairey Swordfish, known affectionately to its crews as the 'Stringbag'. In fact, especially aboard the MAC-ships, the Swordfish was to prove a blessing, especially when needed for anti-submarine patrols. It was also to prove extremely difficult to replace.

Although the Royal Navy had seven aircraft carriers in 1939, of these four were elderly and had been due for replacement, had not the threat of war caused them to be retained in service. The best of the pre-war carriers were needed to operate with the battleships and cruisers on offensive operations. The four ships that had been due for retirement had been too small and too slow to keep up with the fleet, and had been due to be replaced by four new fast armoured carriers of the Illustrious-class, but even though another two ships had been ordered, these would not be ready to meet the immediate need. In any case, there was neither the money nor the resources, but most of all there was not the time, to build a sufficiently large fleet of thoroughbred carriers, which would in any case be wasted protecting convoys, most of which steamed at less than 10 knots, indeed, often much less.

Aircraft Transports and Hybrid Carriers

The Americans started from a completely different premise, and seemed to have started much earlier, during the early 1930s. Their initial thinking was that ships were needed to transport aircraft to overseas territories, with the Philippines being a case in point, and to replenish the air groups of carriers at sea. The Washington Naval Treaty of 1922 had placed upper limits on the total tonnage of aircraft carriers permitted in the navies of the nations that were signatories to the treaty, and it was important not to waste this tonnage but instead reserve it for fast fleet carriers. What emerged was a need for some kind of vessel that might be seen as a transport or part of the fleet train and, therefore, not covered by the treaty which did not take auxiliaries into account.

The Washington Treaty also overlooked any ship that was experimental, including the first American carrier, USS *Langley*, or any ship carrying aircraft that displaced less than 10,000 tons. The irony of this was that the *Langley* had been converted from a supply ship, the US Navy's fleet collier *Jupiter*, and commissioned into the US Navy in 1922. She should have been a reminder to all of what could be achieved in providing a simple but sufficient aircraft carrier. By the outbreak of the Second World War, her role was much reduced, and she was mainly used as an aircraft transport. The role of aircraft transport sounds safe and unglamorous, but it was only as safe as the control of the seas and skies of the fleet in which the ship was a part. On 27 February 1942, as the *Langley* was transporting Curtiss P-40 fighters to Java while the Allies struggled to stem the Japanese tide sweeping across the Pacific, south-east Asia and the

Netherlands East Indies, the elderly carrier was discovered and attacked by Japanese bombers, receiving five direct hits. Listing badly, she had to be finished off by 4-in shells from the USS *Whipple*, her escorting destroyer.

Other possibilities considered by the US Navy included a form of hybrid cruiser-carrier which, under the limitations of the Washington Naval Treaty, could be no more than 10,000 tons displacement and carry either 6-in or 8-in guns, depending on whether it was rated as a 'light' or a 'heavy' cruiser, but with a flight deck that would enable the ship to carry aircraft for reconnaissance and, perhaps, to defend itself. Such a ship would not break the Treaty limitations on total carrier tonnage, since the Treaty did not count as an aircraft carrier any ship that was not used exclusively as such, possibly because of the number of battleships and cruisers that carried aircraft. On such a ship the most likely arrangement would have been for the smokestack and bridge to have been accommodated in a starboard side island, with the flight deck cut short aft of the foredeck, allowing 'A' and 'B' turrets to be left in position. This solution would have been elegant and practicable. On the downside, the design would have meant that the ships would have suffered from a short flight deck in the same way that the three British converted battlecruisers *Furious*, *Courageous* and *Glorious* were so afflicted, although in their case the foreshortened flight deck was to allow a secondary deck for aircraft taking off straight from the hangar.

A less practical solution would have been a ship similar in appearance to the two Japanese battleships *Ise* and *Hyuga*, with the aft turrets removed and replaced by a flight deck, modified by the Imperial Japanese Navy late in the Second World War. Just how successful such a hybrid would have been is difficult to say, since it would seem to suffer problems of turbulence from the superstructure for aircraft landing, and taking off could only have been by use of a catapult.

The short range of many aircraft also meant that fighters in particular had to be shipped rather than flown across the Pacific, and even the North Atlantic, until the advent of the long-range escort fighter, by which time the Allies had secured bases in Iceland.

Desperation led to consideration of some measures that were

9

clearly impractical. Early in the war, one idea investigated was the creation of a large airbase made of ice in mid-Atlantic. It was found that by mixing ice with woodpulp, a concoction known as pykrete by its inventor, Hermann Mark, an Austrian-born chemist, the ice lost much of its brittleness. Tests proved that pykrete was weight for weight as strong as concrete, and did not shatter on being hit by a projectile. But that unless cooled to and kept at a temperature of at least minus 15 degrees Celsius – not something that could be guaranteed – it tended to sag slowly under its own weight. The Fleet Air Arm requirement was for a deck that was 50 feet above the waterline, 200 feet wide and 2,000 feet long. The Admiralty had even higher expectations, requiring it to be self-propelled with a hull at least 40 feet thick to be able to withstand torpedo attack! If this specification seemed to be stretching the art of the possible to breaking point, someone then demanded a cruising range of 7,000 miles. In the end, these requirements added up to a vessel that had a theoretical displacement of 2.2 million tons with a rudder the height of a 15-storey building. Not so much a super aircraft carrier as a floating island with its own propulsion system. The original concept of a simple iceberg had developed to the stage that the US Navy found that the volume of steel needed to freeze sufficient pykrete in a single winter was going to be greater than the amount needed to build a comparable ship of steel. Not surprising, the project was abandoned.

Convoys

Contrary to popular opinion, in wartime convoys were never compulsory, but they were highly advisable other than for those ships that were so fast, such as the big liners *Queen Mary* and *Queen Elizabeth*, that submarine attack was all but impossible. Such ships would have been difficult to escort in the open Atlantic, especially in winter, when their size would have enabled them to maintain a higher speed in heavy seas than the small escort vessels. During the First World War, the argument against convoys was that it provided submarines and surface raiders with a highly concentrated mass of targets, and while this was true, it was possible to allocate ships to protect a convoy, but impossible to do so for individual sailings. The fact that submarines were attracted to convoys was more of a plus than a minus, inasmuch as at first, until the German Enigma codes could be intercepted and broken, finding a submarine was like hunting for a needle in a haystack. If submarines were attracted to a convoy that was well protected, it was as if a moth had been attracted to a flame; fatal.

Excluding coastal convoys around both the British Isles and the eastern seaboard of the United States and Canada, during the Second World War there were to be 2,889 escorted trade convoys sailing to and from the UK, with a total of 85,775 ships. Out of these 654 were sunk, a loss rate of 0.7 per cent. Perhaps it was not surprising that on some convoys, Fairey Swordfish, the biplanes used by the Royal Navy and nicknamed 'Stringbags', for convoy protection, were cheered by the seamen in the merchant ships as they returned from patrol. In addition to ships lost whilst sailing in convoy, there were the losses of ships sailing independently, and in 1942, these accounted for 840 merchant vessels lost to U-boats, against 299 from convoys, and at least sixty of the convoy losses were stragglers; ships that for one reason or another could not keep up with the rest of the convoy.

The Swordfish looked like a museum piece; a large single-engined biplane with a fixed undercarriage and three open cockpits for the pilot, observer (the Royal Navy term for navigator) and the telegraphist/air gunner or TAG. While it could carry up to four depth charges or a large 1,650-lbs torpedo, its own defensive armament was poor, simply a fixed machine gun on the fuselage for the pilot and another rear-pointing machine gun for the TAG, which was never used on convoy escort duty and would have been all but useless if it had been! The affectionate name 'Stringbag' given to the Swordfish reflected the fact that its full range of possible armaments was rather like the pre-war British house-wife's 'stringbag'; a shopping bag that could expand to carry almost anything. Swordfish were not fast – many maintain that they could not manage 100mph when fully armed – but could loiter and seemed to be almost impossible to stall. On the other hand, their low landing speed meant that it could be difficult for one of them to catch up with a carrier in a strong headwind.

So pressing was the need for additional carriers as the threat of war in Europe grew closer that, as mentioned in the introduction, the Admiralty's Trade Department even gave consideration to converting the two Cunard liners *Queen Mary* and *Queen Elizabeth*, pride of the British Merchant Navy, to aircraft carriers. These would have been the largest in the world for many years had it gone ahead, but the objections to this on the grounds that they would be needed as fast troop transports were overwhelming. As it was, the British Army had already lost the use of many other smaller liners as troop transports as these were taken up and converted to armed merchant cruisers for convoy protection.

The Merchant Aircraft Carriers

Originally intended purely as a stop-gap measure while the escort carriers were awaited, for various reasons the merchant aircraft carriers took time to arrive, despite the fact that had they been present earlier, the massive convoy losses of 1942 could have been avoided. Another interim measure was the use of catapult armed merchant ships or CAM-ships, although these had the drawback, as with the fighters flown off lighters towed by destroyers during the First World War, that the aircraft could only make a single sortie and then had to be ditched. The other problem was, of course, that adequate fighter cover really demanded combat air patrols, or CAP, to be flown constantly above the convoy. Until the MAC-ships were available, the convoy war went badly against Britain, and these were strictly anti-submarine measures as fighters could not be operated.

The irony is that some of the aircraft carriers lost in the early years might have been better used as escort carriers, rather than put into situations where they were at the mercy of enemy aircraft, as happened with the small *Hermes*. As it was, only two of the Royal Navy's pre-war carriers survived the war, the two oldest, *Furious* and *Argus*.

Merchant aircraft carriers, or MAC-ships, were always either tankers or grain ships because these ships loaded and discharged cargo by means of a pipeline, with no hatches to open. The tankers could carry three Swordfish while the grain ships could carry four as it was possible to convert one of the holds aft into a small hangar into which aircraft could be struck down with a hoist. Once the superstructure of these ships had been cut down and converted into an island on the starboard side, with their boiler uptakes diverted to the island, a flight deck could be laid over their holds. The grain ships had a shorter flight deck, at between 413 and 424 feet, than the 460 feet of the tankers, but the extra length of the tanker deck was no advantage as it was offset by having aircraft parked on the deck, reducing the take-off run. Regardless of the type of ship, the width of the flight deck was a standard 62 feet. Aboard the tankers, the absence of a hangar naturally made maintenance work difficult, while it was unpleasant and even dangerous in bad weather, and sometimes impossible. At night too, it was difficult to work on an aircraft parked on the deck without showing lights.

With the benefit of hindsight, it seems almost criminal that work on the MAC-ships did not proceed more quickly, and that such vessels were not available until early 1943 rather than within months of war breaking out. The reason for the lengthy delay was that too few at the Admiralty believed that the concept would work. The Naval Air Division convinced itself that 12-knot ships would be too slow to operate aircraft. The Director of Naval Construction felt that it would take more than a year just to design such ships, obviously expecting everything to be just right! The Admiralty and the Ministry of War Transport agreed that it would be far too dangerous for aircraft to land and take-off on a steel flight deck running over tanks containing thousands of tons of highly inflammable fuel.

This impasse was overcome by the director of Merchant Shipbuilding, Sir James Lithgow, member of the famous British shipbuilding family, who sketched out a rough design using the back of an envelope. 'I have two ships about to be built which can be converted without undue delay,' he claimed. 'I am prepared to do this provided I am not interfered with by the Admiralty.'[1]

Work on converting the first two MAC-ships, *Empire MacAlpine* and *Empire MacAndrew*, started in June 1942 and, by October, work had started on ten more, although the original plan to have thirty-two such ships was cut back to nineteen as escort carriers started to arrive. The first two ships were both grain ships, but the October batch included the first tanker, *Rapana*. The simpler tanker conversion took much less time, and ships were converted in as little as five months. This in itself seems rather long given the comparative simplicity of the conversion, and that the first

13

American escort carrier, the USS *Long Island* underwent a more thorough conversion in three months. The tanker MAC-ships could carry 90 per cent of their pre-conversion cargo, giving up some of their hold capacity for aircraft fuel, but the figure for the grain ships was lower with one hold no longer available as it was used as the aircraft hangar.

To suit the capacity of the ships, the Swordfish for these ships were deployed as flights of three or four aircraft each, and belonged to Nos. 836 and 860 squadrons, based at HMS *Shrike*, Royal Naval Air Station Maydown, which had originated as a satellite of HMS *Gannet*, RNAS Eglinton, just outside Londonderry in Northern Ireland, but achieved its own independent status at the beginning of 1944. Maydown later housed the anti-submarine school. The two squadrons were known as the MAC-ship Wing, and of these 836 was the larger squadron and was manned by Royal Navy personnel, while 860 was manned by members of the Royal Netherlands Navy, who operated from two Dutch MAC-ships, MV *Acavus* and *Gadila*. Each MAC-ship flight had a lettered suffix, so that the first flight to be formed within 836 was No.836A, and so on. Eventually, when at full strength with half a dozen spare flights ashore at Maydown in County Londonderry, 836 had no less than ninety-two aircraft, beating even the total of sixty-three for No. 700, the wartime parent squadron for the catapult flights aboard the Royal Navy's battleships and cruisers. Unlike No. 700, which existed for administrative convenience, No. 836 had a commanding officer, although despite the squadron's huge size and tremendous responsibilities, Ransford Slater still only held the rank of lieutenant commander, the equivalent of a major in the Army, while in the Royal Air Force, squadrons could be, and in the case of Bomber and Coastal Commands usually were, led by a wing commander, the equivalent of a lieutenant colonel. Slater himself was very much a working flight commander, leading 836A and so taking his share of time at sea.

Maydown was a convenient base, with ships' flights disembarked to the air station as the convoy approached the Clyde. On the other side of the Atlantic, the MAC-ships used Halifax, Nova Scotia, and their aircraft disembarked to the Royal Canadian Air Force base at nearby Dartmouth.

From May 1943 until VE-Day, MAC-ships made 323 crossings

of the Atlantic and escorted 217 convoys, of which just one was successfully attacked. The Swordfish they carried flew 4,177 patrols and searches, an average of thirteen per crossing, or one per day at average convoy speed. Usually, the mere sighting of an aircraft was enough to force any U-boat to submerge, although there were occasions when U-boats caught on the surface, possibly while charging their batteries, did make a fight for it. No confirmed kills of U-boats can be attributed to the aircraft carried by the MAC-ships, but on the other hand, and what really matters, was that there were no instances of any ship being sunk in a convoy protected by a MAC-ship. In contrast to the escort carriers, none of the MAC-ships was sunk while on duty.

The slow and lumbering Swordfish was to be the ideal aeroplane for convoy protection duties, but at first it was not the only contender. The Fleet Air Arm also took a serious interest in the Vought-Sikorsky Chesapeake, a monoplane known to the wits on the squadrons as 'Cheesecakes'. The Chesapeake looked much more like a modern warplane, with retractable undercarriage, which when lowered also acted as an airbrake, important for an aircraft originally designed as a dive-bomber, and a variable-pitch propeller. After three months being assessed for the anti-submarine role by No. 811 Squadron at Lee-on-Solent, the then home of naval aviation on the south coast between Portsmouth and Southampton, the Admiralty decided that the Chesapeake would not be suitable for operation from escort carriers. The main reason given for this decision was that the engine was not powerful enough, although at least one naval aviator who had flown the aircraft maintained that it had shown no shortcomings, and that reverting to the Swordfish was like 'trying to fly a truck'. On the other hand, would such an aircraft have been able to loiter at well below 100 mph ahead of a convoy, keeping a watch for U-boats?

Operating aboard the MAC-Ships

The first MAC-ship, *Empire MacAlpine*, was ready in April 1943, by which time the first of the mass-produced escort carriers were on their way. The aircraft were painted white, as were the Royal Air Force's Sunderland flying-boats, as this was judged to be the best

15

colour when flying over the sea in daytime. The Stringbags probably remained cleaner on operational service than the Sunderlands whose hulls suffered from the rubbing of the crew launches coming alongside before and after missions.

Some aircrew changed the lettering on the sides of their aircraft from ROYAL NAVY to MERCHANT NAVY, which supposedly led to some eye-rubbing if the aircraft in question landed anywhere other than Dartmouth, Nova Scotia, or Maydown. It could also have led to some unpleasant questions being asked had an aircraft crashed or been forced down leaving the crew to fall into the hands of the Germans. As it was, while training sessions off the Scottish coast and life aboard ship saw considerable informality in dress amongst the aircrew, once in the air battledress tops with gold stripes of rank were worn, essential if any downed aircrew were not to be shot as armed civilians.

Aboard a MAC-ship, a flight of three aircraft would have three crews each with a pilot, observer and TAG, as well as a petty officer in charge of the maintainers, who included four riggers and fitters to look after airframes and engines, three electricians, including one who was a specialist able to look after the ASV (anti-surface vessel) radar, and two air mechanics ordnance, AMOs, to take care of the weaponry. There would also be a batsman – possibly more necessary than ever given the limitations of the MAC-ship flight decks – an air staff officer, ASO, responsible for liaison with the convoy commodore and escort commander as well as briefing the aircrew, and usually a naval surgeon as well.

Even the sturdy Swordfish could not operate in the worst of the Atlantic weather, but such severe conditions were in themselves some protection from U-boat attack.

The need to keep radio silence except in extreme emergencies meant that Morse communications were the norm between aircraft and between aircraft and ships. It was important that signals were brief and so the instructions to aircrew, usually from the convoy commodore's ship, were in code with each pattern of search or reconnaissance assigned its own 'reptile' code-name, shown in Appendix I. This not only kept instructions brief, it also maintained some degree of security if the instruction had to be amended while the aircraft was in the air, and it was not unknown if the aircraft was within sight for this to be conveyed by Aldis lamp.

These patrol patterns were suitable for one aircraft at a time, reflecting the reality that few aircraft were available on an escort carrier or MAC-ship, with just three or four Swordfish. Even if all aircraft were fully operational, the need to re-arm and refuel meant that not all could be in the air at one time. Only the patrols code-named *Cobra* and *Viper* could be used by more than one aircraft.

On a convoy, the merchant ships were controlled by the convoy commodore, usually a senior Royal Navy or Royal Naval Reserve officer, including many who had come out of retirement, even dropping a rank or two, to provide their experience for this demanding and important role. The commodore's ship would be a merchant ship, usually steaming as the leading vessel in the central column of the convoy. The warships providing the escort would be controlled by the senior officer (escort), known as the SOE, in close liaison with the commodore. Flags and Aldis lamps were the preferred means of communication, but VHF radio, which could not be picked up by the enemy at a range of more than a few miles, could also be used. The MAC-ships, hybrid merchant vessels with a naval role to play, came under the command of both the SOE and the commodore, and to ensure that the master had maximum flexibility in operating his ship to provide the best take-off and landing position for her aircraft, the MAC-ship was usually the last vessel in the central column of a convoy. Once all nineteen MAC-ships were operational, and escort carriers had started to arrive in ever greater numbers, often convoys would have two MAC-ships, giving them at least six and perhaps as many as eight Swordfish for protection.

The difficulties of operating safely and efficiently from a MAC-ship were such that Slater insisted that all flight commanders had to have made at least one MAC-ship crossing before being appointed, although in the beginning this rule must have been breached before it could be honoured.

One Swordfish pilot flying from a MAC-ship was the then Lieutenant John Godley, RNVR, who later inherited the title of Lord Kilbracken. Godley was sent to 836, initially joining 836F flight as she waited for the conversion of the tanker *Acavus* to be completed in autumn 1943.

No. 836 and its Dutch sister squadron 860 used Swordfish IIs fitted with radar. This was not the only innovation as the aircraft were all fitted with underwing racks for the firing of rocket projectiles; RPs. Four RPs could be installed under each lower wing, and a single RP was enough to sink a U-boat, with pilots trained to dive at an angle of 20 degrees towards a U-boat and fire their rockets from a height of 800 feet. Godley recalls finding that aiming the rockets was easy, and as the flight spent a month training and working up before joining its ship, he was able to hit a four-foot-square target every time. The only drawback of the RP system was that it required a cloud ceiling of at least 1,000 feet, and if the cloud was lower, depth charges had to be used. This must have posed problems for aircraft actually in the air as the weather changed as the convoy made its steady progress across the Atlantic. Depth charges also remained necessary for U-boats that managed to dive before the aircraft could catch them, but many U-boats spent some time on the surface, both to recharge batteries and also because a U-boat on the surface could overtake a convoy to get ahead into a good position for an attack. A U-boat capable of 20 knots on the surface could only sustain 7 knots submerged, generally too little to keep up with a convoy, although the U-boat packs were often spread out ahead of a convoy, waiting. Part of the role of the aircraft carried aboard MAC-ships and escort carriers was to force the U-boats to remain submerged, while U-boat commanders preferred to wait until they were in a position to attack a convoy before submerging.

The first successful RP attack against a U-boat had been in May 1943, when Sub Lieutenant Horrocks, flying a Swordfish from the escort carrier HMS *Archer*, had sunk *U-752*.

Striking Back at the U-Boats

Attacking a U-boat was not an easy option as by 1943 the AA armament had been much improved compared with the early days. Even a large, well armed and relatively fast moving Sunderland could, and did, fall prey to U-boat fire. To safeguard the limited number of Swordfish and scarce aircrew, Swordfish pilots were given complete freedom over whether to attack or simply report the U-boat's position, using such cloud cover as was available. On receiving a report, all available aircraft would be sent to make a combined attack on the U-boat, and as U-boat defences improved, this procedure became mandatory. Most often, if the U-boat was close enough to the convoy, surface vessels would be sent, and many more U-boats were lost to aircraft cooperating in this way with surface vessels, usually corvettes or destroyers and, later, frigates, once these had been 're invented' by the Royal Navy. The danger was always that it was a finely judged matter over how best to destroy a U-boat. Having all of the aircraft from a MAC-ship or escort carrier in the air at once meant that there was nothing left waiting and that all would be on the deck refuelling at much the same time and with the escort vessels, pulling one away from the convoy could leave a gap in the protective screen.

Radar in the surface vessels augmented that of the Swordfish, but not always with the expected results. One Swordfish crew guided towards a 'submarine' and unable to find it, didn't discover until many years after the war had ended that the radar operator on the senior officer (escort) ship had mistaken the 'blip' of the Swordfish for a submarine, and had vectored the aircraft on to itself!

At first, weather permitting, transfers between Maydown and the MAC-ship had a small ceremonial fly-past both past the small control tower at the air station, and then past the ship. Swordfish were so well suited to landing on even the most limited and diffi-cult carriers that it was normal practice for three aircraft to be able to land aboard a carrier within a minute, but the only time that three or four aircraft would approach a MAC-ship to land on would be as the flight flew aboard from either Dartmouth or Maydown, and it was advisable to leave some time between aircraft if the 'bats', deck handling crew and even the arrester wires were all new – say three minutes to be safe. Given the limited length of the flight deck, the crash barrier, not normally needed for a Stringbag landing, was more important than ever. Smart work by the men on deck was important as the arrester hooks had to be disconnected manually from the wires after landing.

Security was important for the convoys, and those aboard were never given advance notice of their sailing date, but some idea of its drawing near was obviously communicated simply by having all shore leave cancelled.

Convoys were rated according to the minimum speed the ships could make in good weather, usually as 8-, 10- or 12-knot convoys, although 4-knot convoys weren't unknown as every-thing and anything that could float seems to have been pressed into service, such was the shortage of shipping after the ravages of the submarine campaign in 1942. The 4-knot convoy took six weeks to cross the Atlantic – by contrast, a fast troopship would do it in four or five days!

On his first convoy in late 1943, Godley and his comrades flew fewer sorties than might have been expected as the convoy ran into a severe gale, and with wind speeds in excess of 60 knots, faster than the Swordfish stalling speed, flying was impossible. However, the bad weather also kept the U-boats down.

The air staff officer would receive intelligence reports, gleaned from sightings or attacks, or often from intercepted German radio transmissions, and decide when patrols had to be flown. Overlap was important, so on a typical afternoon, with fears that the U-boats might be closing in as darkness fell, patrols would be flown off at 14:20 and 16:20, with aircraft landing at 16:35 and 18:35. The MAC-ship chartroom was used for briefing aircrew. The procedure was for the MAC-ship to reduce speed by 3 or 4 knots to drop some distance behind the convoy, but not too far, so that the master could turn the ship into the wind. With a stiff wind over the deck and the MAC-ship doing her best, giving a wind speed over the deck of 35 knots, a Swordfish with the full length of the deck could be airborne even before reaching the MAC-ship's diminutive island.

With one aircraft in the air, the other two, or three if the ship was a grain carrier, would be on standby, with their crews in full flying gear and the aircraft armed with RPs and the engines warm. Operating a *Viper* patrol, the Swordfish would typically fly at around 90 knots, the pilot using 'Mk I eyeball' to look at the sea ahead, the TAG doing the same astern, while the observer or 'looker' spent his time peering at the screen of the ASV radar. On a *Viper* the Swordfish would be flown around and around the convoy at a distance of around fifteen nautical miles, its crew hoping for a sighting of a submarine. Sometimes, only one aircraft out of three or four might be serviceable, especially if bad weather had given aircraft stuck on a tanker deck a bad battering. On the usual patrols, the convoy was usually within sight, but only just, but if an aircraft was sent in response to a sighting or an intercepted radio transmission, it could entail flying some distance from the convoy.

On one occasion, after a storm that had lasted five days, a convoy commander received a position report of a U-boat sixty miles to the south of a convoy and asked for all available aircraft to be sent. There was only one, and with a forty knot wind beating across the deck, it was airborne in no time. Poor visibility and low cloud meant that six depth charges were fitted rather than rockets. Godley recalls:

> It was the first time, although it became a frequent experience, that I had flown out of sight of any vessel and far out of range of land. This brings a special sense of loneliness, especially when in a relatively small, single-engined aircraft with radio silence in force except in emergency or on sighting of the enemy. On such flights, the monotony and vastness of that unending expanse beneath us becomes so intense that any break is always welcome – a slick of oil, a flight of sea-birds, a large patch of seaweed, a whale perhaps or an iceberg – and we would swoop down to examine it.[2]

It took them more than an hour to get to the U-boat's reported position, after which they spent an hour making a square search. The crew recall not being worried about the dangers of their position, since each had an individual small inflatable dinghy and there was a larger one stored in the upper mainplane large enough for all three of them, while they were confident that their 'mayday' signal before ditching would be picked up and an escort vessel sent to their rescue. In fact, the chances of their 'mayday' being picked up, let alone the escort finding them in time, were slender indeed.

> We completed our search and headed homewards. *Acavus* still pitching badly, her stern rising and falling some fifteen or twenty feet as she rode the long Atlantic swell. But my ground speed would again be so low that instead of landing the Stringbag on the deck I should practically be able to wait for the deck to rise up and catch the Stringbag. I approached with a fair bit of motor and was given the signal to cut, whereupon the deck rose so violently that the impact neatly snapped off my tail wheel.[3]

Fortunately, John Godley then caught a wire and the damage to his aircraft was slight, repaired within an hour. His great regret was that this was his thirty-seventh out of an eventual total of 142 deck landings, and the only one on which he damaged his aircraft in any way. Fortunately, since he had more than another 100 deck landings to go, he eventually qualified for the Centurion Club, for which the aspiring member had to have no less than 100 consecutive safe deck landings. In the extreme conditions, accidents were not unknown and even a relatively minor accident, such as an undercarriage collapsing, could mean that an aircraft had to be written off, literally pushed over the side, so that operations could resume.

Occasionally, SOE could allow an hour for a deck to be cleared, but ten minutes was more usual. One advantage of the escort carriers when they arrived was that they could carry such a range of spares that providing the main part of the fuselage was intact, an aircraft could be completely rebuilt, with a Swordfish receiving a new mainplane, both port and starboard, tailplane, engine and undercarriage in as little as thirteen hours. In fact, in such rebuilds there could be little of the original aircraft left!

The homecoming of a squadron was more than usually welcome. It was usual for Swordfish flying ashore to Maydown at the end of an Atlantic crossing to be heavily laden with duty free goods, and 'goodies from unrationed Canada'. There was always the hope, more often fulfilled than not, that the aircraft could be substantially unloaded before a representative of His Majesty's Customs appeared. One Swordfish crew are believed to have overdone the goodies to the extent that their aircraft broke up. Not all of the smuggled goods were exotic. Wartime austerity measures had meant that birdseed had disappeared from the British market, so this was one of the more profitable, but bulky, consignments. Problems arose when not all of the aircraft were flyable, and this could entail the disappointed crews coming to an arrangement with those whose aircraft were still airworthy.

Maydown was not an unpopular posting. More comfortable and less windswept than Macrihanish or Hatston, it had the added advantage of proximity to the border with the Irish Republic. British personnel were not allowed to cross the border in uniform for security reasons, but a steady supply of meat and vegetables completely 'off ration' at reasonable prices found its way across the border from neutral territory. There was an operational advantage to the Royal Navy in all of this. Aboard the MAC-ships, the Merchant Navy personnel worked strict trade union hours, and while a cup of tea was available at 07:30, there was no breakfast until 08:00 and the last meal of the day was at 18:00. If an early patrol was needed, the aircrew had either to take-off on an empty stomach, and even after arriving back might have to wait cold and hungry for up to an hour for food, or take a primus stove aboard plus eggs and bacon all purchased ashore, and at least take-off warm and replete. This matter of breakfast could have meant the difference between survival and death if the aircraft had to be ditched in the sea for any reason, as experience in harsh wartime conditions showed that those who had taken some nourishment before ending up in the sea were more likely to survive than those who hadn't.

The inflexibility of trade union hours had other drawbacks. When a 'ready use' locker for depth charges and rocket projectiles was smashed in a gale and needed to be repaired, since otherwise re-arming aircraft would be slower and more difficult, and possibly more dangerous as well, it had to wait from Saturday to Monday. No one seemed to have told the British trades unions that there was a war on!

Swordfish from 836 used the British MAC-ships, those from 860 used the Dutch-registered ships, including the *Macoma*, and while transfers did not take place, the squadrons did use each other's ships in an emergency. On his last round-trip aboard a MAC-ship, Godley had reason to 'cross-deck' in this way. He was on patrol in poor weather and with a stomach upset, hoping to be able to reach his own ship, *Adula*, quickly, but as he approached ready to land he saw a red flare indicating that he should not attempt to land. Now in acute discomfort, he spent ten minutes circling, until they received a signal by Aldis lamp:

OUR ARRESTER WIRES UNSERVICEABLE AAA YOU ARE
TO LAND ON MACOMA.

He could see *Macoma* beginning to drop astern from the convoy and turn into wind ready to receive his aircraft, while on the flight deck all three of her Swordfish were moved forward by hand and the safety barrier raised behind them.

23

After landing on a carrier other than your own, there are normally one or two niceties to perform; a friendly word to the aircraft handling party on clambering down from the Stringbag, strolling aft to the island to pay your respects to the Master, then below to the chartroom for debriefing with the ASO (air staff officer). To hell with the niceties, I leap headlong from the Swordfish before the prop stops turning.

'Where are the bleeding heads?'

As bad luck would have it, the Dutch air mechanic to whom I addressed this simple question somehow failed to understand it.

'The heads . . . the shithouse, the jacks, man. *La toilette*.'

Blank incomprehension. Then happily realizing that *Macoma* and *Adula* were in all probability almost identical twins. Finding the same companionway, hence to the haven I was seeking. Ah then, what blessed relief!

Ten minutes later I report to the bridge. Hearty laughter all round. Repairs to the arrester wires took only a couple of hours. After an excellent meal with the Dutchmen, preceded by several Bols, the two carriers turned into the wind together so that in less than a minute I could fly from one to the other. We flew *Vipers* (the codename for a convoy air patrol circling the convoy at the distance of visibility) all next day and kept the U-boats down . . .[4]

Notes
1. *Daily Telegraph*, 19 May 1977.
2. Kilbracken, Lord, *Bring Back My Stringbag: A Stringbag Pilot at War*, Pan Books, London, 1980.
3. Ibid.
4. Ibid.
5. Ibid.

II

THE ESCORTS APPEAR

The struggle to overcome the shortage of aircraft carriers continued on both sides of the Atlantic. It is a popular misconception that the first British escort carrier, HMS *Audacity*, influenced the development of the escort or auxiliary carrier, but this is wrong. The first escort carrier, also known initially as an auxiliary carrier by the US Navy, was the USS *Long Island*, which was commissioned into the US Navy on 2 June 1941, followed shortly after by HMS *Audacity*, on 20 June. The two ships differed considerably, with the most significant difference being that the American ship had a hangar.

The origin of this new class of ship was that the American Moore-Macormick Line was building a substantial number of merchantmen on a standard hull known to them as the C3. Standardization of merchant hulls had been an innovation introduced by the United States Maritime Commission in order to dramatically increase the output of American shipyards, which between the wars had seen launchings fall to as little as fifty merchantmen a year. The Maritime Commission had been set up to increase production at American shipyards and to provide funds for their modernization. A ten year programme stipulated a minimum of fifty ships a year starting in 1937, but by early 1939 when war in Europe looked increasingly inevitable, this was doubled to 100 ships a year, and in 1940, after the fall off France, it was doubled yet again to 200 ships a year. These figures were to be exceeded later once the simpler utility 'Liberty' ships were introduced as the C3 and the other standardized hulls at first favoured by the MC proved to be too complex for high rates of production. Increasingly, under wartime pressures, the labour involved was less experienced and less skilled than that available in peacetime.

Meanwhile, the US Navy had purchased a number of Moore-Macormick Line C3 merchant vessels both for their own use and that of the Royal Navy, with the first of these, the *Mormacmail*, a break bulk dry cargo ship, immediately put into dockyard hands for conversion to a carrier. The President of the United States insisted that the work be completed within three months, far less time than that taken for the supposedly simpler MAC-ship conversions. This was despite the fact that the ship was a 'one-off', effectively a prototype, so the use of prefabricated and standardized components that was to be a feature of the later escort carrier programme was not an option. In the case of the *Mormacmail*, conversion consisted of removing the superstructure and building a hangar aft with a wooden flight deck over the top of this continuing forward for a total length of about 360 feet. A navigating bridge was built under the flight deck. There was no island superstructure, while the ship's diesel propulsion meant that exhaust gases could be discharged horizontally. A single lift provided access to the hangar, itself just 120 feet long, while there were arrester wires aft. For self-defence, the ship had just two single 3-in guns provided forward and a single 4-in aft on the quarter deck. Ample provision of tanks for 100,000 gallons of aviation fuel was also made during the conversion, allowing the ship to provide fuel for escorting destroyers. The resulting carrier had a maximum speed of 16 knots. Aircraft capacity was originally intended to be twenty-one aircraft, but in practice this was reduced to sixteen on operations, but as a transport naturally a far higher figure was possible. Once in service, it was soon clear that the flight deck was far too short, especially given the lack of catapults and the low speed of the ship, and this was extended by a further sixty feet to 420 feet. The bridge was replaced by two sponsons to port and starboard, and five 20-mm Oerlikon guns added to improve air defence, although soon twin 20-mm guns were added and the aft 4-in replaced by another 3-in. After a year in service, a radar mast was added.

Long Island was initially classified as an auxiliary carrier, AVG-1, which strictly meant 'aircraft escort vessel', but this was later changed to ACV-1, 'auxiliary aircraft carrier', and it was not until July 1943 that she was officially classified as an escort carrier and given the designation CVE-1. Despite this, the ship never operated as an escort carrier, but was used as an aircraft transport and as a training carrier which, bearing in mind the rapid expansion of Allied naval aviation during the war years, became a very important role indeed.

If the first American escort carrier was the result of a planned purchase with a programme of conversions very much in mind, by contrast the first British ship was the result of a grudging acceptance of the need for air power at sea. In March 1940, the Royal Navy had succeeded in capturing the *Hannover*, a fast refrigerated cargo ship built for the Norddeutscher Line in 1939, when she was in the West Indies. This 'prize' was brought back to the UK, and in January 1941, permission was given for her conversion to an aircraft carrier. Once again, her superstructure was removed and her diesel engine uptakes altered to discharge horizontally, while the resulting carrier lacked an island, with navigation from a rudimentary platform to starboard that must have made effective conning of the ship difficult. Arrester wires were provided aft with a crash barrier, but there was no hangar, so that the ship's aircraft, just six, had to be manhandled forward of the crash barrier before other aircraft could land, and then manhandled aft again to be ready for operations. Another contrast with *Long Island* was the provision of only 10,000 gallons of aviation fuel. The ship was capable of just 15 knots. Armament was a 4-in gun at the stern, with four 2-pounders forward and aft at the edge of the flight deck, and four 20-mm singles were also mounted forward but behind the forward 2-pounders. There were also a number of Hotchkiss light machine guns, and for anti-submarine protection, four depth charge projectors near the stern.

Commissioned into the Royal Navy as HMS *Audacity* on 20 June 1941 in this form, the ship was quickly deployed on convoy escort duties on the route between the UK and Gibraltar, which had to run the gauntlet of aerial attack by Focke-Wulf Fw200 Condor maritime reconnaissance aircraft based in occupied France. Six Grumman Wildcats were provided, with no anti-submarine protection at all. *Audacity* was to survive for just three operations, but her performance was convincing enough. On her three convoys with just six aircraft, they managed to shoot down, damage or drive-off nine Focke-Wulf Fw200 maritime reconnaissance aircraft and report nine U-boats to the escorting destroyers.

27

No doubt the threat of aerial attack was the greater menace, but it seems entirely unsurprising in these circumstances that when the ship did meet her end while on her third convoy escort duty on 20 December 1941, escorting a UK-bound convoy off Portugal, it was to torpedoes from *U-751*.

By this time, the United States had been brought into the Second World War by the Japanese attack on the US Pacific Fleet at Pearl Harbor. While five escort carriers were being built in the United States for the Royal Navy, the US Navy hastily ordered a further twenty-five, of which twenty-four were intended for their own use and one for the Royal Navy, as it had been decided to hold back one of the first five, *Charger*, to provide carrier deck training for the many British pilots being trained for the Fleet Air Arm in the United States.

Aboard *Audacity*, flying operations had been tough. There were just two arrester wires compared with the six on the larger British fleet carriers, and of these the second had no hydraulic retardation and, if caught, brought aircraft and pilot to an abrupt and brutal halt, but at least it was better than continuing down the flight deck to the crash barrier, which would damage the aircraft, at the very least wrecking the airscrew, and possibly making a mess of the pilot as well. That, of course, was assuming that the barrier was hit head on, but it was not unknown on a pitching, rolling deck for an aircraft to catch the barrier with its undercarriage and somersault over it, with fatal results. Aboard *Audacity*, of course, the forward part of the flight deck was likely to always have aircraft parked, with no hangar deck to be struck down into.

Life for the maintainers was also far from ideal. As on the MAC-ships, they had to maintain aircraft in the open without shelter from the wind and the sea, often wet from rain and spray. The damp sea air was devastating to aircraft left in the open, jamming throttles, corroding gun wells and the electrics. Bad enough in daylight, but at night the maintainers had to struggle to continue working with torches masked by blue filters while a shipmate shielded this tell-tale light with his coat. On the other hand, having been converted in a hurry, especially for the officers, the accommodation aboard had standards of comfort quite out of place aboard a warship, with comfortable staterooms that there had been no time to remove.

If the ship was sadly lacking, a hasty compromise permitted by an Admiralty that was not altogether convinced, the aircraft were quite the opposite and a revelation to British naval pilots accustomed to aircraft that were at best obsolescent. The Grumman Wildcat, known at first to the Royal Navy and the Fleet Air Arm as the Martlet until standardization of nomenclature became highly desirable after US entry into the war, was a thoroughbred carrier fighter. Although still not as fast as contemporary land-based fighters, it was nevertheless described as 'tough and tireless'. On the carrier's final voyage, Sub Lieutenant Eric 'Winkle' Brown's aircraft had a bent airscrew, but he still managed to chase a Focke-Wulf Fw200 Condor into thick cloud, until suddenly he found the aircraft heading straight towards him. Brown, who favoured the head-on attack to compensate for the Martlet's lack of speed, just managed to press the firing button, sending a stream of bullets into the Condor, shattering the windscreen and blasting bits off the aircraft's nose, before he had to pull up to avoid a head-on collision, only just managing to miss the aircraft's tail. He turned back to see the aircraft hit the water so hard that the port wing was torn off. Brown's experience was not unusual, another pilot on the same squadron had returned to *Audacity* with the W/T aerial from a German aircraft wrapped around his aircraft's tail wheel. Post-war, Brown was to make the first planned jet landing on an aircraft carrier when he put a de Havilland Sea Vampire onto the deck of the light fleet carrier HMS *Ocean*. He doubtless found this ship superior to the escort carriers, but no doubt would have liked something bigger and faster than a light fleet on which to land a jet fighter.

The next British escort came from the United States, where one of the six C3 hulls purchased by the US Navy was converted. Originally laid down as the *Mormacland*, HMS *Archer* was designated BAVG-1, 'British aircraft escort vessel', before her transfer under Lend-Lease and commissioning into the Royal Navy on 17 November 1941. A hangar occupied a quarter of the ship's overall length, with the wooden flight deck continued forward on open girders to a point just short of the forecastle. Another difference between *Archer* and the two earlier ships was that she had a hydraulic catapult, known to the Royal Navy at

29

the time as an accelerator, forward, as well as the usual arrester gear aft. A small platform was fitted to the starboard side of the flight deck well forward for navigation and air control. Although designed to carry 85,000 gallons of aviation fuel, the Royal Navy objected to the US practice of replacing used fuel with sea water and determined that permanent ballast be carried to enhance stability, so that her fuel capacity was reduced to around 40,000 gallons. As we will see later, the British practice of using compressed air rather than sea water to force aviation fuel to aircraft was to have serious problems of its own.

The British habit of refining the CVEs sent to them by the US Navy caused considerable irritation, as the US Navy estimated that there were delays of between twenty-four and thirty weeks between delivery of a ship to the Royal Navy and its operational availability. Not only did the Royal Navy not like the layout of the fuel system and also objected to using sea water as compensation for spent fuel, they also preferred to ballast the ships, further reducing their aviation fuel capacity. The way in which the hulls of the escort carriers were broken up into watertight compartments was also regarded as being below British standards. One result was that the Americans reproached the British for making poor use of the carriers supplied at some sacrifice to the US Navy's own interests. The question was, of course, whether the risk to the crews of the carriers or the risk to merchant shipping and escort vessels on the convoys lacking air cover was the greater. Even with hindsight, this cannot be answered.

The outcome of the British alterations to the escort carriers was that these ships were not available on the North Atlantic until March 1943. Even then the ship was the USS *Bogue*, although she was joined by HMS *Biter* in April, and by *Archer* in May. By June, there were four escort carriers operating, and even this small number sufficed to make enough of an impression on the 'Atlantic gap' that the U-boats were forced to change their tactics and start looking for victims in the less heavily patrolled waters of the South Atlantic.

Defensive armament aboard *Archer* consisted of three US-pattern 4-in guns and as with *Long Island* these were mounted with one aft and another on the forecastle, while there were also fourteen 20-mm Oerlikon guns in single mountings in seven positions on each side of the ship, and two twin 20-mm on either side of the flight deck aft. In late 1942, the 4-in guns were replaced by British weapons of the same calibre and two twin 40-mm Bofors installed the following year. Also in 1942, the flight deck was lengthened to 440 feet.

The ship's Achilles heel was her machinery, a complex arrangement of four diesel engines driving a single shaft that proved cumbersome and unreliable. She was also to prove to be unlucky, with the first aircraft to be catapulted off, a Grumman Martlet, dropping into the sea. Within a few weeks, in January 1942, she collided with a Peruvian cargo ship while still on trials, and this led to a further delay of two months while she was repaired. She did not sail for Greenock, on the River Clyde in Scotland, until June 1942, but had not got very far when one of her own bombs exploded aboard causing nineteen casualties and further damage, so she was diverted to New York for yet more repairs. After that, on her first crossing of the Atlantic, she broke down, and returned to the USA. Finally, in November 1942, she sailed with an American convoy to Morocco to cover the Allied invasion of North Africa; Operation Torch. After this, she eventually found her way to Liverpool and further machinery repairs that kept her out of action until March 1943.

Ashore, the squadron assigned to her initially was transferred to other work with its personnel left speculating on what had happened to the ship. This was our friend John Godley again, and he composed a derogatory ditty to the tune of *The Road to the Isles* that expressed their frustration in no uncertain terms:

> There's a squadron going rotten
> For it's waiting for the war
> And the war is waiting for the Admiraltee:
> Eight-eleven's* simply heaven
> If you want to stay ashore,
> For we never, never, never go to sea.

---

* No. 811 Naval Air Squadron – Fleet Air Arm squadrons were numbering the 700 series for non-combatant and support or second line squadrons, and in the 800 series for combat squadrons. No. 811 was a Fairey Swordfish squadron.

31

To Lee-on-Solent and Arbroath
And Machrihanish we may pass,
We have searched the pubs and brothels far and wide.
Oh we've flown until we've grown
A paid of wings upon our arse,
But we'll never find the *Archer* on the Clyde[1]

Their frustration was understandable, for while the escort carriers were awaited, convoys were being mauled by U-boats. Allied merchant shipping losses in the Atlantic and the North Sea soared from 2,451,663 tons in 1940 and 2,214,408 tons in 1941 to 5,366,973 tons in 1942, when these ships were so desperately needed. The German *Kriegsmarine* had entered the war at a disadvantage, having not expected war to break out until 1944–1945, and was far from ready. Most important of all, it had started the war with a fairly small U-boat strength, with just fifty-nine submarines but, by 1942, U-boats were coming into service at an increasing rate. The Germans were also helped by delays in introducing a convoy system along the east coast of the United States. The impact of the escort carriers and of improved maritime-reconnaissance aircraft could be seen the following year, 1943. After June 1943, except for July, when 136,106 tons of shipping were lost, no other month saw more than 50,000 tons lost. The year end figure was a total of 1,764,202 tons, a decrease of more than 67 per cent over the previous year. By the end of 1944, the annual total of Allied shipping lost to the U-boats had slumped to 293,624 tons.

By this time, *Archer* was in service and to her credit one of her Swordfish became the first aircraft to sink a U-boat using rocket fire in May 1943. Even so, her engine troubles remained and she was laid up as a stores ship in August 1943 and decommissioned in March 1945, even before the war in Europe had ended.

Nevertheless, these were no more than teething troubles whose impact would have been lessened had conversions started earlier and been in time for any problems to be resolved. The new infant was essentially the right vessel for the job, and as other ships followed this could be clearly seen. Despite considerable experience of aircraft carrier design on both sides of the Atlantic, the right configuration was also slightly difficult to establish at first.

The solution should have been clear enough, simply build a scaled down and utilitarian version of a full-sized carrier, with arrester wires, catapults, hangars and island. It is impossible to get a new concept right first time, and the real grounds for criticism have to be that the process of experiment and conversion started too late, and the crippling and unsustainable losses of 1942 could have been, if not avoided altogether, much reduced had conversions started earlier. If a dozen of the merchantmen lost in 1942 had been taken up from trade earlier and converted, not only would their fate have been different, but so too would that of other ships, and it is fair to suggest that these would have outnumbered the ships converted several times over. It would have eased pressure on wartime production and the condition of the civilian population in the UK, and saved the lives of countless seafarers. It could even have seen the war end up to a year earlier as Germany struggled to provide yet more U-boats and drained the other services of supplies.

Nevertheless, no matter how belatedly, the tide was beginning to turn with the next batch of escort carriers, known to the British as the Avenger-class. Initially this was to have been a class of five ships, *Archer*, *Avenger*, *Biter*, *Charger* and *Dasher*, but the US Navy, struggling to meet both its own increased wartime demand for naval airmen and also much of that of the Royal Navy, understandably decided to retain *Charger* to provide carrier deck training for the new generation of Fleet Air Arm pilots.

The Avenger-class set the pattern for succeeding escort carriers in many ways, with small starboard islands for navigation and air control and radar for both air and surface threats. These features were a logical development of the first escort, *Long Island*. Once again, in Royal Navy service the fuel storage was reduced to 36,000 gallons primarily on safety grounds. It is a moot point whether the larger US fuel storage reflected a less cautious approach to the hazards of fire and explosion, or whether they wished the escorts to have a secondary 'oiler' role for smaller convoy escort vessels. It could also be simply that the US Navy always planned for longer ranges in its vessels than the Royal Navy, whether this be bunkerage, aircraft fuel or even drinking water. British warships often had notoriously short ranges, a reflection on having a vast empire with refuelling stations seldom far apart. The Americans were also well ahead in replenishment at sea, inventing the abeam method of replenishing and refuelling while the Royal Navy used the in-line method, which not only took much longer but was far more limited in the sea states in which these operations could proceed.

Built on the C3 merchant hulls, the four Avenger-class carriers were commissioned into the Royal Navy between March and July 1942. Armament consisted of three 4-in and nineteen 19-mm guns. On arrival in the UK, their flight decks were lengthened to 440 feet.

The first, *Avenger*, had the distinction of escorting the first of the Arctic convoys to have an escort carrier, PQ18, and carried Hawker Sea Hurricane fighters as well as Fairey Swordfish for reconnaissance and anti-submarine work. The Arctic convoys needed protection from aerial attack as well as from submarines, while the new German battleship *Tirpitz*, moored for most of the time in a Norwegian fjord, was a constant threat, able to outgun and outrun any convoy escort. All three ships also supported the Allied invasion of North Africa, Operation Torch.

With so few escort carriers at first, the casualty rate was considerable. *Avenger* was sunk the month after Operation Torch on 15 December 1942 when she became yet another victim of U-boat attack. The carrier was torpedoed by *U-155* off Gibraltar, and her thin merchantman hull offered too little protection for the torpedo set off a fire from which explosions followed and just seventeen of her crew of 500 survived. The disaster seems to have fitted the American cynics' view of the escort carrier designation of CVE as standing for 'combustible, vulnerable, expendable', since hasty construction – it was intended that they could be converted back to merchant ships after the war – and poor armour protection meant that they were vulnerable in battle. Nevertheless, it was to have a marked impact on Anglo-American relations.

Yet, despite all the effort put into making the escort carriers safer for the Royal Navy, one disaster put in doubt the value of the British modifications. While the fate of *Dasher* was not as costly in lives as that of *Avenger*, it was tragic enough, especially since it was not due to enemy action. Following the North African landings and convoy escort duty in the North Atlantic, *Dasher* was blown apart by an aviation fuel explosion while in the Firth of

Clyde on 27 March 1943. Her loss has been the cause of some speculation, including sabotage by German agents, but a fuel explosion caused either by a leak or during aircraft refuelling has become regarded as the most likely cause. Few German agents remained undetected long enough to do much damage to the British war effort. Some have suggested an alternative explanation, that aircraft were landing on at the time and that an aircraft could have missed the flight deck and hit the aft armament and the 'ready use' ammunition locker, setting off an explosion. But this would have had to cause further explosions to destroy the ship and eyewitness accounts talk of a single devastating explosion with heavy loss of life and, more importantly, confirm that flying had finished for the day.

Once again, an escort carrier had lived up to the American jibe about being 'combustible, vulnerable, expendable'. The ship had exploded into an inferno and only the bows were unaffected. The ship's commanding officer had announced shore leave over the Tannoy and many of the crew were below decks washing and shaving ready for a 'run ashore' once she returned to port, when there was a massive explosion below decks, hurling the aircraft lift, weighing two tons, sixty feet into the air. Fires broke out detonating the anti-aircraft ammunition which in turn tore holes in her hull and in just three minutes she had sunk. One witness to the event was Brian 'Blinker' Paterson, who eventually reached the rank of lieutenant commander. Paterson saved himself by jumping off the flight deck and into the freezing sea, itself alight after leaking fuel caught fire. Traumatized by his experience, he nevertheless found the strength to swim to a destroyer nearby. Out of a ship's company of 528, no less than 379 were either killed by the explosion, trapped by the fires or died before they could be picked up.

The only one of this batch of carriers to survive the war was *Biter*, who after being returned to the US Navy in April 1945 was immediately passed on to the French Navy, becoming the *Dixmude*.

The loss of *Dasher* in an accident merited an Admiralty Board of Inquiry, but this did nothing to resolve the disagreement between the Royal Navy and the US Navy, whose ship *Dasher* remained as she had only been 'on loan' to the British. Once again, the Admiralty came to the conclusion that safety arrangements for handling aircraft fuel in the escort carriers were 'practically non-existent' by British standards. The Americans for their part maintained that Royal Navy officers lacked experience in handling aviation fuel. The American contention seems strange given the fact that the Royal Navy had been involved in the development of the aircraft carrier and even while the Fleet Air Arm was under Royal Air Force control, the ships themselves had been manned by naval personnel. On the other hand, the rapid expansion of the Fleet Air Arm under wartime conditions with many RNVR officers and 'hostilities only' ratings, and the need to take over from Royal Air Force maintainers, could have meant that training and experience was far below the ideal.

British shipyards were by this time busy building escort vessels for the convoys, often working under heavy air attack with those on the south and east coasts especially vulnerable. There was also much repair work to be done, especially on the west coast ports that were used for convoys to turn round. The ability of American shipyards to mass produce ships on standard hulls, using many prefabricated parts, meant that setting up a duplicate production line on the eastern side of the Atlantic was unnecessary. The Lend-Lease terms also made these ships attractive to a nation that was bankrupting itself – effectively the United Kingdom had run out of foreign exchange by the end of 1940 – by the demands of the war, but the Lend-Lease traffic was not one-way for, in what has been sometimes referred to as 'reverse Lend-Lease', British and Canadian-built corvettes were transferred to the US Navy for convoy escort duties.

There were to be a small number of British-built or converted escort carriers, however. One reason for this was that the Admiralty believed that riveted construction was better suited to the demands of the Arctic convoys to the Soviet Union than the welded construction favoured by the Americans. In fact, US-built escort carriers do not seem to have suffered unduly from the low temperatures and violent seas.

One of the first British-built ships was HMS *Activity*, converted from the fast refrigerated cargo ship *Telemachus* before she was completed. She was one of the few escorts to have a steel flight deck, but lacked catapults and also suffered from having a short hangar, less than 100 feet in length, that limited her capacity to just ten aircraft, while just 20,000 gallons of aviation fuel was carried. Commissioned late in 1942, initially she was used for deck landing training before seeing service on convoys to Russia and on the North Atlantic, while after the end of the war in Europe she ferried aircraft to the Far East.

By this time, ships began to have a standard pattern of design, all of them having a small island, sometimes sponsoned out to increase deck space, while full length hangars became the standard. The British received first the US Bogue-class, which became their Attacker-class, and then the similar Ameer-class, sometimes referred to as the Ruler-class. On the other side of the Atlantic, the Americans introduced the Sangamon-class, converted from tankers and which could double up as oilers, then a number of ships of the Bogue-class not handed over to the Royal Navy, and followed this by the fifty ships of the Casablanca-class and then the Commencement Bay-class, like the Sangamon-class based on a tanker hull. Details of all of these ships are given in Appendices III and IV. The impressive output of American ship-yards, part of the 'arsenal of democracy' meant that while these vessels were being built, along with hundreds of wartime utility 'Liberty' merchant ships, the Independence-class light carriers, based on cruiser hulls and the purpose-designed and built Essex-class fleet carriers were also produced. It was not until the end of the war that the British light fleet carriers, the Colossus-class, began to appear, based on a design that could be built by yards without a tradition of warship building, but even so, a purpose-designed carrier. The other achievement was to get all six of the fast armoured carriers, ordered before the outbreak of war, completed plus HMS *Unicorn*, supposedly a maintenance carrier but in fact used on operations from time to time.

The shortage of flight decks felt by the three carrier-operating navies during the Second World War resulted in some unusual compromises. One of these was that the British fast armoured carrier, HMS *Victorious*, second ship of the successful Illustrious-class, went on loan to the US Navy. This was after she had spent much of the winter of 1942–1943 being refitted at the Norfolk Navy Yard. She was given the temporary name of USS *Robin*, until later relieved by the American interpretation of the fast carrier, the USS *Essex*, lead ship of the class of the same name with no less than twenty-five large carriers in all. The *Robin*, alias *Victorious*, operated with the US Pacific Fleet, and no doubt helped to improve inter-operability between the two navies, something which was a matter of some concern. In fact, for a period after the Royal Navy 'returned to eastern waters, HMS *Illustrious* and the USS *Saratoga* operated together for the same reason, and also to ensure that the Royal Navy could get used to the concept of massed air attacks using a combination of fighters and bombers, and with aircraft from more than one carrier.

Apart from the MAC-ship conversions, many of which were not available until after the more capable escorts had started to appear, which hadn't been the object of the exercise, there were four more all-British escort carriers, the *Pretoria Castle*, the two Nairana-class ships *Nairana* and *Vindex*, and *Campania*, the latter resurrecting a name from the First World War.

The urgency of providing more carriers must have been very much in mind when the Admiralty agreed that the *Pretoria Castle*, pre-war a Union Castle liner sailing between the UK and South Africa, which had been converted into an armed merchant cruiser, could be taken over for further conversion into an aircraft carrier. Commissioned in April 1943, she was to be the largest escort carrier in service with the Royal Navy, at 19,650 tons standard displacement, and with a full length hangar and steel flight deck with a single catapult forward, although the design was hampered by having just a single lift forward, close to the small island, that gave problems in handling aircraft. Armament included two twin 4-in guns aft, plus ten twin 20-mm Oerlikons and four quadruple 2-pounders, although much time must have been wasted and the availability of the ship considerably reduced by the order that the 2-pounders were only to be used while in the escort carrier role and that when used as a training carrier they had to be replaced by eight single 20-mm Oerlikons! Aircraft totalled twenty-one, usually fifteen torpedo-bomber-reconnaissance aircraft, the trusty Swordfish, and six fighters.

Nairana and the similar *Vindex* were both converted from fast refrigerated cargo ships, and again had a full length hangar and steel flight deck, although both lacked catapults and once again there was just a single lift. Smaller than *Pretoria Castle* at 13,825 tons, they nevertheless had the same twenty-one aircraft capacity. Aviation fuel capacity was one of the highest for British escorts at 52,000 gallons, which enabled *Nairana* to keep her escort vessels 'topped up' when she acted in the hunter-killer anti-submarine role in the Atlantic in 1944–1945. Both ships commissioned in December 1943. It was an indication of just how adequate convoy protection had become during the last eighteen months of the war that escort carriers could be sent on 'hunter-killer' missions that had been so dangerous that the Royal Navy had lost its fleet carrier HMS *Courageous* on one such operation just a fortnight after war had broken out in Europe. The differences were, of course, that the late war hunter-killer operations, that followed successful US experience of this type of operation in mid and South Atlantic, enjoyed far greater escort vessel protection for the carrier, and constant patrols by radar-equipped Swordfish. Improved intelligence following British breaking of the German Enigma codes coupled with high frequency radio direction finding also meant that information on the whereabouts of U-boats was far better than at the beginning of the war. Both ships survived the war, with *Nairana* becoming the first Royal Netherlands Navy carrier, *Karel Doorman*.

The final British ship, *Campania* was similar to *Nairana*, but with a slightly longer and wider hull despite a lower tonnage at 12,450 tons, but only eighteen aircraft could be carried. The first British escort to have an action information organization, AIO, she was commissioned in March 1944. Her early duties were on the Russian convoys, but instead of heading to the Far East after German surrender, she was deployed to the Baltic. Unlike many of the other escorts, she remained in service post-war until going into reserve in 1952 and then being scrapped in 1955.

Having a single lift presented many problems. The one most frequently encountered was that of sometimes having to range a number of aircraft on the flight deck simply to get the aircraft needed for a sortie out from the back of the hangar deck. This was time-consuming and demanded much exhausting man-handling, often on slippery hangar and flight decks that were pitching and rolling. Worse than this, however, was the problem of having a lift motor fail. The carrier then had to operate like a tanker MAC-ship as if there were no hangar or, more usually, operate the lift manually. When this happened aboard *Vindex*, it took an hour for each cycle of raising and lowering a lift. Repairing such faults was usually beyond the resources aboard, although on *Vindex* the offending motor was swapped for that of one of the aft capstans – not an easy task on a ship at sea, but necessary.

Notes
1. Kilbracken, op. cit.

III

LIFE ABOARD

For those who were more used to merchantmen, life aboard naval vessels came as a nasty shock. The population density aboard a warship was far higher than that aboard a merchant vessel, which had simply to be steamed from the port of departure to its destination, with a ship's company who could be divided simply into those of the deck and engine departments, plus a small catering staff and perhaps a radio officer. By contrast, a warship had to have sufficient manpower to control and operate the weapon systems, possibly a number of marines, while the need to continuously monitor the seas around the ship, and the sky above and the depths below, meant that radar and sonar, or Asdic as it was known during the war years, needed to be manned continuously.

Aboard an aircraft carrier, there was another consideration, the aircraft, which not only took up a considerable amount of space, but needed spare parts and had weapons of their own and fuel as well. They also added considerably to the size of the ship's company and the population density aboard with the need for aircrew and the maintainers. It all became very cramped.

In fact, during the Second World War these differences would have been less obvious than today. Not only was the standard of living much lower at home, merchant ships had far larger manpower requirements than is the case today. Even on merchant ships, a large number of seamen might find themselves messing together in cramped confines and sleeping in hammocks, something known to old hands as a 'glory hole'. On the other hand, despite their utilitarian construction, one positive, saving feature when it came to the escort carriers was that the vast majority of them were American in origin, and reflected the US Navy's ideas of what was suitable in terms of accommodation and facilities.

A comparison between the wartime Royal Navy and the US Navy can be best made by looking at something completely different from an aircraft carrier, the submarines of the two services. British submariners were often noted for their beards, strictly regulated by the Admiralty so that only a 'full set' was acceptable with no goatees or moustaches, and that it had to be grown in the wearer's own time, meaning whilst ashore on leave, and only with the permission of his commanding officer. The growth of a beard in one's own time was probably overlooked under wartime conditions. By contrast, in the US Navy, beards were a relative rarity. Why the difference? It was not a case of differing fashions but simply that supplies of fresh water aboard American submarines were always far more abundant than on British submarines, with none of the latter's need to economize on water. The water shortage aboard British warships meant that often sea water and special soap would have to be used for washing and shaving, with considerable difficulty experienced in raising a good lather. The situation was made even more critical when the numbers aboard were increased by the presence of survivors or of prisoners of war. Increasing aircraft sophistication also played a part, as with the fitting of radar for example, the numbers of maintainers also grew. On the other hand, this was countered to some extent by the abolition of the practice of each aircraft having its own team, usually just two on a Swordfish, and the adoption of a 'garage' system, which meant that an entire squadron's team of maintainers would work on any aircraft as needed.

Accommodation

The arrival of the escort carriers more or less coincided with a change in the catering arrangements aboard British warships, but for the ratings it also preceded by more than a decade a change in accommodation. Primitive and utilitarian the escorts were in one sense, but the American-built ships introduced British sailors to bunks instead of hammocks, although not everyone relished this change. One change that was for the better and generally widely accepted was the change in catering, and the fact that junior ratings no longer had to eat, sleep and entertain themselves in the same cramped space. Naturally enough, the accommodation differed between ranks, as all navies provided better accommodation for senior ratings and for officers, while in any case a certain amount of 'distance' helped in maintaining good discipline.

On the outbreak of the Second World War, two different types of messing arrangements were in use in the Royal Navy; these were 'general messing' and the misleadingly named 'canteen messing'. In general messing, the paymaster or his deputy had the responsibility of drawing up a menu for the lower deck and each mess had to send a 'duty cook', a role that each member of the mess took in turn, to collect the meals for the agreed number of men in the mess. The meals once served would be eaten on wooden tables with the ratings sitting on wooden stools or benches. At night the mess became the sleeping accommodation, but hammocks had to be taken down and rolled up and stored away during the day. The so-called canteen messing was a variation on this. Each mess drew supplies, including a ration of meat, potatoes or rice, and any other vegetables from the ship's provision store and this was prepared in the mess by the duty cook, again chosen in turn from the mess members, and then taken to the galley to be cooked. Later, once the meals were cooked, the duty cook would return to the galley to collect the food, which would then be served as in general messing.

These arrangements had many drawbacks, not the least being the varying qualities of the duty cook in canteen messing. In canteen messing, it was sometimes possible to pay extra for special treats, or if a full allowance was not drawn, the saving could be credited to the pay of the mess members. On one ship, the members of one mess used to enjoy creating what they termed a 'one pound cake', with a pound, or 454 grams, of each ingredient. This would be taken to the mess to be baked as a cake or steamed to make a pudding or desert. The system worked well until a newcomer with no catering experience at all included a pound of yeast in the ingredients. When he went back to collect the result, it burst out of the oven door when it was opened and spread over the galley deck. 'Relations with the cooks were never the same afterwards,' recalled one crew member.

One problem with both of these types of messing on an aircraft carrier was that not every one could be available at meal times, and the system did not take into account those who might be working to get aircraft operational, or into the air or struck down into the hangar deck on return or, of course, they might be flying as there were some rating aircrew, notably the telegraphist/air-gunners on many British naval aircraft. If you were lucky and people remembered, a meal might be put aside, but the hapless rating would find that it was a cold, congealed mess. The one thing that was always saved for the returning mess mate was his 'grog', the ration of rum and water issued daily to all adult seamen in the Royal Navy at the time, and after which one recalled: 'You could eat anything!'

On the escort carriers, the system of cafeteria messing was introduced, with ratings having their meals in a self-service cafeteria as they would have ashore when in barracks. This took food away from the sleeping accommodation. The escort carriers and the new fast armoured carriers also had recreation areas. As the war progressed, the new catering system also made it easier to provide food at different times to suit operational and working requirements.

Pilots and observers were almost always commissioned in the Royal Navy's Fleet Air Arm, and when a major operation was planned, meals would be provided at whatever time of day was required. This could mean breakfast very early in the morning if a dawn attack was planned, and not surprisingly, appetites were dull indeed if an operation against heavy AA fire or fighter defences was anticipated.

Life with the Merchant Navy

By contrast, on the Merchant Aircraft Carriers, the MAC-ships, catering was provided by the Merchant Navy. The problem was that the strict trade union hours worked by the Merchant Navy could mean the three-man crew of a Swordfish departing too early for breakfast on a cold dawn patrol. As mentioned earlier, nothing more than a cup of tea was available at 07:30 with breakfast at 08:00, and it was not until someone had the bright idea of buying food 'off ration' in the Irish Republic or Canada and using a small primus stove to prepare a hot breakfast that the situation became tenable.

The fact that the MAC-ships carried cargo and were operated by Merchant Navy personnel led to some strange situations. For a start, all members of the Swordfish flights had to sign on as members of the ship's company once embarked. This meant that they were supposed to receive a shilling a month and a bottle of beer a day to reflect their status as being under the command of the ships' masters. The shilling seems to have never been paid, but seven bottles of beer were safely deposited in the cabins for each member of the flights every Sunday. For their part, the aircrew were proud to be able to wear the small silver MN badge in the lapels of their uniforms, which not infrequently upset senior officers ashore! A few even had Merchant Navy or shipping company buttons interspersed with those of the Royal Navy on their uniforms!

There were other problems, and as with the Canadian-manned escort carriers, these centred around pay. Merchant Navy ratings were paid far more than their counterparts in the Royal Navy, but when a ship was lost, those in the Merchant Navy had their pay stopped immediately until, hopefully, they were rescued and joined their next ship, while those in the Royal Navy continued to be paid until it was clear that they genuinely were lost at sea.

Aboard the Escorts

Typical of the new escort carriers in many ways was the USS *Guadalcanal*, CVE-60, one of the Casablanca-class. Her new commanding officer, the then Captain Daniel Gallery, described his new command as a 'Cinderella' of ships when he took her over at the Kaiser Yard at Vancouver, upstream on the Columbia River in Washington State, and compared her with the bulk of the Essex-class carriers, also by this time coming into service. Captain Gallery recalls:

> The decision to build these ships caused the greatest argument in naval circles since Noah built the Ark. By pre-war navy standards these ships simply didn't make sense, and anyone with a few years' seagoing experience could tell from a glance that no good would ever come of them.
>
> A lot of people said so in no uncertain terms, too. When

my crew was being formed I found it necessary to assemble them and scotch some of the rumours that began to circulate around the waterfront.

One was to the effect that the ships were structurally unsound, and would break in two in a seaway. I must admit this didn't seem too implausible at the time, especially when you looked around the building-yard and saw the farmers, shop assistants and high-school gals who were assembling the ships.

Strange things must have gone on during the night shifts in the Kaiser Yard when Rosie the Riveter was building aircraft carriers. One day shortly after we went into commission, Earl Trosino, my chief engineer, came up to the cabin gingerly holding a pair of pink silk panties by one corner. He had fished them out of the starboard main condenser. By sundown that day every man in our crew had his own theory as to how this bit of feminine 'twixt-wind-and-water-rigging' had got into our machinery.[1]

Guadalcanal had her fair share of mechanical problems. The start of her shakedown cruise started with the port engine failing, but Gallery decided not to linger in port and ordered his engineers to fix it as he conned the ship on one screw. Gallery again:

Earl Trosino, our chief engineer, never called for time out. . . He kept that ship going in spite of blown-out boiler tubes, scored piston rods, bad brickwork in the fireboxes, and salt in the feed water. On our return from every cruise that we later made in the Atlantic, the Navy Yard foreman came up to the cabin after inspecting our plant and told me, 'You barely just made it this time. If you had to go another ten miles you would have been towed in.' I never argued with him.

One alarming characteristic of our ship was dinned into our ears the moment we crossed the bar and got some motion on her. The thin plates between the hangar deck and the flight deck 'oil-canned' on every pitch of the ship – i.e. the plates would spring in when we were over the back of a wave and the plates were in tension, springing out when we got in the rough and put them under compression. This springing in and out like an oil can was accompanied by a thunderous booming that reverberated throughout the ship and reminded everybody of the predictions that these ships would break in two. Actually, there was no danger of this, but that ominous thunder sounded like the crack of doom.[2]

While many maintain that the Royal Navy fared better for food than the civilian population ashore, the amount and quality of food was not as good as that in the US Navy, but no one would have expected it to be. British warships were also notably short of space, and one effect of this was that after a week or two at sea, potatoes were no longer available and rice was served instead, as this took less storage space. 'Our first carrier was in fact a lucky break for us, for just about everything aboard came with the ship from the US, including stores and certainly some of the food,' recalls Bill Drake, who was a maintainer aboard an escort carrier. 'This was served on the ubiquitous aluminium trays in a cafeteria dining space and when we hit turbulent water in the Mozambique Channel the mess tables and their contents were sent flying.'[3]

Nevertheless, as we will see later, to avoid creating diplomatic problems, when two escort carriers were assigned to the Royal Canadian Navy, it was decided that these would continue to be Royal Navy ships as HMS *Nabob* and *Puncher*. The arrangement was that Canadians would run the ships, while the British would provide the personnel for naval air operations and the engine room personnel, meaning that the ships had 500 Canadians and 300 British. This was almost a recipe for disaster and there were to be many causes of friction. For a start, Canadian rates of pay were much higher than those of the Royal Navy, as was the daily victualling allowance, and despite being outnumbered by the Canadians, since the ship was 'HMS', British victualling rates applied and the food was, by all accounts, terrible. This was a particular shock to the Canadians in the crew as many of them were very inexperienced and new to naval life. A mutiny was only averted on one occasion when the ship had to go to action stations, but when she arrived at Norfolk, Virginia, after passing through the Panama Canal, a number of the crew deserted. In desperation, her commanding officer, Captain Nelson Lay flew to Ottawa and succeeded in obtaining Canadian victualling rates for the entire ship, and Royal Canadian Navy rates of pay for all of the ship's company other than those who belonged to the Fleet Air Arm. Given that they had flying pay, this might not have seemed too bad to the aircrew of No. 852 Squadron, but it was no doubt hard for the maintainers to swallow.

Aboard warships, the communal washbasins often lost their plugs, but on the escort carriers, this problem was solved using an American innovation, which entailed having hinged basins that could be tilted to dispose of their water. It seems that these were intended for certain parts of the anatomy only. However, on one occasion a rating washing his feet slipped and tilted the basin, but when he hopped back to recover, the basin then fell onto a delicate part of his anatomy – a part that was impossible to bandage! This was not the only hazard awaiting the unwary, or the simply inexperienced. 'The US style toilets were open stalls with a trough flowing with seawater,' recalls Bill Drake. 'This did not encourage moments of quiet contemplation and provided opportunities for pranksters with floating paper boats set alight to catch passing "traffic".'[4]

If the toilets were spartan, there were compensations elsewhere, especially in the sleeping accommodation. In any case, it was a step forward not to have to eat and sleep in the same cramped space. Bill Drake explained:

> The US accommodation provided bunks so our hammocks were redundant. Instead each bunk had a mattress inside a waterproof cover, which was opened for use and secured close over the bedding during the day. Typically American and so much more convenient, it seemed as if we Brits were determined to make our lives hard work. I shared a small 2-bunk cabin off one squadron ratings' mess deck with my workmate, Leading Air Mechanic (Electrical) Hawkins. This was deep in the stern and the sea could be heard lapping the thin steel plates outside; not a lot of protection as we were later to find out.[5]

Bill was not the only one to discover that the thin plating of a utility conversion offered little protection. Two naval airmen being carried as passengers on an escort carrier crossing the North Atlantic were thrown out of their bunks when a passing destroyer launched her depth charges. On the other hand, by the standards of the day, for two ratings to share a cabin was luxury indeed. On the purpose-built British fast armoured carriers, three officers could find themselves sharing a cabin.

There were limitations to the comforts available. Even at sea, the heat was intense, and ships at the time lacked air conditioning. Many found it difficult to sleep below, and many of those belonging to the embarked air squadrons used to sleep on the flight deck using the mattresses from their bunks and tucking themselves under an aircraft wing. One night while doing this, Bill Drake was caught in a tropical rainstorm. He closed up the water-proof cover of his mattress and at first was dry inside, but he had not reckoned on the heavy downpour and soon water seeped inside and forced him to retreat. Fortunately, he was able to dry his bedding out in a hot space by the funnel casing.

Working in such conditions was difficult, although the short time spent away from base on operations meant that major maintenance was left until the squadron was ashore. Even so, with such sweaty bodies, electrical resistance was much reduced and changing a battery in the rear fuselage of an aircraft could result in the unwary being given an unwelcome shock! Even American-built ships, capable of producing far greater quantities of water than their British counterparts, could not keep up with the demand for fresh water as personal consumption soared in the heat, and eventually water had to be rationed by limiting the amount used for showering. Water was turned on for limited periods each day, which was a problem for those suffering from prickly heat, for which the remedy was to wash as often as possible using mercury-based soap and who had to be alert for the 'wet' spells in order to get a shower or wash down.

The fact that the escort carriers were based on merchant hulls also brought difficulties when attempting to work on aircraft or move them in the hangar. At the ends of the hangar deck, the deck sloped upwards. Another problem was that the deck opened directly onto sponsons on the side of the ship, following the usual American practice, and as a safety measure at night, the doors leading from the hangar deck to the sponsons were fitted with switches that cut out all lights and power points if any of the doors had to be opened. Fine in theory and a feature that ensured the safety of the ship from passing enemy warships, submarines or aircraft, but the feelings of those working upside down inside an aircraft when suddenly all power went and they were plunged into complete darkness can well be imagined.

Notes
1. Gallery, Rear Admiral Daniel V., USN, *Clear the Decks!*, George G. Harrap, London, 1952.
2. Ibid.
3. Drake, C.S. 'Bill', *A Bit of a Tiff*, Platypus Books, Bishops Waltham, 2004
4. Ibid.
5. Ibid.

IV

THE AIRCRAFT

Given their small size and low speed, while not all of them had catapults, the variety of aircraft that were flown from escort carriers was impressive. The Vought Corsair was initially rejected by the US Navy as being too large and too heavy for carrier operation, but United States Marine Corps and Royal Navy pilots did fly Corsairs from escort carriers. Escort carriers also operated the Grumman Avenger, probably the best naval strike aircraft of the war, and while it was a moot point whether the Corsair or the Grumman Hellcat was the better carrier fighter, Hellcats were also present aboard these ships.

There was a wide variation in performance between the aircraft embarked in these ships. There was also a considerable variation in appearance, with at least one aircraft type looking as if it belonged to a different age, and had ended up in the wrong war.

Fairey Barracuda

The first attempt at a successor to the Fairey Swordfish was another biplane with a fixed undercarriage, the Fairey Albacore, albeit one with enclosed cockpits. But the Albacore was unreliable and few if any were embarked in escort carriers.

Next was the Fairey Barracuda, a high-wing monoplane of unsurpassed ugliness and 'a maintenance nightmare' in the words of one naval maintainer. It did at least have a retractable undercarriage. With a maximum speed of 150 knots, the Barracuda was hardly fast. It was mainly used as a torpedo-bomber or as a dive-bomber, and amongst its 'battle honours' could be counted a number of successful attacks on the German battleship *Tirpitz*. Its war load was not much different from that of the Swordfish, while power was provided by a Rolls-Royce Merlin XXXII engine of

1,620-hp, and maximum range was almost 600 nautical miles, or 1,000 nautical miles with a 116 gallon extra tank. The crew was just two.

The Barracuda proved difficult to fly, having an unfortunate tendency not to pull out of a dive. Barracudas were among the aircraft sent east when the Royal Navy returned to the Far East in force but, given the low speed of the escort carriers and the gentle breezes of the Indian Ocean, the aircraft could only just get airborne without any bomb load at all and even when using RATOG, rocket-assisted take-off gear. In fact, after leaving the flight deck, the aircraft would sink alarmingly towards the surface of the sea and then struggle to climb away, leaving a wash in the sea from its slipstream.

Fairey Swordfish

In 1939, the main striking force of the Fleet Air Arm was built around a biplane, while biplane fighters were also to see service aboard British warships in 1939 and 1940, but the fighters did not remain in service long enough to see the escort carriers arrive.

Because all British service aviation was controlled by the Royal Air Force for most of the time between the two world wars, it was the Air Ministry, rather than the Admiralty, that was responsible for the specification of the Fairey Swordfish. It was not simply the biplane configuration and fixed undercarriage that marked the Swordfish down as an anachronism, other features added to the impression, including the three open cockpits, one for the pilot, another for the observer, as the Fleet Air Arm designated the navigator, who in truth had to do much more than simply navigate, and a third for the telegraphist/rear-gunner, or TAG in naval parlance, with communication between the crew being by means of a simple tube, known as a Gosport tube, dating from before the First World War. Instruments were primitive, little better than the basics of compass, altimeter and air speed indicator, ASI, although the aircraft could home in on the carrier's beacon for a safe return. Checking the fuel in the air meant the pilot gaping through a hole in the instrument panel to see the fuel indicator, which was situated some distance ahead over the engine. It was not always reliable, and the best method of actually being sure of how much fuel remained was to use a dipstick, something that could only be done on the ground or on the deck. Later aircraft did have blind flying panels for operations at night, but flying through cloud in formation remained risky. Also to be found on some later aircraft were enclosed cockpits, especially for the observer manning the radar set.

Later versions didn't simply have stronger mainplanes and more power, they also introduced airborne radar, making the Swordfish the only biplane to be so fitted – a museum piece with the latest technology.

The spartan open cockpits may well have saved one Stringbag. One pilot wishing to give his aircraft a test flight after repairs offered his rigger what would today be called an 'air experience flight'. Wearing only his cotton overalls, as the aircraft gained height the rigger slunk down inside the cockpit to avoid the cold, and discovered that the floor of the cockpit was sticky from leaking oil – he immediately alerted the pilot and they were able to make an emergency landing back on the carrier before the engine seized up.

If communication between the crew was primitive, on the early versions so was that with the ground or the ship. There was no voice communication for Stringbags for the first couple of years of wartime flying, when Morse transmissions remained essential, so perhaps it was a blessing that often radio silence was ordered. Communications between aircraft were often by means of an Aldis lamp, especially at night when a gesture from a pilot or observer could not be seen. By 1944, nevertheless, radio was available.

The performance of the 'Stringbag' was far from sparkling. Many maintained that it couldn't manage 100 mph when carrying a torpedo, although official figures suggested that it could be much higher. Range was 450 nautical miles, but this could be increased to almost 900 nautical miles with a ninety-three gallon tank, either in the observer's cockpit when carrying a torpedo or large mine, or strapped under the fuselage when in bomber configuration. The aircraft could carry a 1,620-lb torpedo or four 250-lb depth charges or three 500-lb bombs, or six 60-lb anti-submarine rockets.

The slow speed may well have been a major advantage. Faster aircraft with a higher wing loading would have had difficulty in loitering ahead of a convoy on the look out for submarines.

Grumman Avenger

There could be no doubt that the Grumman Avenger was one of the aircraft that the Royal Navy would have liked to have had during the early years of the war, but the first flight wasn't until August 1941, and examples did not reach the Fleet Air Arm until April 1943. Although the role was officially that of TBR, torpedo-bomber-reconnaissance, the same as that for the Swordfish, there was little else that the two aircraft had in common. The 1,600 hp, boosted to 1,800 hp on take-off, of the Wright GR-2600-8 Cyclone engine gave a maximum speed of 232 knots and a range of almost 1,000 nautical miles that could be extended to 2,200 nautical miles with two eighty-three gallon drop tanks. As with the Swordfish, a crew of three was carried, with the telegraphist/air gunner or TAG having a single 0.50 Browning machine gun, while four more of these were placed in the wings. A 1,620-lb torpedo could be carried, or a single 2,000-lb or two 1,000-lb bombs. In British service, bombs were carried more often than torpedoes and the aircraft saw most service in the Far East.

Grumman Hellcat

Although the Grumman Hellcat was in service with the Fleet Air Arm comparatively quickly after its first flight on 26 July 1942 (the first examples arriving about a year later) many of the aircraft were allocated to the fleet carriers, although a number did embark in escort carriers and saw service over Norway and in the Far East. The Hellcat obtained a maximum speed of 330 knots and a range of 950 nautical miles, which could be extended to 1,340 nautical miles with a 125 gallon drop tank, from its 1,675-hp Pratt & Whitney P-2800-10W. Armament was four 0.5-in and two 20-mm cannon, while two 1,000-lb bombs could also be carried.

The Hellcat's long range meant that it was the natural choice for fighter escort work in the Far East, where most of these aircraft were to be found. A useful feature was that the wings folded backwards and upwards, leaving the armament facing deckwards, thus reducing the risk of guns blazing into aircraft parked forward of the aircraft on a crowded flight deck or in the hangar, the cause of some spectacular and costly accidents aboard British carriers in the Pacific.

Grumman Wildcat

Known initially to the Fleet Air Arm as the Martlet until names had to be standardized to prevent confusion after the United States entered the war, the Wildcat was a revelation to the Royal Navy, an aircraft designed as a single-seat carrier-borne fighter. The tendency for British naval fighters to have two seats had crippled performance, while the first single-seat monoplanes were adaptations from land-based aircraft and the shortcomings inherent in this also had to be suffered. The extent to which British equipment had lagged behind can be judged from the fact that the Wildcat had first flown in September 1937, although the first examples were with the Royal Navy in September 1940. The single 1,100-hp Pratt & Whitney R-1830-86 Twin Wasp engine could have its power boosted to 1,200-hp on take-off, and provided a maximum speed of 278 knots, not to be compared with the landplanes of the day, but better than anything the Royal Navy had at the time. Armament consisted of either four or six 0.5-in machine guns, while two 100-lb bombs could also be carried under the wings.

For the most part, members of the Fleet Air Arm liked their American equipment, with the maintainers enjoying the standardization of the location of the components, which made switching from one aircraft type to another so much easier. One slightly dated aspect of the Wildcat was the fuselage mounted undercarriage, which often resulted in the aircraft appearing to 'dance' from one wheel to another if the carrier was rolling heavily. On the Royal Navy's escort carriers, Wildcats served mainly with convoy escorts on the Atlantic and Arctic runs.

Hawker Sea Hurricane

The Hawker Sea Hurricane was the Royal Navy's first British-built single-seat monoplane fighter and was modelled on the Hawker Hurricane fighters of the Royal Air Force that had borne the brunt of the Battle of Britain in 1940, although most accounts centre on its newer and more streamlined counterpart, the Supermarine Spitfire, of which there were relatively few in service at the time. The Hurricane soon became displaced as the Royal Air Force's front-line fighter, unable to cope effectively with a Messerschmitt

Bf109 fighter in air-to-air combat, although its tighter turning circle did give the very best pilots a fighting chance against the faster German aircraft. Few British naval officers pre-war believed that aircraft carriers could operate high performance fighters, although the attitude changed somewhat after Royal Air Force pilots, without any deck landing experience and without arrester hooks on their aircraft, flew their Hurricanes to land safely aboard the carrier HMS *Glorious* during the Anglo-French withdrawal from Norway in spring 1940.

The Sea Hurricane was a single-seat fighter adapted in haste from the Hurricane and lacking folding wings. Several different marks of the Rolls-Royce Merlin were used, giving at least 1,030-hp, a maximum speed of 268 knots and a range of 482 nautical miles. Armament on the earlier versions consisted of eight .303-in Browning machine guns, but later aircraft had four 20-mm cannon. While the first examples had entered service with the Royal Air Force in 1938, the Royal Navy did not receive this aircraft until July 1941.

On the Malta convoys, Sea Hurricanes struggled to cope with Axis fighters and even some bombers, but the aircraft marked a massive improvement in the air defence of the fleet and did much useful work on the Arctic convoys in particular. It was easy to repair, and escort carriers would often carry replacement aircraft which could be assembled as replacements as aircraft were shot down or suffered deck landing accidents. Altogether some 800 saw Fleet Air Arm service. In addition, many were deployed aboard the catapult-armed merchant ships, the CAM-ships, but apart from a handful, most of these were flown by members of a special Royal Air Force unit since, of course, they had no need for carrier deck landing skills.

Supermarine Seafire

Like the Sea Hurricane, the Seafire was yet another naval adaptation of a land-based fighter. It was notable amongst naval maintainers as being the first aircraft for which they were given proper training, being sent to the manufacturer on a course, while with earlier aircraft they had simply been given an instruction manual and left to get on with it! The Seafire was not in naval service until June 1942, but offered much improved performance with its 1,415-hp Rolls-Royce Merlin XLVI engine providing a maximum speed of 352 knots and a range of 440 nautical miles, rising to 600 nautical miles with a single forty-five gallon drop tank. Armament was four .303-in Browning machine guns and two 20-mm cannon. In the fighter-bomber role providing close air support, three 500-lb bombs could be carried.

The Seafire saw service in the Mediterranean, especially covering the landings in North Africa, at Salerno and the South of France. Opinions varied on the Seafire. One pilot had good cause to love it after the armoured bulkhead behind the cockpit saved his life during an encounter with a Vichy French fighter. Others hated the way it bounced on landing, and being nose heavy tended to often end up nose down on the flight deck. The undercarriage offered insufficient protection and durability for rough carrier landings. One comment that summed up the aircraft succinctly was that 'It was too genteel for the rough house of carrier operations.' A very attractive aircraft, but not rugged enough.

Supermarine Walrus

Known affectionately as the 'shagbat', the escort carriers never carried more than one Supermarine Walrus amphibian, and the aircraft bore no resemblance at all to the elegant Spitfire and Seafire, despite coming from the same source. The Walrus had the all important role of search and rescue, and would have been very welcome aboard the Atlantic and Arctic convoy escort carriers, but this facility was clearly regarded as a luxury until the last year or so of the war when these aircraft were detached from a squadron at Ceylon (now Sri Lanka) aboard the escort carriers in the Indian Ocean. Yet another biplane, the Walrus had a single 775 hp Bristol Pegasus engine driving a pusher propeller. Its successor, the Sea Otter, with a more conventional tractor propeller does not seem to have reached the escort carriers. Early versions had a metal hull, but the MkII built by Saunders-Roe had a wooden hull, which doubtless saved on scarce materials but would have been far less practical for tropical conditions. Maximum speed was just 135 mph, and range 600 miles.

Vought Corsair

Originally intended for the US Navy who considered it too large and too heavy for carrier operation, the Vought Corsair was eagerly snatched up by the Royal Navy, desperate for any aircraft with a decent performance, although the first examples didn't enter service until June 1943, just over three years after the first flight. The aircraft was also used extensively by the United States Marine Corps. Despite reservations over its deck landing capabilities, both the Royal Navy and US Marine Corps used the aircraft from escort carriers while the former deployed them aboard its fast armoured carriers in the Indian Ocean and the Pacific.

A large single-engined crank wing monoplane, the 1,700-hp Pratt & Whitney P-2800-18SW engine gave a maximum speed of 393 knots and a range of just over 1,000 nautical miles, or 1,300 with two 125 gallon drop tanks. On later versions, power rose to 2,000 hp while a two stage turbocharger, with first stage engaged at 10,000 feet and second stage at 19,000 feet, meant that the later aircraft could fly at more than 400 knots. Armament was six .50-in machine guns and two 1,000-lb bombs could be carried.

As with the Seafire, opinions differed and again pilots either loved it or hated it. One pilot described it as 'the best naval fighter of the war' and another said 'everything about it was high class'. Features that were liked were the cockpit layout, so much better than on British aircraft of the day, and what would now be described as many 'fail-safe' features, with tail hook dropping ready for a safe landing if the hydraulic system failed, while the undercarriage, which had to remain up as long as possible if speed and range were to be maintained, could be blown down in an emergency by the use of a CO_2 bottle. Others described it as 'the bent wing bastard from Connecticut', because this aircraft shared the Seafire's tendency to bounce on landing and noses and propellers were often the unfortunate victims of deck landings. Perhaps the best description of all was that from the Japanese, who called it 'whispering death' because little was heard of it until it had roared overhead and away.

During the final year of the war, Corsairs were used against targets in the Netherlands East Indies and in the Marianas.

American aircraft brought with them Stromberg injection

carburettors, which meant that during flying a loop the engines wouldn't cut out.

One British naval pilot wrote of the Corsair:

> The Corsair was a rugged machine which could take any amount of punishment on the flight deck and appeared to make light of it. Everything about it was high-class and great attention to detail proclaimed itself wherever one looked. The cockpit was meticulously arranged with all dials readily visible and every lever and switch comfortably and conveniently to hand, without any need to search or grope. (Infinitely superior, I may say, to the cockpits of British aircraft of the time which suggested, by comparison, that they had been designed by the administrative office charwoman (cleaner).[1]

These were just the main aircraft types operated from the escort carriers. In their role as aircraft transports, many other types would have been carried, and craned on and off at the beginning and the end of voyages, while some United States Army Air Force aircraft were flown off on at least one occasion. The United States Marine Corps also flew light air observation post and liaison aircraft on and off carriers – no need to use arrester wires or catapults with these – in the closing stages of the war in the Pacific, until land bases became available. The problem for these aircraft with their undemanding take-off and landing requirements was not so much a runway, as a beach or jungle clearing would do, but the need for a secure base.

Note
1. Hanson, Norman, *Carrier Pilot*, Patrick Stephens, Cambridge, 1979.

V

WINNING THE BATTLE
OF THE ATLANTIC

War broke out in Europe on 3 September 1939, after Germany had rejected an Anglo-French ultimatum to withdraw its forces from Poland. The period that followed has often been termed 'the phoney war', which came to an end only with the German invasion of Denmark and Norway, followed by the push westwards through the Low Countries and into France. The German term for this period was the 'sitting war', meaning that the opposing armies merely sat and waited. There was no 'phoney war' at sea, however, for on the very first night of war at 21:00, the 13,500 ton liner *Athenia*, outward bound for the United States, was torpedoed with the loss of 112 lives, including twenty-eight US citizens. The Germans claimed that a bomb had been planted on the ship by the British to prejudice US-German relations. On 5 and 6 September, three more British merchantmen were sunk off the coast of Spain, with only the crew of one of them saved and the other two going down with all hands.

This was not the official start of the Battle of the Atlantic, however. That had to await the fall of France that enabled the *Kriegsmarine* to move its submarines to bases on the Atlantic coast of France, such as Brest and St Nazaire, cutting out the long and hazardous passage from the Baltic around the north of Scotland and the north of Ireland, that took the U-boats close to the British naval bases at Scapa Flow in Orkney and Londonderry in Northern Ireland, and then Devonport in the south-west of England. The Battle of the Atlantic is generally regarded as lasting from July 1940 to May 1945. It can be fairly said to have been the single longest running battle of the war.

In 1939, the British could still count their Merchant Marine as the largest in the world, at some 21 million tons of shipping. This was about the same figure as in 1914, due in part to the poor state of world trade between the wars, but the ships were larger and so there were fewer of them. Almost immediately, some 3 million tons were earmarked for use by the armed forces, mainly to supply the Royal Navy and support the British Army abroad, but also including a number converted to naval use, that could include anything from an armed merchant cruiser through minesweeping, anti-submarine trawlers and hospital ships down to motor fishing vessels on humble harbour duties. After taking into account the shipping needs of the British Empire, that left some 15.5 million tons to continue to carry Britain's foreign trade, a cut of more than a quarter over normal peacetime requirements.

Generally, the Battle of the Atlantic can be divided into four distinct phases:

1. The period from July 1940, after the fall of France, until December 1941, when the United States entered the war after the Japanese attack on Pearl Harbor.
2. January 1942 to March 1943, when the German U-boats reigned supreme, with numbers increasing more quickly than the Allied countermeasures could destroy them.
3. April and May 1943, when the arrival of escort carriers and MAC-ships combined to inflict heavy and unsustainable losses on the U-boats, which were temporarily withdrawn, many of them for re-equipping.
4. The period from June 1943 to May 1945, with the closure of the 'Atlantic Gap' by escort carriers and ever longer-range maritime reconnaissance aircraft, with growing losses by the U-boats.

At the outset of war in Europe in September 1939, Germany had just fifty-nine submarines, but the war years saw a total of 785 U-boats sunk, while in the North Atlantic alone, no less than 2,232 ships totalling 11,899,732 tons were lost. It is simply worth considering what would have happened if the famous German Plan Z had been carried out, calling for 223 U-boats by 1948, although Doenitz, later to become head of the German Navy and subsequently Hitler's successor as Führer, planned an extension of the submarine arm to 300 boats.

German successes early in the battle could have been far higher but for the fact that the *Kriegsmarine* initially suffered problems with its torpedoes in combat conditions. This was a problem also suffered by the US Navy during the war in the Pacific. Many commentators have wondered at this weakness given the German reputation for engineering excellence, but it could be that the problem was at least in part the result of the Führer 'system' in which intrigue played a part and any admission of weakness or under-achievement was perceived as a damning failure. Later, new 'electro' U-boats were delayed when they could have countered the reverses suffered by the *Kriegsmarine* in 1943, while effort was wasted on the hydro-peroxide Walther U-boats, which were to prove fatally unreliable.

While German naval strength included a considerable number of surface raiders, for the most part the Battle of the Atlantic was a submarine war. The raiders were generally used in other theatres of war, including the South Atlantic, the Indian Ocean and the Pacific, far away from Germany and, more important, from British bases. The battleship *Bismarck* and her escort the cruiser *Prinz Eugen* were intended to mount such an offensive in Operation Rhine Exercise, but the early dispatch of the *Bismarck* by the Royal Navy put paid to this idea. Later, the two battle-cruisers *Scharnhorst* and *Gneisenau*, with *Prinz Eugen*, posed a threat while they remained in harbour at Brest, and caused a considerable amount of British bombing effort to be devoted to these ships, with little real result. These too were removed from the scene during the so-called 'Channel Dash' of February 1942, that saw them return safely to Germany. At the time this operation was a source of considerable embarrassment to the British, but in the end the outcome was favourable to the balance of naval power.

Sea power was not the only means available to the Germans. The fall of Norway and then France also freed air bases, and the long-range Junkers and Focke-Wulf maritime-reconnaissance aircraft operated from these bases over the Bay of Biscay, while others flew from France to Scandinavia via the west coast of Ireland, in almost a maritime-reconnaissance variant of British and American 'shuttle' bombing, posing a menace to convoys as they approached or departed the Irish coastline.

Land-based maritime-reconnaissance aircraft were among the most effective anti-submarine measures during the war years, but the aircraft of the day had limited endurance. Despite experiments by the British with air-to-air refuelling in the late 1930s, this had been for commercial flying-boats and was not available for military operations during the war years. The result was that there was a significant stretch of the North Atlantic over which land-based air cover could not be provided, and this was the celebrated 'Atlantic Gap', also sometimes referred to as the 'Black Gap'. The gap might have been shrunk earlier had the bases in the west of Ireland to which the British were entitled by treaty been made available, but it would not have disappeared altogether. The question of the Irish bases has remained controversial to this day. Did the loss of them add to the toll of lives of Allied seafarers, or would protecting these from possible German invasion and, more probably, Irish nationalist terrorists have been more trouble than they would have been worth?

The Royal Navy was not left entirely on its own. In September 1941 American warships began to escort convoys to a mid-ocean handover point, officially to ensure that neutral shipping was not engaged by German submarines, although the United States was officially neutral from the outbreak of war in Europe until the Japanese attack on the US Pacific Fleet at Pearl Harbor just over twenty-seven months later. Inevitably, a U-boat eventually attacked an American warship, when the destroyer USS *Greer* found a German torpedo heading for it on 4 September 1941, while on passage from the United States to Iceland carrying mail and passengers. In response, the destroyer attacked with depth charges. Although a second torpedo was fired, neither the destroyer nor the U-boat was damaged.

After the United States entered the war, the Royal Navy made facilities available to the US Navy at Londonderry in Northern Ireland. The new commander of US naval forces in the Atlantic, Admiral Ernest King, had remarked on taking up his post that it was like being given a big slice of bread with 'damn little butter', reflecting on the shortage of ships. After the battleships *Idaho*, *Mississippi* and *New Mexico* had been transferred with the aircraft carrier *Yorktown* from the Pacific to the Atlantic, the President of the United States, Franklin Roosevelt, asked King how he liked the butter he was getting. Came the reply: 'The butter's fine, but you keep giving me more bread.'

By the time the Battle of the Atlantic began in earnest, the Royal Navy had already lost two of its seven aircraft carriers, the sisters HMS *Courageous* and *Glorious*. While not the newest ships and of obsolescent design, these converted battlecruisers were nevertheless still among the best and most modern of the British carriers at the time, with only the new *Ark Royal* more modern. The loss of *Courageous* to torpedoes from *U-29* on 17 September 1939 while she was 'trailing her cloak' hunting for submarines, was especially wasteful. *Glorious* was sunk by gunfire from *Scharnhorst* and *Gneisenau* during the withdrawal from Norway, effectively caught napping without radar, aerial reconnaissance patrols or even having a lookout in the crow's nest. Both ships could have mounted offensive operations or been better employed escorting convoys.

The First Phase

In 1940 from the end of August to the end of September, U-boats sank twenty-two ships from four convoys, a loss of 113,000 tons of shipping. At the outset of this period, between 29 August and 2 September, six U-boats sank ten ships totalling 40,000 tons from three convoys, HX66, OA204 and OB205. Later in September, five U-boats sank twelve ships totalling 73,000 tons from convoy HX72 that had set sail from Halifax, Nova Scotia. This was just a start.

There were two main areas for the U-boats. The first was the 'Atlantic Gap', that part of the mid-Atlantic out of reach of shore-based maritime-reconnaissance aircraft from either the British Isles or North America. Convoys from the United States and Canada, and from the Caribbean, some of which would have come through the Panama Canal from the Pacific, were the targets in this vast area of ocean. The other was the Bay of Biscay and the Atlantic off Portugal. On this route passed convoys to and from Gibraltar, which itself was the dividing point from where convoys would either proceed across the Mediterranean or south to the African territories of the British Empire. Often, a Mediterranean and a South Atlantic convoy would sail as one from the UK as far as Gibraltar. As the situation in the Mediterranean became increasingly desperate, convoys for the Middle East and Australia were forced out of necessity to route past the Cape of Good Hope, avoiding the Suez Canal. During 1941 and 1942, the chances of convoys successfully crossing the Mediterranean were so slight that British forces in Egypt were also supplied by way of the Cape route and the Suez Canal.

October 1940, saw the situation worsen. In the North Channel between Britain and Ireland, during the four days from 17–20 October, nine U-boats found the convoys SC7 and HX79 with a total of seventy-nine ships. Between them, the U-boats sank no less than thirty-two of the ships with a total of 155,000 tons, and would have continued but for the fact that they had exhausted their torpedoes. Just a few days later, on 23 October, just two U-boats accounted for twelve ships, a total of 48,000 tons, from convoys SC11 and OB244. A further nine ships, 53,000 tons, were sunk from convoy HX90 by U-boats in December. To put the losses into perspective, during 1940, the average number of U-boats at sea in the operational zones each day was around a dozen. The massive build-up to 100 or so U-boats patrolling daily was some time away.

The U-boats were far from the sole predators. Armed and camouflaged merchantmen were deployed as auxiliary cruisers as early as April 1940, with *Atlantis, Orion, Pinguin, Thor* and *Widder* operating against Britain's trade routes, while in August the *Komet* managed to reach the Pacific by sailing north of Siberia. The term 'auxiliary cruiser' was hardly appropriate, as these vessels were disguised as merchantmen, sometimes from neutral countries, and only displayed their true colours, and intent, at the last minute, making their operations more akin to piracy. During that second winter of war, the battlecruisers *Gneisenau* and *Scharnhorst* and the heavy cruiser *Hipper* operated in the Atlantic, and with the heavy cruiser *Scheer* in the Atlantic and Indian oceans, managed to account for forty-nine ships, or 271,000 tons of shipping, between October and March.

Overall, Allied shipping losses, which meant British and French, totalled 509,320 tons during the final four months of 1939, concentrated entirely in the Atlantic and North Sea. The

65

following year, the total rose to 2,451,663 tons in the Atlantic and North Sea, with a further 13,170 tons in the Mediterranean and 12,223 tons in the Indian Ocean. Most of the North Sea was to be closed to convoys as a result of Germany holding the entire coastline of mainland Europe from the North Cape to the Bay of Biscay. The two worst months were June, with 356,937 tons lost in the Atlantic, a further 8,029 tons in the Mediterranean and 8,215 tons in the Indian Ocean, and October, when 361,459 tons were lost in the Atlantic. To put this into perspective, the loss for the year was almost a sixth of the available tonnage of merchant shipping, although this would have been boosted by new construction and by vessels that had fled from the German occupied territories, with Norway and the Netherlands both maritime nations having considerable tonnages of merchant shipping, and continued to operate with the British. Despite reaching a new monthly peak of 363,073 tons in May 1941, the overall total for the year fell to 2,214,408 tons in the Atlantic, but the figures for the Mediterranean rose to 54,200 tons, and while those for the Indian Ocean fell from 12,223 tons to 9,161 tons, no less than 40,666 tons were lost in the Pacific as Japan entered the war.

Denied the use of the 'treaty ports' in the Irish Republic, or Irish Free State as it was known at the time, the Allies used Londonderry in Northern Ireland, although it was less well-placed for this role than ports in the south and the west. More important than these ports, however, would have been the airfields that extended the area of the Atlantic that could have been patrolled by land-based maritime-reconnaissance aircraft.

The year 1941 saw more than 117,000 tons of shipping lost in January, but it was in February that major action was seen, with a convoy battle off Cape St Vincent, at the extreme south-west of Portugal, between 8 and 11 February. The term 'battle' was not too strong for this action, which involved U-boats and German air and surface units. Action started on 8 February when *U-37* spotted convoy HG53 and promptly sank two ships, before her reports prompted the Luftwaffe to send five long-range maritime-reconnaissance aircraft to attack the convoy, sinking five further ships. *U-37* then turned to a third ship, sinking that and then calling for the heavy cruiser *Hipper*, which sank a number of stragglers. Now active in the area and with no comparable British warship to stop her, *Hipper* found convoy SLS64 and sank seven ships.

In April and May, two more convoys were savaged by the U-boats. Between 2 and 4 April, six U-boats sank nine ships in convoy SC26, while between 19 and 22 May, HX126 was attacked by nine U-boats which sank another nine ships. Nevertheless, even without escort carriers to defend the convoys, the U-boats did not always have everything their own way. When convoys HX133 and OB336 were attacked by no less than fifteen U-boats between 20 and 29 June, with the loss of nine ships, the escort vessels were able to account for two of the U-boats and eventually drive away the remainder. Again, between 9 and 19 September, when the large convoy SC42 with seventy ships was attacked by fifteen U-boats with the loss of eighteen ships, two U-boats fell prey to the convoy escort. The size of the convoy was in itself some protection, attracting a heavier escort and also forcing the U-boats to divide their fire. Between 19 and 27 September, convoy HG73 lost ten of its twenty-five ships off Cape St Vincent, and worse was to come between 21 and 24 September when just three U-boats accounted for seven out of the eleven ships in convoy SL87.

Some of the pressure was taken off the Royal Navy and Royal Canadian Navy in that month when US Navy ships started to escort convoys as far as the mid-ocean meeting point. One of the first convoys to enjoy this protection was convoy SC48, which was attacked by nine U-boats between 15 and 18 October, losing nine of its thirty-nine ships plus two escorts.

The escort carrier first became involved in convoy protection with Convoy HG76 which sailed from Gibraltar to Britain on 14 December 1941, with thirty-two ships, including the CAM-ship *Darwin*, escorted by the Royal Navy's first escort carrier, HMS *Audacity*, two destroyers, four sloops and nine corvettes, which together made up the 36th Escort Group. The 36th was commanded by the then Commander F.J. 'Johnny' Walker (later Captain Walker, VC), the Royal Navy's leading anti-submarine commander in the sloop HMS *Stork*. Against this convoy were the seven U-boats of the *Seerauder* Group, which were guided onto the convoy by the Focke-Wulf Fw200 Condors of *1KG40* based in Bordeaux. At dusk on 15 December, the most southerly of the

U-boats discovered the convoy and was soon joined by a second boat. On the morning of 16 December, *U-131* was attacked by Wildcats flying from *Audacity*, before being attacked and sunk by destroyers. On 17 December, the destroyer *Stanley* was torpedoed by *U-434* and blew up, and in the frantic counter-attack led by Walker, *U-434* was depth-charged and forced to the surface, and then rammed and attacked by further depth charges. The convoy escorts had by this time also sunk *U-567*, commanded by *Kapitänleutnant* Engelbert Endrass, one of Germany's most experienced U-boat commanders. Nevertheless, the escort themselves suffered a bitter blow on 20 December when *Audacity* was torpedoed and sunk by *U-751*. However, despite the loss of the carrier, a destroyer and one of the merchantmen, four out of the seven U-boats were sunk.

It seems strange in retrospect that the ship carried Grumman Wildcats, known as Martlets to the Royal Navy at the time, rather than the Fairey Swordfish that were to prove the saviour of so many convoys when faced with U-boat attack, but passing through the Bay of Biscay, German maritime-reconnaissance aircraft were also a threat, and one against which the Swordfish were useless. An idea of how slow convoys could be when faced with bad weather and heavy attack can be gained from the fact that the convoy did not reach the UK until 23 December. Stranger still that while an escort carrier could be provided so early in the war, even in 1942 these ships were to be scarce when they were most needed and it would not be until 1943 that escort carriers and MAC-ships became commonplace.

Audacity had been a British prize, having started life as the Norddeutscher Line cargo ship *Hannover*, 5,500 gross registered tonnage, and captured by the British in the West Indies in March 1940. The Admiralty was under pressure to provide additional carriers and concerned less pressure grow so that much-needed battleships and cruisers might have to be converted, so approval was given in January 1941 for the captured ship to be converted to act as an escort carrier. The conversion was quick and distinctly rough and ready, as the ship had no hangar, meaning that her aircraft had to remain permanently on deck, while only the most rudimentary platform on the starboard side was available for both navigation and air control.

On 7 December, the Japanese had attacked the US Pacific Fleet in its forward base at Pearl Harbor in Hawaii, bringing the United States into the war. This was followed by Germany declaring war on the United States, something that would probably have happened anyway, but it seems incredible that Hitler should have drawn the USA into a European war prematurely, thus vastly increasing the resources that could be thrown against Germany. The one advantage to the German war effort was that immediately convoys in US home waters could be attacked. The lack of a convoy system off the US coastline at first, coupled with the lack of a blackout that meant that at night ships were shown in silhouette against the lights of American coastal towns and cities, meant that at first the U-boats enjoyed a high kill rate.

The Second Phase

Bringing the United States into the Second World War was the most dramatic move of the entire conflict, completely altering the strategic position. It formalized the unofficial alliance between the United States and the British Empire, and while the vital Lend-Lease supplies continued, it also opened the way for what some have described as 'reverse Lend-Lease', with a number of corvettes fitted with Asdic, or sonar, as it is now known, supplied to the US Navy from the British and Canadian fleets.

Nevertheless, the Germans were anxious to strike while the US Navy was still relatively weak with its available resources divided between the Atlantic and the Pacific. On 13 January 1942, the *Kriegsmarine* launched Operation *Paukenschlag*, or Operation Kettledrum Beat, against US shipping. Between January and March, they accounted for 1.2 million tons of Allied shipping in the Atlantic, with losses reaching a monthly total of 628,074 tons in June. The figure for the year was to be 5,366,973 tons for the Atlantic alone. Added to this, however, were figures for the Barents Sea at 234,158 tons, while in the Mediterranean losses had almost quadrupled to 193,644 tons as Malta began to starve to death, and 666,003 tons in the Indian Ocean, against which the Pacific losses of 85,494 tons faded into insignificance. The latter were undoubtedly a reflection of both the way in which the US Navy bounced back so quickly, taking the war to the Japanese and putting them on the defensive within six months of Pearl Harbor, and also Japanese inability to take the war to American convoys and merchant shipping.

The losses were increased by the decision during the winter of 1941–42 that the Allies should send convoys to the Soviet Union. There were three routes to the USSR, of which the most famous was the Arctic route off the coast of Norway and round the North Cape to Archangel and Murmansk, mainly carrying supplies from the UK but also including *matériel* from the United States, so that many of these convoys were routed via Iceland. This is given a chapter of its own. The other two routes included the main route from the United States via the South Atlantic and the Indian Ocean to the Gulf, with consignments offloaded in Iran for onward delivery to the USSR. A third route was from the West Coast of the USA and Canada to Vladivostok, but this was the least important in terms of equipment supplied, largely because the Trans-Siberian Railway was the only viable route to the battle-fronts and this had severe limitations on its capacity. The USSR did not need massive deliveries of supplies in the Far East as it would not declare war on Japan until shortly before the Japanese surrender in August 1945. Arctic convoy losses appeared in the Atlantic and Barents Sea figures as the route embraced both sectors.

Notable convoy actions in the Atlantic in early 1942 included convoy ONS67, which lost eight merchantmen to six U-boats between 21 and 25 February without any losses among the U-boats. Then, on 12 and 13 May, just two U-boats sank seven ships from convoy ONS92. One of the worst convoy losses of this desperate year was that of convoy SC94, whose thirty-six merchantmen were attacked by seventeen U-boats between 3 and 11 August, with eleven ships lost for just two U-boats. The following month, between 10 and 14 September ON127, whose thirty-two merchantmen had just six escorts, was attacked by thirteen U-boats, who accounted for seven merchantmen and one of the escorts, a destroyer, without any loss to themselves. October was little better, with SC104 losing eight ships between 12 and 14 October, with *U-221* accounting for five of the merchantmen, although on this occasion three U-boats were sunk. Later, on 27–29 October, HX212 lost six ships in attacks by four U-boats.

Convoy SL125 was another convoy that suffered a cruel fate when off Morocco during 27–31 October 1942, with just four escorts to look after thirty-seven merchantmen. Ten U-boats found the convoy and sank eleven merchant vessels. It is hard not to believe that this convoy was a 'tethered goat', there to attract the wolf pack, as the rush of U-boats to the convoy enabled the troop transports for the Allied landings in North Africa to pass completely unscathed. The landings were also significant as the first to be supported by escort carriers, strategic considerations giving the landings higher priority for these ships than convoy protection. This was sensible, as seizing North Africa ensured safer passages for ships through the Mediterranean, and released the equivalent of a considerable volume of shipping through once again allowing the Suez Canal to be used for its intended purpose, providing a short cut between Europe and the Indian Ocean.

The losses continued. Holding North Africa could only have a marginal impact on the Atlantic. Between 1 and 6 November, convoy DC107 lost fifteen out of forty-two merchantmen to attacks by thirteen U-boats, although two of these were sunk by the escorts. Then twenty U-boats were sent against ONS154 between 24 and 31 December, with the loss of another fourteen ships, some 70,000 tons of shipping, out of a total of forty-five.

Worse was to come in the New Year. Between 8 and 11 January 1943, convoy TM1, the first tanker convoy from Trinidad to North Africa, lost seven out of the nine tankers with their valuable fuel, necessary to push the Axis out of Africa. Once again twenty U-boats were deployed between 4 and 9 February to attack convoy SC118, sinking eleven ships totalling 60,000 tons, although three of the U-boats were sunk by the escorts. Later that same month, between 21 and 25 February, ON166 with forty-nine merchant-men was attacked by a large wolf pack of U-boats, with ten boats getting within firing range to sink fourteen ships totalling 88,000 tons for the loss of one U-boat. One of the largest U-boat packs came between 6 and 11 March, when SC121 with fifty-nine ships was attacked by twenty-seven U-boats, losing twelve ships while the U-boats escaped unscathed.

This period saw the U-boats at their maximum strength in the North Atlantic, when, from September 1943 to March 1944, there were more than 100 craft in the area at any one time. Hitler had by this time decided that the *Kriegsmarine*'s surface fleet was a waste of resources, and the entire burden of pursuing the German naval offensive fell to the submarine, but despite the U-boats building up for what was to be the largest convoy battle of the Second World War, a decisive naval engagement could not be found.

Two convoys sailed from New York. The first, SC122, departed on 5 March with fifty-four merchantmen, to be followed by the faster HX229 with forty ships on 8 March, which was scheduled to catch up with SC122 on 20 March. Speed was, of course, a relative term, since the large ocean liners could cross the Atlantic in five days. It also has to be recognized, however, that defensive measures against the U-boats did not simply consist of surface escorts and aircraft, whether carrier-borne or shore-based. The British had broken the German Enigma codes and by this time it was easier, although not always successful, to divert convoys away from the waiting patrol lines of U-boats.

The attacks started on 16 March, when up to forty U-boats found HX229 and over two days, the convoy lost ten ships. On 17 March, U-boats started to attack SC122. Plans for the two convoys to pass close together were abandoned and they spread out. In the days up to 20 March, twenty-one ships were lost to both convoys with a total of 141,000 tons, and just one U-boat sunk. The attacks stopped once the convoys were within range of shore-based maritime-reconnaissance aircraft from Northern Ireland.

This disastrous performance nevertheless marked the peak of the U-boat campaign. It would never be as effective again and losses would begin to mount, and bring with them a loss of experienced personnel so that the life of a U-boat and its crew began to shorten dramatically. The arrival of the MAC-ships and the escort carriers were behind this complete change in the fortunes of the German submariner. Indeed, some would argue that the great convoy battle of 16–20 March 1943 had in itself marked the start of the decline of the U-boat as the massive fleet of 100 submarines had been at sea for some time without finding and sinking a single merchantman. In fact, the entire U-boat campaign showed the same kind of missed opportunities that bedevilled the operations of the German surface fleet during the war years. Poor air-sea coordination was one feature, but poor strategy and bad tactics also played a part.

One authority on the wartime German Navy, Jak Mallman Showell, maintains that two-thirds of the U-boat fleet, some 800 craft, never got within reach of the enemy, and that half of those that did only attacked four or fewer Allied ships. Most of the Allied losses were down to just 131 U-boats.

On 23 March, just a few days after the heavy losses suffered by the convoys SC122 and HX229, another convoy left Canada for the UK, but despite repeated attacks by U-boats, crossed safely to arrive on 8 April without a single ship being lost. This was despite the 'Atlantic Gap' still being some 500 miles wide.

The Birth of Canadian Naval Aviation

As the convoy war raged, the evidence was growing that air power at sea was vital. In Canada, plans for a Royal Canadian Naval Air Service dated from 1918, but had, in the words of one Canadian historian, 'been stillborn'. Post-war, in 1920 Admiral Lord Jellicoe had drawn up plans for a Canadian fleet, including aircraft carriers, but the Royal Canadian Navy barely survived post-war, and even the Royal Canadian Air Force had a difficult and prolonged birth. By 1942, it had become clear that aviation had to be part of any navy that wished to or needed to engage the enemy on the high seas or in distant waters. Many Canadians had managed to make their way to the UK and join the Fleet Air Arm. Further pressure on the Royal Canadian Navy to play a part in naval aviation came in December 1942, when the Admiralty in London asked for more Canadians to train as aircrew for the Fleet Air Arm while remaining in the Royal Canadian Navy. This could be viewed as a cheeky way for a hard-pressed Imperial power to ask the Canadian taxpayer to pay for those of their fellow countrymen assigned to the Fleet Air Arm, but it was also the case that none of the dominions took defence seriously between the two world wars, leaving much to the United Kingdom.

Captain Nelson Lay, RCN, Director of Operations, and Captain Harry de Wolf, Director of Naval Plans, pressed Vice Admiral (later Admiral) P. W. Nelles, Chief of the Canadian Naval Staff, to send senior officers to obtain up-to-date information on naval air operations, and the escort carriers in particular. They also proposed that Canada should have four escort carriers, one for each of the four escort groups provided by Canadian ships in the Atlantic.

De Wolf left to command a warship shortly afterwards and it was not until spring 1943, that Lay was able to visit both the United States and the United Kingdom, spending two weeks with the US Navy and two months with the Royal Navy. The greater amount of time spent with the Royal Navy was a reflection of attitudes at the time, when the 'British' model was usually taken rather than the American one. He made a report in August, proposing a Royal Canadian Naval Air Service modelled on the Fleet Air Arm. By this time he recommended that two escort carriers be obtained to be manned and operated by Royal Canadian Navy personnel, while shore-based long-range maritime-reconnaissance would remain the preserve of the Royal Canadian Air Force, again following United Kingdom practice rather than that of the United States. One difference between Canadian and British practice, however, was that the Royal Canadian Air Force would also provide support for Canadian naval aviation at shore bases, and this was to have longer term post-war implications for Canadian naval aviation.

The two escort carriers soon proved to be *Nabob* and *Puncher*, commissioned in September 1943 and February 1944 respectively. These were built in Seattle and moved to Vancouver in nearby British Columbia for the modifications, including installing additional watertight sub-divisions, that the British regarded as so necessary and so irritated the Americans. The Royal Canadian Navy wanted the carriers for anti-submarine operations in support of convoy escort groups, but the Royal Navy had decided that these were to be strike carriers, and won the argument because, so that Canada did not appear to be receiving Lend-Lease aid from the United States, the ships remained on the Royal Navy's strength and were commissioned as HMS rather than HMCS. Captain Lay took command of *Nabob*, while Captain Roger Bidwell took command of *Puncher*.

If the Canadians were unhappy that *Nabob* was to operate in the strike role rather than hunting submarines, at least she was involved in some of the more notable operations of the war, attacking the German battleship *Tirpitz* cowering in a Norwegian fjord. For *Puncher* at first the war was irksome and boring, for after she went to sea for the first time in April 1944, her initial role was that of an aircraft ferry and occasional troopship. It was not until February 1945 that an operational role came to her, when four-teen Grumman Wildcats of the Fleet Air Arm's No. 881 Squadron were flown on with four Fairey Barracudas of No. 821. Then those aboard had plenty of action, again off the coast of Norway, but in her case her first action was against German surface convoys. Then she joined HMS *Premier* and provided fighter escorts for that ship's Grumman Avengers on minelaying operations, something known earlier in the war to the Royal Air Force as 'gardening', no doubt because minefields are 'sown'. The next operation was to cover more minelaying but also to protect British minesweepers. In early April, *Puncher* was to be part of a four carrier group to attack a U-boat base at Kilbotn in Norway that had been menacing the Arctic convoys, but bad weather caused the operation to be cancelled. With five operations under her belt, and the Royal Navy not needing her in the Pacific, Captain Bidwell's final task was to take the ship home to Norfolk, Virginia, where he handed her back to the US Navy in January 1946.

The Third Phase

Naturally, the change in the fortunes of both the convoys and the U-boats did not happen overnight, although the change was spread over a fairly short period. The third phase of the Battle of the Atlantic started with two successes for the U-boats.

Between 4 and 7 April 1943, fifteen U-boats sank six ships, 41,000 tons of shipping, from convoy HX231, although this cost two U-boats. Then on 30 April and 1 May, *U-515* found a convoy off Freetown in Sierra Leone, and sank seven ships totalling 43,000 tons with nine torpedoes. The success of *U-515*, while outstanding, was by this time the exception. In 1940, each U-boat on patrol sank an average of six merchantmen per month, but by 1942–43, it took more than two U-boats to sink a single merchantman.

Nevertheless, April and May 1943 are regarded as being a turning point in the Battle of the Atlantic. From this time on, the U-boats would be on the defensive. The successes of March and April became a disaster in May when more than forty U-boats were lost, many of them to aerial attack, while others were the result of collaboration between aircraft and surface escorts. Technical innovation would not be enough to ensure the survival of the U-boats. Schnorkels were progressively introduced from this time onwards to enable U-boats to recharge their batteries without surfacing, and indeed to run on diesel power under water. Heavier anti-aircraft armaments were also progressively introduced, although often at the cost of reducing speed while submerged still further. In fact, attacking a U-boat that elected to remain surfaced in an aircraft such as a Fairey Swordfish, the obsolescent biplane operated from MAC-ships and the anti-submarine aircraft of choice for the British and Canadian escort carriers, took some nerve. On the other hand, a fast well-armoured aircraft such as those operated by the Royal Air Force and US Navy was a different matter altogether and for most U-boat commanders, the crucial factor was just how fast they could dive, known to them as the 'Battle of the Seconds'. Even so, there were a small number of instances of a U-boat inflicting fatal damage on a landplane, but the odds were against it, as the armament was too light and the firing platform unstable in the heavy Atlantic swell.

Between them, the MAC-ships and the escort carriers closed the 'Atlantic Gap', the 500 miles or so of mid-ocean that lay beyond the range of shore-based aircraft, forcing the U-boats to abandon their pack tactics. The impact on merchant shipping losses was dramatic, falling from fifty ships in August 1942 to just sixteen between September 1943 and May 1944, and only another five between then and VE-Day a year later.

Life aboard the escort carriers was hard and often uncomfortable, while aircrew were often waiting for hours in the ready room as the ship, single screw and hence more likely to roll, plodded at convoy speed across the Atlantic. Nevertheless, there were distractions and one visitor, spotting aircrew squatting on the deck in the ready room playing dice or poker, thought that they looked 'like a lot of thugs out of *The Rake's Progress* gambling in a graveyard'.

The Fourth Phase

The fourth phase of the Battle of the Atlantic was marked by continual German technical innovation pitched against growing Allied aerial superiority.

Allied tactics started to change during this period, with a return to 'hunter-killer' operations as intelligence on U-boat operations improved. The early 'hunter-killer' groups were in the mid and South Atlantic and operated by the US Navy, although later British and combined British-Canadian groups were formed. One reason for the creation of the 'hunter-killer' groups was that as the Atlantic gap was closed by the escort carriers, U-boat tactics changed. The *Kriegsmarine* ordered the U-boats away from the North Atlantic shipping lanes and into the mid and South Atlantic.

On 11 June 1944, *U-490*, the last of the supply U-boats that had acted as *milch* cows for the fleet during extended operations, was sunk. Too late, on 12 June 1944, *U-2321*, a class XXIII boat and the first of the much needed electro-submarines, was commissioned, to be followed on 27 June by *U-2501*, the first large electro-submarine of class XXI. The pennant numbers give a false impression of the numbers of U-boats built – there were just under 1,200 commissioned altogether and the '2000' series pennant numbers indicate a step-change in capability.

Amongst the changes introduced as the war progressed were acoustic torpedoes, but these seem to have been more of a hindrance as they failed to work successfully, and the explosions heard by the U-boat crews convinced them that the convoy escorts had been destroyed when they hadn't. Direction finding anti-convoy torpedoes also seem to have failed to meet expectations.

Allied anti-submarine operations also underwent a radical change during the fourth phase. Convoys continued to be escorted and to enjoy the close protection of one or two escort carriers, but now anti-submarine sweeps by 'hunter-killer' forces of escorts with one or two escort carriers also re-appeared following American success with these techniques in the mid and South Atlantic. To say that anti-submarine sweeps 're-appeared' is simply to recognize that this was the technique that had fallen into disuse following the loss of the British fleet carrier HMS *Courageous* in September 1939, but this time the techniques were different. *Courageous* had just two escorts to protect her, and by this time between four and six per carrier was more usual. More important, *Courageous* had been hoping to find a submarine, but the late war task groups knew where they would find U-boats refuelling and taking on supplies from the supply submarines, replacing hope with a high degree of certainty. Direction finding could detect the radio 'chatter' between U-boats, including their signals to base, while the breaking of the German Enigma codes also meant that the location of the ocean refuelling and re-supply points became known. The submarines were now the hunted. Refuelling a U-boat at sea was difficult enough, transferring stores and ammunition between two low lying craft rolling and pitching in a heavy mid-ocean swell was much more so, with the problems compounded by hatches that were too small for efficient stowage of supplies, but big enough for large waves to enter.

VI

HUNTER-KILLER FORCES

A significant feature of the fourth and final phase of the Battle of the Atlantic was that the Allies switched to completely different tactics. It was still wise to provide protection for convoys, but instead of waiting in effect for the U-boats to come and find Allied shipping, the emphasis switched to searching for enemy submarines. One reason for the change was that the location of the U-boats was known to the Allies, thanks to Ultra intelligence, intercepts of the German Enigma codes. One weakness of the German submarine campaign was the regular reports sent from U-boat commanders, and the instructions from the centre, so necessary for the wolf packs to operate successfully. Even so, the chances of finding a U-boat were far from certain.

The Capture of *U-505*

One of the most spectacular successes of these groups occurred on 4 June 1944, when the escort carrier USS *Guadalcanal*, commanded by Captain (later Rear Admiral) Daniel Gallery, US Navy, operating with the destroyer escorts *Chatelain*, *Jenks* and *Pillsbury*, managed to force the large Type IXC U-boat *U-505* to the surface north-west of Dakar in West Africa, and then board her and take her captive.

A Casablanca-class CVE, *Guadalcanal* had already a creditable record of anti-submarine warfare, both leading 'hunter-killer' groups and as a convoy escort. Built at the Kaiser Shipyard in Vancouver, Washington, *Guadalcanal* had been laid down on 5 January 1943, launched on 5 June of that year, and commissioned on 25 September at Astoria, Oregon. Sailing through the Panama Canal she had arrived at Norfolk, Virginia, on 3 December, leaving on her first war 'cruise' or patrol on 2 January 1944 with four destroyers and her air group, VC-13, to form Task Group 22.3. On 16 January, her Grumman Avengers had used rockets and bombs to sink *U-544*. This was lucky, as many escort carriers made three or four patrols before sinking their first U-boat. The patrol was marred by an accident one day as an Avenger returned from an anti-submarine patrol, missed the arrester wires and bounced right over the barrier, landing in the middle of the last five operational Avengers parked forward on the flight deck, damaging them. It was simply fortunate that nobody was injured, but it was the end of the first cruise.

Guadalcanal was one of the first US escort carriers to place considerable emphasis on night flying, the reasoning being that U-boats were more likely to be found on the surface at night charging their batteries. This was obviously far more fruitful from the sub-hunting aspect, but also far more dangerous for the aircrew, and indeed for many others on board as well. On one night landing, an Avenger made a bad approach and missed the arrester wires, so the pilot opened up the throttle to go round again but, as he was too far to starboard, he hit the bridge with his wing, the aircraft spun around and ended up at the base of the island, blocking the only way out for those on the bridge, leaving them trapped and spilling aviation fuel which burst into flames. By some miracle, the three crewmen got out of the aircraft with just minor injuries, but amidst the burning wreckage were five live depth charges. Captain Gallery recalled:

> We knew that if those depth charges behaved the way the Navy Department claimed they would they could stand a petrol fire for about three minutes before blowing up. In about two and a half minutes our flight deck crew got the fire put out, and heaved the depth charges overboard.[1]

Her second operation, leaving the United States in March, with VC-53 embarked, as a convoy escort had been even more successful, on the homeward leg from Casablanca to the United States, on the night of 8 April, off the Azores, one of the Avengers caught *U-515* on the surface outward bound from the French port of Lorient and made a depth charge attack, although these exploded too far from the submarine to do serious damage. The next day, her aircraft and the destroyers *Chatelain, Flaherty, Pillsbury,* and *Pope* used rockets and depth charges to destroy *U-515.* The following day, after dark, they caught *U-68* on the surface in bright moonlight re-charging her batteries 300 miles south of the Azores and once again attacked with depth charges and rocket fire, sinking her. The convoy arrived safely at Norfolk on 26 April 1944.

It was after the sinking of *U-515* that the idea occurred to Gallery of the capture of a German submarine. The feeling was that they had come close to being able to do this, with *U-515,* and that an opportunity had been missed. This was not the first time that a submarine had been boarded and captured as the latest German Enigma codes had been captured after a German submarine, *U-570,* had been captured by a British escort vessel south of Iceland in August 1941.

On her third operation, *Guadalcanal* left Hampton Roads on 15 May, heading a 'hunter-killer' group. No doubt morale was affected adversely by the news that a sister carrier, the USS *Block Island,* had been torpedoed and sunk on a similar operation. After a fruitless two weeks patrolling the North Atlantic, on 4 June, 1944, Captain Daniel Gallery in command decided to head for North Africa to refuel. Just ten minutes after changing course, the destroyer *Chatelain* detected a submarine, which turned out to be *U-505,* and immediately launched a depth charge attack. A second depth charge attack was assisted by Grumman Wildcat fighter aircraft from *Guadalcanal,* which circled the spot where she had dived, marking this by firing their machine guns onto the water. The second attack blew a hole in the outer hull of the submarine, and rolled the U-boat on its beam ends. Her commanding officer was inexperienced and hearing shouts from the conning tower, decided to blow his tanks and surface, appearing just 700 yards from *Chatelain.* A torpedo from the destroyer missed the submarine, but the escorts, *Chatelain, Pillsbury* and *Jenks,* all opened fire and were sooned joined by the *Guadalcanal* and the two remaining escorts, *Pope* and *Flaherty,* while aircraft joined the attack, encouraging the U-boat's crew to abandon ship.

This was just the opportunity that Captain Gallery had planned for, having already prepared boarding parties for such an eventuality. He ordered a boat from the destroyer *Pillsbury* to head for *U-505* and board her.

> As the sub surfaced it flashed through my mind, 'Here is exactly the situation we were hoping for. This is where we came in on the *U-515*!' So I grabbed the mike on the bridge and broadcast, 'I want to capture this bastard if possible.'[2]

Under the command of Lieutenant JG (Junior Grade, with one-and-a-half rings on his uniform) David, *Pillsbury*'s boarding party went across to the submarine, by this time completely unmanned but running slowly on the surface in circles, leapt onto the submarine and found it abandoned. David and his men quickly dived below decks, anxious to at least capture the boat's papers and codes, in a repeat of an earlier incident in which a British destroyer had gained the key to the German Enigma codes, while others started to close valves. They eventually managed to stop the engines to allow *Pillsbury* to get a tow-line to the submarine. Next on the scene was a larger salvage party from *Guadalcanal*, helping to stop the leaks and prepare the U-boat for towing. Once the towline was secured and the German survivors picked up, the carrier started for Bermuda, towing the submarine until the fleet tug *Abnaki* could take over this task. The entire group arrived without further incident in Bermuda on 19 June. The submarine eventually reached the United States, yielding considerable valuable information about German submarine technology. To keep the Germans unaware of what had happened, the entire affair was kept secret until the end of the war. Captain Gallery explained:

> David and his party of eight took their lives in their hands when they boarded that U-boat. They had every reason to believe they would be greeted by a blast of machine gun bullets when they started down the hatch. They also knew that all German subs were fitted with fourteen time-fused demolition charges, but they didn't know what time it was by the German's clocks. This made no difference to David and his boys.
> David got the Congressional Medal of Honor for this job.

Only one other was awarded in the Battle of the Atlantic. His two principal helpers, Knispel and Wdowiak, should have got it too, but they had to settle for Navy Crosses.[3]

The German crew had started to scuttle the U-boat and she was rapidly filling with water. When the boading party pulled the switches to stop the main motors, she started to go down by the stern, so that they had no option but to start the motors again to maintain headway and keep the stern up. In fact, once they had time to look over the U-boat, they found that the damage had been confined to her external ballast tanks and that the pressure hull was intact.

U-505 was the first enemy warship captured on the high seas by the US Navy since 1815. *Guadalcanal* and her escorts shared a Presidential Unit Citation.

Hunter-Killer Groups

Another escort carrier that saw service on a hunter-killer group was the British conversion HMS *Vindex*. This ship had been laid down as the fast cargo liner, *Port Sydney*, but was commissioned in late 1943 as an auxiliary aircraft carrier intended for service on the Arctic convoys to Murmansk and Archangel. *Vindex* left the Clyde on 9 March 1944 to conduct operations against U-boats threatening transatlantic convoys. The intention was that she would operate with a second carrier, the Attacker-class US-conversion HMS *Striker*, but escorts were still in short supply and *Striker* was needed for a convoy from West Africa to Gibraltar. Initially, *Vindex* was to be supported by a destroyer, two frigates and two corvettes of the 6th Escort Group, a Royal Canadian Navy flotilla.

While the initial US Navy operations had been daylight only, *Vindex* carried six Sea Hurricanes and twelve Swordfish, but with just eight complete Swordfish crews, and was able to operate by day and by night. While the risk of enemy air attack diminished as the task group steamed further west into the mid-Atlantic, the fighters were able to operate daylight patrols, looking for U-boats, while the Swordfish would handle the night patrols.

Aboard, a chart of the North Atlantic showed the position of

Allied ships and convoys, and U-boats, indicated by little black swastika flags. Between Fastnet Rock, off Ireland, and Cape Race, Newfoundland, there was an area where the little black swastikas were thickest; the main concentration of U-boats. On 10 March, *Vindex* and her escorts were well on their way, and at dawn she went to action stations and began to zigzag, only breaking off to fly off or receive her aircraft. The decision was taken to use the fighters to fly patrols during the hours of daylight, reserving the Swordfish for night operations.

The first of the nocturnal Swordfish operations was flown-off at 20:25, with a second at 20:40. Just forty minutes later, one of the escort vessels had a U-boat contact, and *Vindex* herself turned northwards to investigate, at the same time flying-off a third Swordfish. The contact was lost and the last Swordfish was recalled, and then after a further thirty minutes, the carrier had to turn into the wind again to receive one of the original Swordfish that had developed engine trouble. Just before midnight, two more Swordfish were put into the air before the duty Swordfish could be landed. A further patrol of two Swordfish was sent off at 01:30 on 11 March, and these in turn landed on after the dawn patrol of yet another two Swordfish was dispatched at 04:00, with one of the observers, Lieutenant (A) Paul House, RNVR, having only landed from a patrol just before midnight. At 06:30, the Sea Hurricanes took over the task of patrolling. At this stage, the carrier stopped her zigzag pattern.

The return of daylight did not mean that the Swordfish were stood down with the exception of an aircraft kept on standby. There was also a difference in patrol patterns as the Sea Hurricanes, like most British fighters of the day, were markedly short on range and could only patrol for an hour or so, in contrast to the three hours or more of the Swordfish. At noon, two Swordfish were scrambled to investigate an empty Carley float – no doubt evidence of an earlier sinking – and while the investigation was made, *Vindex* resumed zigzagging. The zigzags ended on confirmation that the Carley float was not a threat, and the Canadian destroyer HMCS *Qu'Appelle* then came astern of the carrier to refuel. While refuelling astern was the standard practice for the Royal Navy in the Second World War, on this occasion it was a particularly lengthy operation, taking more than six hours, as it had to be interrupted twice for aircraft alarms while the carrier resumed zigzagging. During refuelling, a Royal Air Force Short Sunderland flying boat attacked a U-boat 250 miles west of Rockall, while another was discovered and disabled by bombing 350 miles off Valentia on the west of Ireland. Shortly after 19:30, just as the refuelling hose was recovered, the carrier's Asdic had a contact 400 yards off the port bow. *Vindex* turned in the direction of the contact, around which underwater explosions could be heard as she was attacked by one of the escorts.

By this time it was 20:00 and the first of the Swordfish patrols resumed as two aircraft took-off into a clear moonlit night. The first of these, flown by Lieutenant (A) Gordon Bennett, RNVR, spotted a U-boat running on the surface shortly before they were due to return to the carrier, and dived to the attack, dropping two 250-lb depth charges that straddled the submarine, but both failed to explode. Another U-boat on the surface was detected by the other aircraft's ASV radar, and the observer guided the pilot, Sub Lieutenant Peter Cumberland, towards it. As they dived into the attack, the submarine rather than dive decided to counter with AA fire, and as they dropped their depth charges, both Sub Lieutenant Frank Jackson, the observer, and the TAG, John Stone, were wounded. Again there had been no sign of an exploding depth charge, and expecting the submarine to dive, Cumberland dropped a marker flare and returned to the ship. Jackson's injuries were not serious, his parachute pack had suffered the worst of it, but the AA shell that had caused the damage had passed through the soft silk of the parachute to kill Stone, although his crewmates did not know this until after they had returned to the carrier. A third Swordfish had used Cumberland's flare to home in on and then attack the U-boat, again dropping depth charges which in this instance bounced off the casing causing sparks, but no explosion.

It soon became clear that *Vindex* had depth charges that would not explode. It was not until flying was largely suspended during bad weather on 17 March that consideration could be given to the reasons for the depth charges failing to explode. Investigation soon showed that this was caused by a manufacturing fault, slight in itself but enough to ensure that the risks taken by the Swordfish crews together with the hazarding of a valuable aircraft were in vain.

This was not the only risk to the Swordfish crews, for it was easy to become lost in the dull grey reaches of the Atlantic. One Swordfish on patrol after taking-off at 02:45 on 12 March was directed to the *Qu'Appelle* which had reported a contact. Finding the destroyer zigzagging furiously, the Swordfish observer asked if the destroyer would be able to give him a course to steer to the carrier once the search was finished, allowing him to concentrate on using the ASV radar for his search. The destroyer agreed, and the Swordfish crew then spent two hours searching the ocean with the destroyer until finally the ship radioed that contact with the U-boat had been lost. Deciding to return to the carrier, the observer asked for a course, only to be told that the destroyer's officer of the watch had no idea where his ship was, and suggested that the Swordfish ditch. The Swordfish pilot, Sub Lieutenant Norman Sharrock, climbed to 3,000 feet, at which point his observer, Sub Lieutenant Brian Jones, was able to pick up the carrier and her escorts some thirty miles away, and also give the destroyer her position.

The Swordfish continued to patrol, however, and the Canadians were joined on 13 March by the five sloops of the 2nd Escort Group. The following morning shortly before noon while re-fuelling *Qu'Appelle* a torpedo was spotted heading for the carrier, her CO ordered the rudder hard to starboard with emergency full speed ahead, and successfully combed the torpedo, while the destroyer continued to take on fuel.

In fact, 14 March turned out to be an eventful day, having started with a Swordfish achieving the rare feat for this aircraft of hitting the crash barrier. That night, Sharrock took off, and almost as soon as he left the deck, his engine failed and the aircraft crashed into the sea. The precious carrier, vulnerable to U-boat attack, sailed on, leaving the Swordfish crew to be picked up by a Canadian frigate. They were lucky – the aircraft sank quickly with its four depth charges, which once again failed to explode, although whether this was because these too were duds once again, or because the safety device that by this time prevented depth charges still attached to the aircraft from exploding worked, was a question that could never be answered. The bad news was that the engine failure seemed to be due to water in the aircraft's fuel.

Fuel was also becoming a problem for *Vindex*, and for her escorts. Unless the carrier could be refuelled herself from a passing tanker in a convoy, the choice was between reducing the carrier's own time at sea or refusing to refuel the smaller escorts. Fortunately, some of the escorts cut out the carrier as the 'middle man' to refuel themselves from a tanker. Meanwhile, the weather worsened, so that on 17 March there was little flying.

Having regained the carrier, Sharrock and his crew must have felt more comfortable aboard the larger ship, having felt slightly 'green' aboard the destroyer. They seemed to be fated, however, as the weather became worse, and on 22 March, flying became impossible once again and all aircraft had to be struck down into the hangar. That night, the carrier's gyros failed and then so did the steering, leaving her to be steered by engines alone. Many of the compartments, or flats, and mess decks were flooded. The steering gear was repaired quickly enough, but even emergency power was threatened by flooding of the aft switchboard.

Flying resumed at 09:00 on 23 March, even though the flight deck was pitching forty feet. Sharrock and his crew were once again amongst the aircraft waiting to take-off, a finely judged operation ideally conducted just as *Vindex* was beginning to lift herself out of a trough. Commander Flying gave Sharrock the green light as the carrier's bows moved to the top of a crest, but by the time the Swordfish reached the end of the flight deck *Vindex* was pointing down into the next trough and the aircraft flew slap into a large wave. The TAG, Chris Williams, was not wearing his safety line, the 'monkey chain', and was catapulted out of the aircraft into the sea. In the days before angled flight decks, such a situation could result in the aircraft being run down by the carrier, but Captain Bayliss acted promptly to turn his ship hard to starboard, so hard in fact that she almost looked as if she was about to fall over.

Sharrock and his observer, Brian Jones, struggled to the surface and found themselves clear of the ship, but as he came to the surface, Williams could hear a booming sound, which he thought might have been the depth charges going off. It wasn't, it was the sound of the sea hitting the ship, and he had come right up against the carrier's hull. He heard someone shout, 'Watch for the screws!' and struck away from the ship, and when he next turned, he saw *Vindex*'s stern disappearing over the crests of the waves. Meanwhile, Sharrock had managed to inflate his own personal dinghy. Williams spotted the crew dinghy while lifted upon the crest of a wave, and swam to it, only to find that it had only partially inflated. Just as he was trying to repair a small hole and complete inflation, he heard Jones, a poor swimmer who had been unable to inflate his Mae West, shouting. Williams wanted Jones to cling to the side of the dinghy while he pumped it up, but by this time Jones was in a bad way, and instead clambered on to the dinghy which promptly folded up. Only when Sharrock joined them in his one-man dinghy, did they manage to keep afloat. Shortly afterwards, one of the escorts steamed past them, seeming not to see them, but they were soon rescued by another Canadian frigate, *Waskesieu*.

Theirs was not the only accident. At 01:25 the following morning, a returning Swordfish missed the arrester wires as the ship pitched badly, and the undercarriage was then torn off by the safety barrier, leaving the aircraft to pancake heavily on the deck, grinding to a halt as fuel gushed from a broken pipe. The aircraft still had two depth charges on the rack under the lower mainplane. Pilot and observer undid their harnesses and jumped out, but the TAG had forgotten to undo his 'monkey chain' and didn't realize this until he was brought up short. He quickly dashed back to undo it. Meanwhile, he was joined by the observer, anxious to save his dividers, by which time the aircraft was on fire. The duty flight deck party then came forward with hoses, and played a hose on the one depth charge that could be seen, but at 01:45 a depth charge on the other side of the burning aircraft exploded, punching a hole eight feet by four feet in the flight deck and a smaller hole in the hangar deck, sending a thin sliver of metal to kill a young seaman asleep in the forward recreational space which was used by the off-duty flight deck party in case they were needed in a hurry. The fire was brought under control at 01:55, and by 02:30 the carrier was able to receive the other Swordfish of the patrol that had had to remain in the air, hoping that the fire would be put out while their fuel lasted. The charred remains of the wrecked Swordfish were

1. Intended to be the forerunner of the escort carrier, the merchant aircraft carriers or MAC-ships, did not enter service until 1943, by which time the escorts were also arriving. Here is *Adula* with a Fairey Swordfish taking off. *(via Lord Kilbracken)*

2. Here is a Swordfish about to land on *Adula*, with little room for any mistakes. *(via Lord Kilbracken)*

3. One of the early escort carriers was HMS *Avenger*, which saw service on the first Arctic convoy to have air cover, PQ18. She is seen here with six Hawker Sea Hurricanes on her flight deck. *(IWM FL1268)*

4. The lack of any folding wings on the Sea Hurricane was a problem, taking up space and reducing a carrier's aircraft capacity. This Sea Hurricane is on the lift of HMS *Avenger*. *(IWM A10982)*

5. One of the earlier US escort carriers was the USS *Altamaha*, CVE-18, one of the Bogue-class, known in Royal Navy service as the Attacker-class. Here she appears to be on transport duties in the Pacific. *(US Naval Institute)*

6. Another of the Bogue-class was the USS *Breton*, CVE-23, which was used exclusively as an aircraft transport in the Pacific theatre. *(US Naval Institute)*

7. The Bogue-class ships in British service under Lend-Lease were the Attacker-class; here is HMS *Attacker* herself, with aircraft ranged aft ready for operations.
(FAAM CARS A/216)

8. One of the few British conversions was HMS *Campania*, seen here in the hands of tugs as she enters port. *(FAAM CARS C/213)*

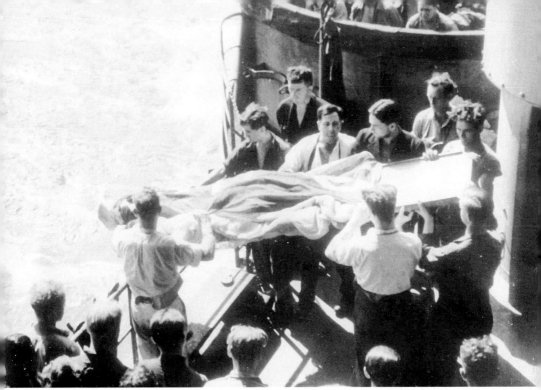

9. Apart from the weather and enemy attack, accidents could and did happen. Here is the funeral of a young rating killed when he was struck by the propeller of an aircraft whilst working on the flight deck of HMS *Attacker*. *(FAAM CARS A/238)*

10. The escort carriers arrived at a time when the Royal Navy was changing over to cafeteria messing, rather than having men eating and sleeping in the same confined space. This is aboard HMS *Avenger*. *(IWM A10960)*

11. This is the wardroom or officers' mess aboard another escort carrier, HMS *Atheling*, one of the class variously known as the Ruler or Ameer-class, which were actually laid down as carriers using a merchant ship hull design. This ship seems to be in port as there are lady guests in the background. *(via Mrs M.J. Schupke)*

12. Two British escort carriers *Biter* and *Avenger* in line astern seen from the flight deck of the fast armoured carrier HMS *Victorious*. The aircraft in the foreground are Supermarine Seafires. *(FAAM CARS B6)*

13. Landing on any carrier could be difficult in bad weather, especially as aircraft weights increased and carrier sizes dropped as with the escort carriers. This is a fire aboard HMS *Tracker* whilst on Arctic convoy duty, with added urgency given to the fire fighting to stop the flames reaching the ready-use ammunition locker for the aft AA armament. *(IWM A22863)*

14. The need for more naval pilots meant that two lakes steamers were converted so that the urgently-needed escort carriers were available for operational duties. This is the USS *Wolverine*. *(US Naval Institute)*

15. The USS *Natoma Bay*, CVE-62, was one of the Casablanca-class ships, seen here in the Pacific, where she operated initially on transport duties before a spell helping in pilot training, and then returning to support the advance towards Japan.

(US Naval Institute)

16. A sister ship was the USS *White Plains*, seen here being assisted by the yard tug *Wenonah*, YT-148. The carrier has just been repainted in Measure 33 camouflage.

(US Naval Institute)

17. Another of the Casablanca-class, the USS *Kitkun Bay,* CVE-71, was used initially as an aircraft transport before moving to combat duties in the Pacific, where she was badly damaged in a kamikaze attack. *(US Naval Institute)*

18. When the Royal Navy returned to the Pacific, British aircraft markings had to change with the red inner of the roundels changed to pale blue to avoid confusion with the Japanese 'rising sun' markings. Here are Hellcats flying past HMS *Ruler.* *(FAAM CARS R6)*

19. Despite wartime, many of the traditions were maintained, such as courtesy visits, but only if operational considerations allowed it. Here are senior British officers aboard HMS *Khedive* with King Farouk of Egypt during a call at Alexandria whilst on passage to the Far East. The aircraft is a Seafire. *(IWM A28114)*

20. A more usual carrier group posing for a photograph were these maintainers aboard HMS *Striker*. *(via S.H. Wragg)*

21. The USS *Makin Island,* CVE-93, with aircraft ranged aft ready for operations. This carrier was present at Lingayen Gulf, Iwo Jima and Okinawa. *(US Naval Institute)*

22. By contrast, another Casablanca, the USS *Bouganville*, CVE-100, is seen here in the role of an aircraft transport, showing just how many more aircraft can be crammed onto a flight deck when operational flying is not needed. *(US Naval Institute)*

23. The USS *Munda*, last of the Casablanca-class, lying at anchor. Originally to be named *Tonowek Bay*, by this time the names of recent actions in the Pacific were being assigned to escort carriers. *(US Naval Institute)*

24. HMS *Nabob* was manned by a mixed ship's company of Royal Navy and Royal Canadian Navy personnel, which led to many problems at first. *(Canadian Armed Forces)*

25. Nevertheless, when a crisis came, the crew pulled together well. This is HMS
Nabob after being torpedoed, down in the water at the stern, but safely back at
Scapa Flow, the anchorage on the mainland of Orkney.   *(Canadian Armed Forces)*

26. High performance fighters such as the Grumman Hellcat could operate from
escort carriers, and did so providing cover for strikes against targets in Norway and
the Far East. This one has just caught the wire.   *(Northrop Grumman)*

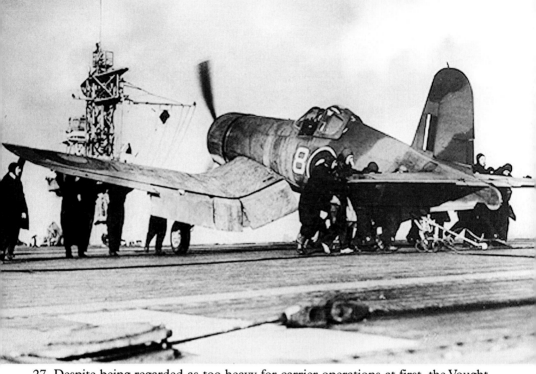

27. Despite being regarded as too heavy for carrier operations at first, the Vought Corsair found its way onto both fleet carriers and, as seen here being unhooked, escort carriers. Many regarded this as the best naval fighter of the war.

(Vought Aircraft)

28. This is HMS *Ameer*, one of the British ships that made it east of Suez towards the end of the war for operations against the Japanese in Burma and Malaya.

(C.S. 'Bill' Drake)

29. One role that fell to the escort carrier on many occasions was that of refuelling escort vessels on convoy protection and anti-submarine 'hunter-killer' groups. On this occasion, HMS *Ameer* is refuelling her plane guard destroyer, a case of enlightened self-interest as the destroyer is there to rescue aircrew.   *(C.S. 'Bill' Drake)*

30. HMS *Empress*, another of the escorts supporting British operations against Japanese forces in Burma and Malaya.   *(C.S. 'Bill' Drake)*

31. The Commencement Bay-class was the ultimate in escort carrier development, with most having a long post-war stay with the United States Navy, sometimes in reserve, but also as anti-submarine carriers. This is the USS *Commencement Bay*, CVE-105, herself. *(US Naval Institute)*

32. Another of the Commencement Bay-class ships was the USS *Vella Gulf*, which entered service shortly before the end of the war. Originally laid down as *Totem Bay*, she served as a training carrier from spring 1945 until some time after VJ Day. *(US Naval Institute)*

pushed over the side at 07:00, and by 11:15, temporary repairs to the damaged flight deck meant that the carrier was able to resume flying-off aircraft.

Flying continued throughout the day, but at 22:00 it was decided that the weather was once again too rough for flying, and the next aircraft did not take-off until 07:00 on 25 March. That afternoon, the sole casualty of the Swordfish fire was committed to the deep. A hard lesson had been learnt, and returning aircraft were ordered to drop unused depth charges before landing. While it had been intended to keep *Vindex* on station for three weeks, on 27 March, after fourteen days on patrol, the last sortie was made and the carrier turned for home. Overall, four Swordfish had been lost and several more were unserviceable, all for a half share in one sunk U-boat. The squadron might have accounted for three more U-boats had it not been for the defective depth charges. The Swordfish of No. 825 had flown 235 hours and made 100 deck landings, '. . . an outstanding achievement . . .' according to C.-in-C. Western Approaches.

It is worth noting that despite more than four years of war, at first the routine aboard *Vindex* was not altered to cater for the needs of naval airmen engaged on operational flying round the clock. The wardroom (naval parlance for an officers' mess) served three meals a day, breakfast, lunch and dinner. Those flying patrols that took off after midnight were expected to fly on an empty stomach in the cold of the North Atlantic – so cold that on at least one occasion when flying was suspended, the enforced idleness saw many aircrew rolling a giant snowball on the flight deck. This was in addition to the constant threat of torpedo attack from a U-boat, or the risk of ditching once water was found in the aircraft fuel, when the time since the last meal could have a profound effect on the ability of the ditched airmen to survive. There was also the not unimportant fact that there were just eight crews to fly the Swordfish. It took a near mutiny on 17 March with a senior observer telling the ship's Commander (F), (Commander Flying, now known as Commander Air), Lieutenant Commander Percy Gick, that they would refuse to fly unless they were properly fed. The Commanding Officer, Captain Bayliss, defused the situation, quietly stressing the importance of their role in the war, while equally quietly arrangements were made for more flexible meal-times for aircrew.

It is also significant that it was not until comparatively late in the war, 1943, that the Royal Navy introduced an aviation medicine course at HMS *Daedalus*, the Royal Naval Air Station Lee-on-Solent, on the Hampshire coast almost equidistant between Portsmouth and Southampton.

On the Clyde, *Vindex* was refuelled on 1 April and re-victualled the next day, but did not receive fresh ammunition until 4 April. While the ship remained in port, Gick took the opportunity to press for his Sea Hurricanes to be fitted with rocket projectiles so that they could attack any U-boat found on the surface instead of having to call up the duty Swordfish or an escorting destroyer, frigate or corvette, by which time the enemy could be relied upon to have dived deep and run quiet to evade detection – almost impossible for a Swordfish anyway. After some inter-service wrangling with the Royal Air Force, which had enjoyed considerable success with RPs against Axis tanks in the North African campaign, he got his way and the Sea Hurricanes were authorized to have this weapon fitted. In fact, five of the Sea Hurricanes aboard *Vindex* retained their four cannon as well as having the RP racks fitted, while the remaining aircraft lost two of its cannon in the interests of having two marine markers installed to allow rapid investigation of U-boat bearings.

Other changes were in the air for the Swordfish. Getting the aircraft airborne when fully laden and in light wind conditions was difficult, given the slow speed of the escort carriers. One solution was the Robinson Patent Disengaging Gear that *Vindex* and many other British escort carriers had at the after end of the flight deck. An aircraft would be attached to this by a strop, the pilot would open up to maximum rpm, at which point the strop would be released and the aircraft thunder along the flight deck. This was only sufficient for an extra knot or knot and a half.

Later, rocket assisted take-off gear became available, known appropriately enough as RATOG. Between one and four of these rockets were placed under the lower wing on each side of the aircraft. The technique of using these safely was to have the aircraft start its take-off run normally, with the aircraft kept straight as once RATOG was fired, lateral control was difficult. The rockets were fired just before becoming airborne, otherwise premature firing could force the aircraft up into the air before full flying speed had been gained. If all rockets fired, and especially if they fired equally on each side, all was well and the rockets and their mountings could be ditched after the four second burst of extra thrust. Using this technique, a full load of four depth charges could be carried safely.

Safety was another important consideration. Many of the relatively inexperienced pilots were seen to be dragging their aircraft into the air as soon as possible, which was not a difficulty in itself with the tolerant Swordfish. The problem arose if the ship was not facing directly into the wind, or if the wind suddenly veered, when the aircraft suddenly lacked control speed. Pilots were ordered to use the full length of the flight deck and only pull the stick back at the last minute.

Vindex's First U-Boat

It was not to be until 6 May that *Vindex* was to gain her first U-boat victory. The carrier left the Clyde late on 24 April, and used the hours of darkness to allow 825 Squadron's Swordfish to practice night take-offs and landings. There were many new faces amongst the squadron's personnel, with replacements for losses on the first hunter-killer patrol, and of course a number of others moved on, including some being 'rested', usually as instructors.

This time the 'hunter-killer' group was to include three frigates of the First Division of the 5th Escort Group, as well as the carrier's close escort, the Royal Canadian Navy frigates *Matane*, *Stormont* and *Swansea* of the 9th Escort Group. Having six ships to support *Vindex* was both a comfort and a problem. The Canadian ships were diesel-powered and had a relatively low fuel consumption, but the three British ships were thirsty steam-powered vessels patrolling the horizon, and to keep them refuelled would mean that at the outset the carrier would use 20 per cent of its total fuel capacity, at a time when Captain Bayliss had no idea how long he would need to remain at sea. After a few days, the Canadian 9th Escort Group left for other operations and were replaced by the remaining ships of the 5th Escort Group.

On the previous patrol, the carrier had gone more or less where Bayliss had decided, aiming for the greatest concentration of swastikas on the map. This time, the Admiralty directed the hunter-killer group using intelligence. *Vindex* arrived in the designated area at 08:00 on 2 May 1944. Shortly afterwards, one of the escorts obtained a bearing on a U-boat that appeared to be transmitting meteorological intelligence. The last of the night patrol Swordfish had landed on, but three aircraft fitted with the new ASV (anti-surface vessel) Mk XI radar were flown off immediately and spent a fruitless morning on a thorough search of the area. Everyone came to the conclusion that an inexperienced HF/DF operator had given them the reciprocal position. Further searches followed until midnight, by which time the weather had closed in and further flying was impossible.

The following day, further flying by the Swordfish continued since the weather was too rough for the Sea Hurricanes – this was a problem with British-built high performance fighters adapted for carrier operations, as they proved too delicate and nose heavy for the heavy landings that came with a carrier deck rising and falling forty feet. Further Enigma interception was by this time reinforced by further HF/DF reports so that the general area in which the U-boat was operating was known. The tactic adopted was to mount saturation sweeps shortly before the next weather report was likely to be made, at roughly twelve hour intervals. This started a game of cat and mouse, as the Germans were fully aware of the use of direction finding by the British.

Flying was normally suspended when a carrier was refuelling her escorts, but on 5 May, *Vindex* was to conduct refuelling while two aircraft landed on. This second patrol was to be dogged once again by the loss of aircraft and, on 5 May, loss of aircrew when a Hurricane ditched due to water in the aircraft fuel.

Later that day, after dark, three Swordfish were flown off in what had become known to the hunter-killer group as Operation Swamp to find the U-boat, whose area had by this time been identified as a strip of around twenty miles wide. One aircraft, flown by Sub Lieutenant (A) Ron Huggins RNVR, had been in the air for around forty minutes when it picked up a contact on its radar, some ninety miles from *Vindex*. The aircraft's observer, Sub Lieutenant (A) Pat Calcutt, RNVR, held the target and fired a flare to draw the other aircraft towards it, but flying at just 350 feet because of low cloud, the flare splashed into the sea without igniting. In any case, the others might not have seen it given the poor visibility, down to around one mile by this time. As they made a run towards the target, it disappeared, so Leading Naval Airman Frank Smeeton signalled the position to the ships of the 5th Escort Group and then marked the spot with a float. By this time fuel was running low, and realizing that he would have to return, Huggins requested permission to drop the aircraft's two depth charges. No sooner had he done this than he saw ahead of him the U-boat on the surface. He could only try to bait the U-boat to remain on the surface by continually flying across it and providing a tempting target. He did this and succeeded in keeping the U-boat on the surface for a full fifteen minutes while the spot was marked with a smoke float and *Vindex*'s radar operators were able to get a fix on the position. The other two Swordfish of the same patrol were vectored in towards the U-boat, while another Swordfish was flown off. Before they could reach the now submerged U-boat, darkness had descended, and so too had fog, giving the airmen considerable problems in getting back to the ship, for although they could detect her on their radar, fuel was running short and the crew of the last aircraft could not see to land. The carrier aimed her searchlight into the sky to try to draw the stragglers home, but only succeeded in blinding the pilot, then suddenly the fog cleared and ahead they could see the carrier, with all lights blazing. They approached, caught the wire and bounced onto the deck, seconds before the engine cut out!

There was no further flying until 03:30 on 6 May, when an aircraft was flown off to support a frigate hunting the U-boat in dense fog. At 04:00, the frigate HMS *Keats* got a radar contact and approached, firing star shell, but the U-boat dived. The frigate began a depth charge attack as soon as an Asdic ping was picked up, but the U-boat had released a submarine bubble target or SBT, and the frigate ended up attacking this. At 05:18, one of the other ships, *Bickerton*, picked up an Asdic ping, and started to direct another frigate, *Bligh*, in a creeping attack. This eventually worked, and at 06:05, they saw *U-765* surface, her conning tower 'twisted, buckled plating . . . evidence that at least one depth charge had found its mark'. At this point, 825's CO, Lieutenant Commander (A) Freddie Sheffield came onto the scene. As the U-boat put up AA fire, which damaged his centre section and starboard mainplane, he dived his aircraft towards her, reaching 120 mph and dropping his depth charges at seventy-five feet. The depth charges straddled the conning tower, and within seconds of their exploding, the U-boat broke in two, leaving a dozen or so of her crew in the water, of whom just eight survived to be picked up by the frigate *Bickerton*.

The U-boat's identity was confirmed by one of the survivors. She had been about to be relieved when attacked, and there was the possibility that the earlier U-boat detected by the hunter-killer group had been her relief. It was not until later that day that the ships and aircraft were able to go hunting for the second U-boat, but by 16:00, *Bickerton* picked up what seemed to be weather signals on her HF/DF, and two Swordfish were flown off to help the search. Eventually the presence of a second U-boat was confirmed, but a depth charge attack by one of the ships just missed, and hopes that the submarine had been badly damaged were dashed the following day when once again signals were transmitted. The hunt continued, interrupted by bad weather and the breakdown of the lift machinery that meant it had to be cranked up and down by hand, until the night of 10–11 May. At 03:30 on 11 March, a Swordfish returning to the carrier, which was pitching and yawing violently, hit its starboard wing on the deck as the ship rolled. The wing snagged a wire and the aircraft skidded sharply to starboard, and then plunged overboard immediately behind the island. The ship immediately steered hard to starboard to avoid the wreckage and the frigate *Goodson* on plane guard duty headed for the spot, seeing two men clinging to an empty dinghy in the rough seas. With her whaler, the frigate spent two hours searching the seas for survivors, but none were found.

The problem of water in aircraft fuel was one that occurred again and again throughout the war years. In many cases, contamination was due to faulty handling or water getting into the system through a leak. The preparations for the famous raid by Swordfish from the fast armoured carrier *Illustrious* on the Italian fleet at

Taranto in November 1940 had been plagued by this problem, which cost at least two aircraft ditched.

Commander Hector Weir, RNR, chief engineering officer of *Vindex* spent much time pondering the problem. His thoughts were that the water could not be in the aviation fuel when it was piped into the ship, so something must be happening in the storage tanks. He knew that fuel was pumped from the tanks to the six aircraft refuelling points in the hangar by compressed air. Compressing air makes it warm, while the inter-connected storage tanks were surrounded by cold water as a safety measure. This meant that any compressed air that passed into the storage tanks cooled rapidly and condensed into moisture, and it was this that was occurring in the fuel. Weir decided to dispense with the cold water surrounding the tanks, and fill the entire aviation fuel system with sea water, driving out all air. The system would remain air tight while replenishing the tanks from the refuelling lighter by opening the outlet valves to allow the sea water to be displaced into the sea by the delivery of aviation gasoline. The light avgas would not mix with the heavier salt water, leaving the tank completely uncontaminated. When fuel needed to be pumped up to the refuelling points, sea water would be taken on again, displacing the light fuel upwards to the refuelling tanks or into the aircraft.

Weir convinced Captain Bayliss, the commanding officer, of his discovery, but Admiralty permission was needed to convert the fuelling system to the new arrangement. As it happened, there was sufficient time to do this while the carrier was on the Clyde.

Lieutenant Commander Percy Gick, the Commander Flying, also had work done while the ship was on the Clyde. His problem was that with just eight Swordfish crews, ensuring not just their availability but their fitness for continuous operations required considerable attention to their welfare. On any carrier, there is the problem that crews on night flying operations suffered from noise during the day. Gick had a special compartment, fully sound-proofed, built next to the crew room with comfortable bunks, each having a reading light. As crews returned from a sortie, they were debriefed, fed and given time to wash, then put to bed. A tally board contained their names and the number of each man's bunk, so that the amount of rest that each had had could be shown, and hence their availability for the next operation. Bayliss and Gick would, whenever possible, allow one crew at a time to relax and unwind in what Gick described as a 'carefully controlled piss-up' in the wardroom every four or five days, or whenever foul weather prevented flying for a reasonable period.

Notes
1. Gallery, op. cit.
2. Ibid.
3. Ibid.

VII

THE ARCTIC CONVOYS

It has often been said that on the Arctic convoys, the weather was as much an enemy as the Germans, since the only route for the Arctic convoys lay around the northern tip of occupied Norway to the Soviet ports of Murmansk and Archangel. In summer, almost constant daylight left the ships open to attack from the air, as well as from U-boats and surface raiders. In winter, with almost constant darkness and just three hours of weak twilight in the middle of the day, the weather was worse, with extremely low temperatures and high seas with freezing snow. Ships could be overwhelmed as the build-up of ice made them unstable. One officer having difficulty eating a meal as his cruiser rolled to angles of 30 degrees consoled himself with the thought that life must have been even more difficult in the destroyers and corvettes, which rolled 50 degrees or more! The cold meant that airmen tried to wear as much as possible, limited only by the need to get into and out of the cockpit. Metal became so brittle that tail wheels could, and did, break off on landing.

The bad weather was a friend in one sense, since at the very height of the winter storms, not only were German aircraft grounded, but U-boat action also became difficult. The weather was such an important factor that, together with the long hours of daylight in the summer months, convoys had to be suspended at the height of summer, especially in 1943. Convoys were also suspended at the time of the Normandy landings in June 1944 as the number of escort vessels available was insufficient to cover the demands of the Allied armies in France and the convoys to North Russia. The shortage of escort vessels meant the destroyers and corvettes that were the staple of convoy protection as aircraft carriers were not involved in covering the Normandy beachheads, although many Fleet Air Arm squadrons were based ashore under the control of Royal Air Force Coastal Command for operations to protect the landings from submarines and motor gun and torpedo boats; the E-boats.

A total of 811 ships sailed in the Arctic convoys to Russia, of which 720 completed their voyages, another thirty-three turned back for one reason or another, and fifty-eight were sunk, giving a loss rate of 7.2 per cent. Of the ships that reached Russia, 717 sailed back (some were being delivered to the Soviet Union), and of these twenty-nine were sunk, a loss rate of 4 per cent. This was the price of delivering to Russia some 4 million tons of war stores, including 5,000 tanks and more than 7,000 aircraft. It is worth reflecting that the sinking of a 10,000 ton freighter was the equivalent, in terms of lost equipment and ordnance, of a land battle. First Sea Lord at the Admiralty, Admiral Sir Andrew Cunningham recalled:

Although much of the *matériel* from the United States to the Soviet Union went via the South Atlantic and Indian Ocean to what was then known as the Persian Gulf, and was offloaded at an Iranian port and taken overland, for aid from the United Kingdom, the main convoy route was from Scotland, often via Iceland, especially when some of the ships were also coming from the United States. This route involved sailing off the coast of enemy-occupied Norway and around the North Cape, calling for the larger aircraft capacity of the escort carriers, for both anti-submarine and fighter protection was needed. CAM-ships also appeared on the Arctic convoys. The convoys were looked after by Royal Air Force Coastal Command, operating from bases in Scotland, Iceland and the Soviet Union, and in British coastal waters often aided by Fleet Air Arm shore-based squadrons under Royal Air Force control.

If the surface escorts and merchant ships suffered in the heavy gales and the bitter cold the young men of the Fleet Air Arm operating from the frozen flight-decks of the carriers took their lives in their hands every time they took off. The conditions in which they worked were indescribable. The aircraft patrols might be flown off in clear weather but when the time came to land on again with petrol nearly exhausted the carrier herself might be invisible in a lashing snowstorm. This happened many a time, and the number of close shaves in the recovery of these valiant young naval pilots is unbelievable. Many, numbed with cold, had to be lifted out of their cockpits. Their work was beyond all praise.[1]

Convoy PQ18

After the terrible fate that had afflicted the ill-fated convoy PQ17, the last Arctic convoy to be without its own air cover, the first Arctic convoy to have an escort carrier was PQ18 in September 1942. This was an indication of the impact of the mauling given to PQ17 as escort carriers were an innovation, even a novelty, at this early stage of the war.

Convoy PQ18's escort carrier was the US-built HMS *Avenger*. She carried three radar-equipped Swordfish from 825 Squadron for anti-submarine duties as well as six Sea Hurricane fighters, with another six dismantled and stowed beneath the hangar deck in a hold, for fighter defence. The fighter aircraft were drawn from 802 and 883 squadrons. The CAM-ship, *Empire Morn* carried another Hurricane, one of the expendable standard aircraft operated by the Royal Air Force's Merchant Service Fighter Unit. Other ships protecting the convoy included the cruiser *Scylla*, two destroyers, two anti-aircraft ships converted from merchant vessels, four corvettes, four anti-submarine trawlers, three minesweepers and two submarines. There was also a rescue ship whose presence meant that the escorts would not be distracted from their work to rescue survivors, an urgent matter in such cold seas. Three US minesweepers being delivered to the Soviet Union were also assigned to act as rescue ships.

Even getting to the convoy assembly point off Iceland was difficult. Rough seas swept a Sea Hurricane off *Avenger*'s deck, while steel ropes failed to stop aircraft breaking loose, crashing into one another and into the sides of the hangar. Fused 500-lb bombs stored in the lift well broke loose, and had to be captured by laying down duffle coats with rope ties, to be quickly tied up as soon as a bomb rolled on to the coats! On her way to the assembly point,

Avenger suffered engine problems due to fuel contamination. Even Iceland was not completely safe, with the carrier bombed by a Focke-Wulf Fw200 Condor long-range maritime-reconnaissance aircraft, which dropped a stick of bombs close to the ship, but without inflicting any damage.

The engine problems meant that the convoy, already spotted by a U-boat whilst on passage to Iceland left without the carrier. On 8 September, PQ18 was discovered by another Condor. By 12 September, *Avenger* had caught up with the convoy, only in time for a Blohm und Voss Bv138 flying boat to appear through the clouds. The carrier promptly launched a flight of four Sea Hurricanes, although not quickly enough to catch the flying boat before it disappeared.

The fighters' role was not limited to protecting the convoy from aerial attack. They also had to provide air cover for the Swordfish whilst they were on patrol, and vulnerable to attack by German fighters. Typical of the work of the Swordfish were general reconnaissance patrols, which in at least one instance found Bv138s dropping mines ahead of the ships. Sometimes, U-boats were discovered on the surface, but attempts to attack them were foiled by heavy AA fire from the U-boats.

At 04:00 on 13 September, Sea Hurricanes were scrambled after Swordfish on anti-submarine patrol were discovered by another two Luftwaffe aircraft, a Blohm und Voss Bv138 and a Junkers Ju88 reconnaissance aircraft, but these disappeared into the low cloud before the fighters could reach them. Later that day a formation of Ju88 medium-bombers made a high-level bombing attack on the convoy. Again, the convoy's fighters were unable to shoot down a German aircraft, largely because the early Sea Hurricane's machine guns could not concentrate enough fire on the bombers to have any effect. While the fighters refuelled and re-armed, the Luftwaffe attacked at 15:40. As twenty Ju88s flew over the convoy in a high-level attack, distracting the defences and causing the ships to take evasive action, twenty-eight Heinkel He111 and eighteen Ju88s made a low-level torpedo attack, followed by a second wave of seventeen Ju88s. Sweeping in at around twenty feet above the waves, the attackers ignored the escorts and concentrated on the merchant vessels, the correct strategy. The Sea Hurricanes were still on the carrier's deck and could not take off.

A mass 45 degree turn was attempted, but the inexperience of many of those aboard the merchantmen, and the large size of the convoy, meant that not all of the ships managed this manoeuvre. Inexperience also showed in the wild anti-aircraft fire against the low-flying aircraft which exposed the anti-aircraft crews on other ships to fire from shells and bullets. Pressing home their attack with considerable courage, the Germans sank eight ships, the more fortunate crews being able to jump direct from their ships onto the ice-encrusted decks of the escort and rescue vessels. The less fortunate had minutes in which to be rescued or die in the cold sea. The temperature of the sea was academic for the unfortunate crew aboard the *Empire Stevenson*, loaded with explosives, as they disappeared with the ship in one huge explosion. During this attack, the convoy's combined AA fire accounted for five aircraft. The Sea Hurricanes drove off a later attack by Heinkel He115 floatplanes, but one was shot down. A change of tactics saw the Sea Hurricanes rotated, each spending twenty-five minutes in the air before landing to refuel, keeping a constant CAP over the convoy.

On 14 September, the first Swordfish of the day found *U-589* on the surface, but she dived leaving the Swordfish to mark the spot with a smoke flare. Once the aircraft had gone, the submarine surfaced and continued charging her batteries. Alerted by the Swordfish, the destroyer *Onslow* raced to the scene. Once again, *U-589* dived, but she suffered for her impertinence when the destroyer attacked with depth charges and destroyed her.

The Germans also changed their tactics. Reconnaissance Bv138s and Ju88s were sent to intimidate the Swordfish, forcing them back onto the convoy, until the Germans were driven away by heavy AA fire. The Swordfish would then venture out, only to be found and driven back again.

A further attack by Ju88s later that day saw *Avenger* herself become the target, moving at her maximum 17 knots. The Sea Hurricanes broke up the attack, and no ships were lost, but eleven Ju88s were shot down, again mainly by AA fire. Further attacks that day, including dive-bombing, saw another German aircraft shot down without any losses to the convoy. In a final attack, three of the four patrolling Hurricanes were shot down by friendly fire, although all three pilots were saved, after five Luftwaffe aircraft were shot down and another nine damaged beyond repair with five of these credited to the Sea Hurricanes. In this attack, *Avenger*'s commanding officer, Commander Copeland, successfully managed to comb the torpedoes dropped by the Germans, but the ammunition ship, *Mary Luckenbach*, blew up, again with the loss of all of her crew, but taking her attacker with her as the aircraft had flown so low to ensure accuracy that it was caught in the explosion.

The following day, the remaining Sea Hurricanes and the Swordfish were again in the air, with the former breaking up further attacks. The day after, 16 September, the Swordfish were relieved of their patrolling by shore-based Royal Air Force Consolidated Catalina flying-boats operating from Russia. The break was short-lived as later that day, the convoy crossed the homeward convoy, QP14, with the survivors of the ill-fated PQ17, and *Avenger*, with her aircraft and some of the other escorts transferred to this convoy. The brief interval after shore-based aircraft had started to provide cover was used by the ship's air engineering team to assemble five Sea Hurricanes, more than replacing the four lost on the outward convoy. All in all, the Sea Hurricanes had accounted for a total of five enemy aircraft and damaged seventeen others.

Keeping the Convoy Route Open

Convoys were also suspended in mid-March 1943 as the battleship *Tirpitz*, battlecruiser *Scharnhorst* and heavy cruiser *Lutzow* were all based in northern Norway. The Allies were concerned that this powerful striking force would break out, and the US Navy hastily assembled Task Force 22 at Portland, Maine, to reinforce the Royal Navy's Home Fleet and protect the Atlantic convoys in case of a breakout. Heavy losses in the North Atlantic, problems in cooperating with the Soviets, and the longer hours of daylight, all meant that later, at the height of summer, convoys to the USSR had to be suspended until the darker days of winter.

In summer 1944, the Normandy landings, Operation Overlord, took up the available escort and heavy units of the Royal and US Navies, needed not only to protect the invasion fleet but also to bring much-needed supplies from the United States and Canada.

Once again, convoys to the Soviet Union had to be suspended. Operation DC saw three destroyers sail on 29 June with supplies for the escorts stranded in Soviet ports, starting their return on 4 July. Nevertheless, convoys were kept operational even up to and beyond the end of the war in Europe. There were two reasons for this. Hitler kept Norway well defended after its occupation believing, as the threat of invasion emerged, that this would be Churchill's preferred route back into Europe. The second reason was that the Admiralty feared that some rogue U-boats might continue to attack convoys even after German surrender while Japan remained undefeated.

Despite Admiralty objections to the welded hulls of the American-built escort carriers, these ships did perform sterling service on the Arctic convoys whenever this was expected of them. Apart from *Avenger* mentioned earlier, other ships included HMS *Tracker*.

Before the Normandy landings, the assault on the U-boats continued at full pace. In March 1944, aircraft from HMS *Chaser* sank U-boats on three successive days. The following month, aircraft from *Activity* and *Tracker* worked with the surface escorts to sink three U-boats in as many days. On a homeward bound convoy in May, aircraft from *Fencer* sank three U-boats in just two days. Later in the year, once the convoys resumed after the Normandy landings, there were successes by aircraft from *Campania* and *Vindex*. Cunningham noted that throughout 1944, at least twenty-three U-boats were sunk by convoy escorts on the Arctic route alone, with nine by carrier-borne aircraft and another three by carrier aircraft cooperating with surface vessels, and another six by surface vessels plus one sunk by a British submarine, and four by Royal Air Force Coastal Command.

On 1 April 1944, *Tracker* had been escorting the Arctic convoy JW58 when aircraft from her embarked composite squadron, No. 846 with Grumman Avenger bombers and Wildcat fighters, collaborated with the destroyer HMS *Beagle* to sink *U-288*. On 3 April, they had then joined aircraft from the British-built escort, HMS *Activity*, to sink *U-355*, and then went on to sink another U-boat, damage three more and shoot down six enemy aircraft during the convoy's passage. As Admiral Cunningham recollected:

The inclusion of escort carriers in our Russian convoys paid ample dividends, as they did also in the Atlantic. Our losses in the Arctic convoys, which until VE day remained one of our major and most difficult commitments in fulfilment of our pledge to our Russian allies, were greatly diminished.[2]

After a spell 'poaching' – attacking enemy convoys – it was time for *Nairana* to become gamekeeper again, providing air support for a convoy to Murmansk. Some might argue that these ships were better off on this work than attacking enemy shipping, especially taking considerable risks for such slender rewards as had occurred on the two carrier mission at the end of January, but wars cannot be won, cannot be brought to a conclusion, by defensive measures alone.

Nairana sailed for Murmansk from Scapa Flow in Orkney after nightfall on 5 February 1945, joining the convoy codenamed JW64 that had sailed from Greenock on the Clyde on 3 February. The convoy itself consisted of twenty-six merchantmen, and the initial escort from the Clyde to a point ninety miles north-east of the Faeroes was three destroyers, four corvettes and three sloops, as well as a vessel from the Royal Fleet Auxiliary, the Royal Navy's fleet train manned by the Merchant Navy. *Nairana* was part of the First Cruiser Squadron, CS1, along with just one cruiser, HMS *Bellona*, and once again was paired with the escort carrier *Campania*, as well as eight destroyers. In contrast to PQ18, this meant that the convoy would have twenty-eight Swordfish and twelve Wildcats. The escort was commanded by Rear Admiral Rhoderick McGrigor, a Scot, who paid the carriers the compliment of flying his flag in *Nairana*, something for which no doubt the escort carrier was never designed.

The convoy's route was to keep it 200 miles off the coast of Norway until the last two or three days, when the need to avoid the southern edge of the Arctic ice pack would take it to within 100 miles. At first, the weather was good, very good for the time of year, and the convoy assembled and set off at 13 knots, which could have taken it the 1,300 miles to the Kola Inlet in just five days, if it could have been maintained. The burden of defending the convoy was to be shared between the two carriers, with one providing CAP while the other provided anti-submarine and surface vessel reconnaissance at any one time, and then switching roles. In addition, both ships had all their Swordfish ready to be scrambled in an emergency at any time, while the Wildcats not in the air would also be ready to be scrambled during the hours of daylight. There was an attempt to give this convoy some night fighter protection with the addition of a Fairey Fulmar to *Campania*'s aircraft, although the Fulmar had never been able to compete with contemporary fighters even at the outset of the war, and was certainly obsolete by 1945.

The hope was always that the position of a convoy, indeed its very existence, would remain hidden from the enemy for as long as possible. Luck played a part in this, as discoveries were often made by accident, and JW64 was no exception, being discovered by a high-flying Luftwaffe aircraft on a routine weather flight early on 6 February. Later that day, as evening drew in, radar showed that the convoy was being shadowed by a Junkers Ju88, loitering at a distance of some twenty or thirty miles. The Wildcats were scrambled from *Campania* within seven minutes and directed to the Ju88 by radar, shooting it down, but one of the fighters failed to return to the carrier for reasons that were never established. As darkness fell, the convoy was without night fighter cover as the Fulmar was unserviceable.

Inevitably, a fresh shadower arrived even before dawn on 7 January, and without a night fighter to contend with, was able to operate unmolested until first light. Daybreak found the weather worsening. The convoy had crossed the Arctic Circle during the night, and was soon in a moderate gale with snow showers and the cloud base at less than 1,000 feet. As the weather continued to deteriorate throughout the day, the convoy's speed fell to 8 knots.

Attack by German bombers or submarines, or both, was expected, and the first air attack came at 07:40, with the aircraft flying so low that they were just ten miles away when *Nairana*'s radar picked them up and her fighters were scrambled. This first attack was not pressed home in the face of heavy AA fire from the escorts, which shot one aircraft down while several 'probables' were also claimed. There was a similar result when Ju88 torpedo-bombers attempted to attack at 09:30, except that on this occasion the fighters were from *Campania*. Later, a shadower was shot down by Wildcats from *Nairana*. Expecting U-boat activity, round-the-clock Swordfish patrols were ordered. In the seventy-two hours between nightfall on 7 January and nightfall on 10 January, there were more than seventy such patrols by 813 and 835 Squadrons. Each patrol lasted between ninety minutes and three hours, with two Stringbags in the air at any one time.

The strain of such operations was compounded not only by the cold, but by the motion of the ship that made proper sleep impossible. Godley, with the responsibility of running a squadron as well as flying, had a cabin at *Nairana*'s stern, in which sleep was almost impossible in bad weather due to the motion of the ship, and no doubt too whenever the stern lifted, the racing of the screws as they came out of the water.

The Swordfish sorties were meant to force U-boats to remain submerged, below periscope depth, at which they would have great difficulty getting into position to attack the convoy or mounting an attack even if the convoy steamed past them. On 9 January, shortly after 20:00, two U-boats were detected by their radio signals, one to the south and the other to the south-east of the convoy. It was essential that they should be forced down to prevent them reaching the convoy, and if possible the U-boats should be destroyed. Six Swordfish from 835 Squadron were sent, two to fly *Crocodiles* and four to fly *Lizards* (see Appendix I), two over the reported position of each U-boat. In such conditions, rocket projectiles could not be used and the aircraft were armed with depth charges. Godley recalls:

I flew a night *Croc* later and it was just about the most unpleasant flight I ever made. The temperature was far below zero Fahrenheit with a wind gusting to over 50 knots and in our open cockpits we were as exposed as ever to the elements. It was an absolutely pitch dark night and I was forced to fly almost the whole mission on instruments, just as George (his observer, Sub Lieutenant George Strong) had to keep his eyes glued to the radar screen. The ceiling was under 1,000 feet. I flew as high as I could without entering cloud, though there was little chance of locating the U-boat visually, to give George the best chance of finding her by radar. Just from time to time I'd catch a blurred glimpse of

106

the whitecaps as we buffeted through the night . . . *Nairana* was pitching like crazy when at last we approached to land, but I've never seen anything more welcome than the heaving lights of her flight deck as we came in, guided as ever by Bob Mathe's inspired batsmanship. Our ground speed at touchdown must have been under 10 knots and the landing was uneventful.[3]

Not the least of the worries for the aircrew was that engine failure in such conditions would have been fatal. Even if they had managed to ditch successfully in the dark and such stormy conditions, getting out of the aircraft and into a dinghy, even if the dinghy inflated properly, would have been very difficult, and it would have been unlikely that they could have survived very long in an open dinghy. Worse still, the storm would have swept them further out to sea towards Greenland. In such extreme conditions, anxious eyes continually swept over the instrument panel, checking the oil pressure and temperature gauges, while anxious ears listened out for any slight change in the engine rhythm, but the faithful 'Peggy' (Pegasus) droned on through the night. The weather was so bad by this time that the convoy was making a mere 5 knots.

On the morning of 10 February, Godley and Strong were once again airborne, taking off before sunrise with a fresh gale blowing, although this was better weather than they had encountered on their previous sortie. On this occasion, the cloud was in two layers, with six to seven-tenths nimbostratus at 500 to 800 feet, and eight-tenths cumulous and cumulonimbus above 4,000 feet. After taking off using RATOG into the strong headwind that saw their aircraft in the air with half of the deck left, they flew a *Crocodile* as no U-boat fixes had been made overnight. Another of 835's aircraft was in the air flying a half-*Viper*. Godley was to the south of the convoy, believing that any attack would come from that quarter, the direction of Norway.

Flying as high as possible, using breaks in the nimbus, he saw low cloud ahead and dived down to fly beneath it, only to find himself flying towards a formation of Ju88s heading northwards towards the convoy at just above wave height. He found himself wishing for some rockets, even though they were not intended for air-to-air combat, as Strong signalled the fleet: 'Beeswax from Topaz Able. Tally-Ho ten eighty-eights position 180ZZ30. Heading for convoy, Over.' Then came a brisk acknowledgement: 'Able from Beeswax. Roger. Out.'

By chance, with visibility of half-a-mile or less, they had been able to give the convoy an extra four minutes warning of a low level attack, and identify the aircraft and the number which the radar operator would not have been able to do. This was just one of several attacks pressed home despite heavy AA fire that morning, but once again, no ships were hit as they successfully combed the torpedoes. *Nairana* herself shot down one of the Ju88s with her AA fire, while two aircraft were shot down by 835's Wildcats and another three claimed as 'probables' by 813. The escorts and the merchantmen shot down another five Ju88s and damaged eight.

Meanwhile, Godley was unable to land on during the attacks, and had to remain on station. Still looking for U-boats, he suddenly spotted a lone enemy bomber heading for the convoy, and just for the 'hell of it', turned and dived towards the Ju88. A Stringbag threatening a Ju88 sounds most unlikely, but one of the enemy crewmen must have spotted a strange aircraft diving at them and not recognizing it, but expecting a fighter, alerted the pilot, for the Ju88 suddenly went into a steep climbing turn and headed back towards Norway!

The excitement wasn't over. With the attacks over, Godley descended through low cloud intending to land on, and appeared above a 'box' of four destroyers, who managed to mistake his single-engine biplane for twin-engined monoplane bombers, and opened fire. He quickly climbed back into the cloud and sent an indignant signal to the rear admiral. When he did get back aboard the carrier, Godley found that 'friendly fire' from a merchantman had shot down one of 813's Wildcats, although the pilot had been rescued, while several other fighters had been damaged, including two from 835. When the next attack developed just twenty minutes after the previous one had ended, there were just six or seven serviceable Wildcats between the two ships, but fortunately these were enough to fend off the attack.

By late on 10 February, there had been another fix on a U-boat. Although they did not know it at the time, no less than eight

U-boats were waiting for the convoy, and by this time the weather was improving, useful for friend and foe alike. Then, unexpectedly, an aircraft on patrol radioed that they had encountered fog, conditions in which neither aircraft nor U-boats could operate. Ahead of the convoy lay a fog bank, and the decision was taken to order the four aircraft in the air to land straightaway, while those ready for take-off would be delayed, leaving the convoy without air cover for the time-being. A change such as this was no easy matter, with the aircraft ranged on the deck ready for take-off having to be manhandled forward of the barrier so that the returning aircraft could land on.

Emerging into clear weather on 12 February at 01:30, the convoy changed course for the Kola Inlet, at 200 miles to the south less than a day's steaming. Shortly after dawn, the convoy rendezvoused with a small group of Soviet warships – the Soviet Navy played virtually no part in protecting the convoys – while occasional appearances of Soviet aircraft were meant to help chase off the U-boats, except that the aircraft were Bell Airacobra fighters, wholly unsuited to the task. Having got through repeated air attacks safely and kept the submarine at bay, at 00:29 on 13 February, the convoy suffered its only loss, when the corvette HMS *Denbigh Castle* was struck by a torpedo fired from one of four U-boats lurking close to the shore. Her commanding officer managed to beach his ship, but she was a total loss. In fact, the crew were lucky, as a torpedo hit on such a small vessel could have resulted in massive loss of life.

For the weary Godley, sleep beckoned.

Convoys back to the UK were almost as important as those to the Soviet Union. In running a convoy system, it was always important never to neglect the 'empties', and for the Germans, a ship sunk sailing homeward was a ship lost to the Allied cause, even if she was empty. The omens for the return voyage were not good. Having lost the *Denbigh Castle*, news now came in that two merchantmen under Soviet escort from Archangel to join the homeward convoy had been torpedoed and sunk, again by U-boats lurking close to the Soviet shore, an exercise that should have been extremely dangerous for the U-boats. In fact, a pack of a dozen U-boats had assembled at the entrance to the Kola Inlet

109

and were eagerly awaiting the departure of the homeward convoy. Five escorts were sent to the mouth of the Inlet, and succeeded in sinking *U-425* at 01:07 on 17 February, the date for the convoy to sail. This was good news, but somewhat spoiled by the fact that the escort force was able to confirm the presence of a number of U-boats.

Meanwhile, in an attempt to improve aircraft recognition standards, John Godley and his comrades produced a 'Valentine' card (see plate section) for the escorts, although he later felt that this may not have been much appreciated.

Departing homeward on 17 February, with the same escorts as before, but with *Campania* down to nine Swordfish and two Wildcats, 813 and 835 were ordered to maintain continuous air cover for as long as the weather permitted. As usually happens in warfare, one defensive measure prompts a new countermeasure, and the presence of ASV radar was countered by growing use of the snorkel by German submarines at this time, allowing them to remain under the surface at periscope level almost indefinitely. The small 'snort' was too small to be picked up by the radar of the day, and could only be seen with the naked eye at distances of up to two miles in good visibility, which did not exist with the four hours of daylight north of the Arctic Circle in February. Night patrols would have to be flown, but unless a U-boat obliged by coming to the surface, they would be useless and simply done to boost the morale of the crews aboard the thirty-seven merchantmen, making it seem that something was being done.

Leaving the Kola Inlet at 07:45, the first air patrols were by Swordfish, with three aircraft launched from *Nairana*, one flying a *Viper* and the other two flying *Crocodiles*. The patrols between them believed that they had spotted a snorkel five or six times, but on closer inspection discovered these sightings to be scraps of wreckage or oil slicks. Continuous air patrols meant exactly that and, so as not to leave the skies clear, replacement patrols were flown off half-an-hour before the previous patrols were due to land on. Just nine minutes after these replacement aircraft had taken off and before they had reached their designated patrol areas, an acoustic torpedo from *U-968* blew the stern off the sloop *Lark*, causing a number of casualties, although the ship herself was saved and taken in tow by a Russian tug to Murmansk for repairs.

110

It was clearly *U-968*'s day, for despite the convoy taking evasive action, with an emergency turn to north-north-east, and aircraft being sent to the location of the submarine, the merchantman *Thomas Scott* was next to be torpedoed. Her crew immediately abandoned ship, but re-boarded as there seemed to be no immediate danger of her sinking. She went down before she could return to the Kola Inlet.

In an attempt to get away from the U-boat wolf pack, the convoy turned due north at 14:50, but instead this led them directly towards *U-711*, and at 15:23 one of her torpedoes struck the Flower-class corvette HMS *Bluebell*, setting off her magazine so that she simply disappeared. Just five of her crew were taken alive from the cold waters, but only one, a petty officer (the naval equivalent of a sergeant) survived. No aircraft were close enough to attack, but several escort vessels mounted a heavy, but completely unsuccessful, depth charge attack. A considerable number of radio fixes were obtained after dark, and a further emergency turn was made to avoid the position of a U-boat, but overall the wolf pack was being left behind as the presence of the Swordfish forced the submarines to remain submerged and unable to keep up with the convoy.

An idea of the many hazards facing the convoy came when a Stringbag crashed during take-off. The pilot had started his take-off run at 23:30 for a night patrol and failed to realize that he was not heading straight along the flight deck, so that when he fired his RATOG his aircraft struck *Nairana*'s island and then somersaulted over the side. Both the pilot and observer managed to escape, but this still left the danger of the depth charges blowing up, which could have severely damaged the carrier. By this time, depth charges were fitted with a device that stopped them exploding if they were still attached to the depth charge rack on the aircraft, but it was known to be unreliable. A corvette on plane guard duty snatched the two men from the icy waters, unquestionably placing the small ship at considerable risk, but fortunately, there was no explosion.

The weather worsened and by 15:30 on 18 February, the order was given for flying to cease. By midnight, the storm was so bad that the convoy began to scatter as winds hit Force 10. The inevitable Luftwaffe shadower appeared before dawn on

19 February, but nothing could be done to discourage this unwelcome guest as winds remained at over 60 knots, too high to launch a Wildcat. As the weather worsened, even the Luftwaffe had to suspend operations until almost midnight, after which the weather eased and an attempt was made to regroup the convoy, so that by 08:00 on 20 February there were only four stragglers.

Four Wildcats remained serviceable aboard *Nairana*, but with winds gusting at up to 55 mph, it was not clear whether these could be launched because of the difficulty in landing. At 10:00, radar picked up an attacking formation, which soon proved to be Ju88 torpedo-bombers, and the Wildcats were scrambled. Despite penetrating the defensive AA fire to launch their torpedoes, the attack was unsuccessful, with one Ju88 shared between two Wildcats, another rated as a 'probable', while the AA gunners claimed two confirmed hits, one probable and four aircraft damaged. The Germans had failed to find the four vulnerable stragglers. The first three Wildcats landed on safely, but the fourth bounced over the wires and into the barrier.

In fact, seven Luftwaffe aircraft failed to return from this attack, and the pilots who did get back claimed to have sunk two cruisers, two destroyers and at least eight merchantmen, despite the convoy having had just one cruiser. Three German U-boats ordered to search for survivors or for signs of wreckage, naturally enough found nothing.

While the weather remained bad, it was decided to keep the Swordfish on deck, although flying would have been possible in the Force 8 gale. Nevertheless, the poor conditions meant that the convoy covered just 600 miles in its first four days at sea. By 16:00 on 21 February, another two stragglers had caught up with the convoy, and it was decided to send four Stringbags to search for the two ships still missing. They located one ship twenty miles to the south-west and guided it back to the convoy, but there was no sign of the other ship. As the weather worsened again that night, radio fixes were made on two U-boats, but it was felt that the chances of finding them in the dark were so low that it did not justify the risk in sending off patrols. Nevertheless, aircraft were ranged on deck ready to be scrambled at first light, triple lashed, but eventually even these had to be struck down to the shelter of the hangar as the ship began rolling heavily, so much so that it was becoming difficult for the crew to maintain their footing on the flight deck and it took twenty men to move each aircraft, and hold them in position in the lift while they were struck down into the hangar. At noon, the convoy was struck by a hurricane, with the anemometer stuck on its maximum registerable wind-speed of 80 knots and kept there for twenty hours. Spray whipped up by the storm froze on the flight deck, which was now impossible for anyone to step onto. Below in the hangar deck, work on the aircraft was impossible. Officers trying to sleep found the deck a better place than their bunks. The convoy started to scatter again, and then during the early hours of 23 February, the convoy broke in two, with most of the merchantmen and *Nairana* struggling on at 4 knots, while a number of others, including *Campania* and three or four destroyers, turned into the wind and simply maintained steerage way.

While it was still dark, Godley was awoken from an uneasy slumber, more of a state of half sleep, by a massive crash from a deck above. Still dressed, he made his way up the companionway, hearing another massive crash as he went, to the hangar deck to find a scene of devastation. The small tractor used to move the aircraft around the deck, bright yellow and weighing around a ton, had broken free from its triple lashings, supposed to keep it tight and secure against a bulkhead, and was now careering from one side of the deck to the other. The massive crash that had alerted Godley had occurred as it slammed against the starboard bulkhead for the first time, the second had been while it crashed into the port bulkhead. In between, as it slid across the deck, it demolished any aircraft that happened to be in the way.

Hangar decks were, and no doubt still are, notoriously difficult to keep truly dry and clean, quickly becoming covered in a thin film of oil. Godley was alone in the hangar at first, but he was soon joined by several others. He ordered them to get as many hands together as possible so that they could attempt to catch the wayward tractor that had already struck six aircraft, two of them possibly beyond repair. One man slipped on the deck, laughing at first as he slid along on his backside on the slippery surface, but his joy was short lived as he suddenly saw the tractor sliding towards him and only just managed to scramble out of the way in time, avoiding being crushed between the tractor and a bulkhead.

Having assembled a team of twenty men with ropes, Godley led them in an attempt to catch the tractor, but each time they caught it, the ship rolled and the ropes parted, leaving the tractor to continue to ricochet between the bulkheads, damaging yet more aircraft. Leaving a junior officer in charge in the hangar to do the best he could, Godley raced up to the bridge in an attempt to get the commanding officer to turn into the wind, just for fifteen minutes, to give them a chance to catch the tractor. *Nairana*'s CO, Captain Villiers 'Strawberry' Surtees, refused, insisting on staying with the convoy, despite the desperate pleadings of 835's squadron commander. On returning to the hangar, he found sixty men with rope and steel cable, and organized them into teams, each under an officer or a chief petty officer (the naval equivalent of a staff sergeant), and they resumed their efforts to catch the tractor. After a further five minutes of struggling, the ship suddenly hit a patch of calmer water, lasting for just a few minutes. This respite enabled them to catch the tractor, throwing ropes around it and every man grabbing at the machine, then as the ship rolled, they used the movement to edge the tractor to starboard and out of harm's way.

The cost of this episode was considerable. Out of thirteen Swordfish left, seven had been damaged, four of them beyond repair. One man suffered a broken leg, but there were no other injuries. Somehow, all six Wildcats parked at the forward end of the hangar, had escaped damage.

Reporting to the bridge, Surtees warned Godley that he would have to be prepared to fly off at dawn if conditions permitted as the convoy had become badly scattered.

Dawn found conditions still too bad for operations, with the wind still at 70 knots. *Nairana* was in company with the cruiser *Bellona*, most of the escorts and a dozen merchantmen, while *Campania* was with her destroyers some twenty miles to the north. The escorts now had the additional task of finding the stragglers, rounding them up and getting them back to the convoy, without any help from the Swordfish. *Campania* caught up shortly after midday, and at 14:00 was able to scramble two Swordfish, signalling *Nairana* to have Wildcats ready. At 14:20, came a distress call from the merchantman *Henry Bacon*, one of the stragglers some fifty miles east of the convoy, caught by nine

Ju88s. Fighters were immediately flown off, but by the time they reached the stricken ship, the attackers had departed leaving her burning. A destroyer was guided to the ship by the Wildcats. The *Henry Bacon*'s gunners claimed two Ju88s as probables, but she had the unwanted distinction of being the last ship to be sunk by German aircraft in the Second World War.

Luckiest of all was the merchantman *Noyes*, the straggler from an earlier storm that had failed to be spotted on the searches and for which all hope had been give up, but which had, in fact, fallen no less than 300 miles behind the convoy yet still managed to reach Loch Ewe in the west of Scotland on 29 February.

On 28 February, *Nairana* with *Campania* and *Bellona* and four destroyers reached the safety of Scapa Flow.

Flown ashore to Hatston in Orkney on 5 March, 835 found itself sent on another anti-shipping strike off Norway that had to be abandoned due to bad weather. It was a sad end to the career of the Fairey Swordfish as after that, only 836 was left operating the aircraft off MAC-ships, while elsewhere, they were replaced by the Barracuda and, in the Far East, by the Grumman Avenger.

Notes
1. Cunningham, Admiral of the Fleet Lord, *A Sailor's Odyssey*, Hutchinson, London, 1951.
2. Ibid.
3. Kilbracken, op. cit.

VIII

TAKING THE WAR
TO THE ENEMY
I – Europe and North Africa

In North Africa, the British Eighth Army inflicted a major defeat
on the German *Afrika Korps* at the Battle of El Alamein, which
lasted from 23 October to 5 November 1942. This was to be the
first major British victory on land, although the Japanese were to
be held in Burma, but it was also the last in which Britain fought
alone.

By this time, even before El Alamein, the Allies had planned
landings in North Africa, to squeeze the Germans between
British and American forces. The North African landings were
known as Operation Torch, and involved landing almost 100,000
men in Vichy French territory, on the Atlantic coast of French
Morocco and in Algeria. In between these two large areas of
Vichy territory lay neutral Spanish Morocco. Responsibility for
the operation was divided between the British, with the Eastern
Task Force, and Americans, with the Western Task Force. The
Allies now had General Dwight Eisenhower as Supreme
Commander while Admiral Sir Andrew Cunningham was Allied
Naval Commander. Force H under Vice Admiral Syfret, with the
aircraft carriers *Victorious* and *Formidable*, and three battleships,
including the new *Duke of York* defended the eastern flanks of
the invasion force from the Italian fleet and German U-boats.
The Eastern Task Force, under the command of Rear Admiral Sir
Harold Burrough, with three cruisers, sixteen destroyers and the
elderly aircraft carriers *Argus* and *Furious*, and the escort carrier
Avenger, covered sixteen transports and seventeen landing craft
to put ashore Major General Ryder's 33,000 British and

American troops near Algiers. The landings to the north and south of Casablanca in French Morocco were covered by Rear Admiral Hewitt's Western Task Force, TF34, from the United States which had twenty-three transports to land 34,000 troops commanded by Major General Patton, protected by three American battleships, seven cruisers and thirty-eight destroyers, with air support provided by the USS *Ranger* and the four American escort carriers *Chenango, Sangamon, Santee* and *Suwannee*.

In between these two major task forces was a Centre Task Force that had sailed from England under the command of Commodore Troubridge, with the two escort carriers *Biter* and *Dasher*, two cruisers and thirteen destroyers escorting twenty-eight transports and nineteen landing craft to put 39,000 men ashore at Oran in Algeria under the command of Major General Frendall.

Landings started at around 01:00 on 8 November at Oran, and then a little later at Algiers, while those in Morocco started at 04:30, with further landings at Safi, almost 200 miles to the south of Casablanca. In the days that followed, there were additional landings further east in Algeria at Bougie on 10 November, and after troops fighting east from Algiers joined up, at Bone on 12 November. The Algerian coastline extended well over 500 miles, while the landings in French Morocco were separated from those in Algeria by some 350 miles of Spanish Moroccan coastline. Coordination was helped by Troubridge maintaining a signals team of more than 100 personnel using a dozen radio wavebands located in a former armed merchant cruiser, *Large*. An idea of the tight timescale in which this, the first big Allied invasion, had been put together can be gathered from the fact that *Large*'s staff officers had to use umbrellas when sheltering in what was supposed to be their accommodation aft of the bridge!

Despite the size of the operation, almost complete surprise was gained. Nevertheless, the rapid expansion of both navies also meant that there were problems with inexperienced aircrew. Aboard the American escort carrier USS *Santee*, there were just five experienced pilots, and she was to lose twenty-one out of her thirty-one aircraft during Operation Torch, with just one of the losses possibly due to enemy action.

Onto the Mainland –
The Salerno Landings

If carrier borne aircraft had been useful, but not essential, for the invasion of Sicily, they were vital for the next stage, the invasion of mainland Italy with landings at Salerno. Although Salerno was within range of aircraft operating from airfields in Sicily, it was only just within range for fighter aircraft, leaving a Spitfire with just enough fuel for twenty minutes on patrol above the beachheads, and far less if engaging enemy aircraft. The obvious solution was to station aircraft carriers off the coast to provide fighter cover.

Salerno was an attempt to shorten the war in Italy, and in this, as we shall see, it was unsuccessful for reasons that might not have been fully foreseen at the time. Montgomery's Eighth Army had already crossed the Straits of Messina into Calabria on 3 September 1943, a relatively easy operation but one that left them at the very tip of the 'toe' of Italy with some considerable distance to move through hilly terrain fighting German and Italian rearguard actions. Salerno was some 200 miles further north. The prospects at first seemed extremely bright, for on the same day that Montgomery moved into Calabria, an armistice was signed in secret at Syracuse with Marshal Badoglio's new Italian government, formed after Mussolini had been deposed in July. Negotiations for the armistice had been prolonged as at first the Allies were suspicious of Italian objectives, but this did at least give the Allies time to plan their assaults on Salerno and Taranto, fully recognizing that the Germans were likely to continue to resist whatever the Italians decided. This was another reason for choosing Salerno, the hope that a substantial number of German troops would be cut off and unable to withdraw. The armistice was announced on 8 September, on the eve of the Salerno landings, but it might have been as well to have waited another twenty-four hours as the Germans were able to move quickly to seize Italian airfields, although the Italians for their part were able to move most of their fleet to prevent it falling into German hands. Had the Germans not known about the armistice in advance, the landings at Salerno could have been easier.

The Salerno landings, Operation Avalanche, on 9 September

were coordinated with a British airborne landing at Taranto to seize the port and enable enemy shipping there to escape to Malta. Vice Admiral Henry Hewitt USN landed Lieutenant General Mark Clark's US Fifth Army in a landing fleet covered by an Independence-class light fleet carrier and four escort carriers, as well as eleven cruisers and forty-three destroyers, while Force H, still under Vice Admiral Willis, had the battleships *Nelson* and *Rodney,* the aircraft carriers *Illustrious* and *Formidable*, as well as Force V with the maintenance carrier *Unicorn* operating in the combat role with another four escort carriers, known in the Royal Navy as auxiliary carriers, *Attacker, Battler, Hunter* and *Stalker*. Force V was under the command of Rear Admiral Sir Philip Vian. Meanwhile, the Mediterranean Fleet had escorted Italian warships to Malta before supporting the Taranto landings with heavy gunfire from the battleships *Warspite, Howe, Valiant* and *King George V,* after which *Warspite* and *Valiant* were redeployed to provide heavy gunnery support for the Salerno bridgehead. While the two large armoured carriers were intended to defend the fleet and look for enemy shipping, the carriers in Force V were solely concerned to provide fighter support, with each escort carrier carrying a single squadron of thirty Supermarine Seafire L.C2s, with their engines tuned to provide maximum power at 5,000 feet instead of the usual 15,000 feet, making it a very different aircraft from those at the North African landings almost a year earlier. *Unicorn* carried two squadrons with a total of sixty Seafires. As in the North African landings, the aircraft would be used to provide air cover and also to provide ground attack against German troops and airfields.

The Seafire was a big improvement in performance over anything that the Fleet Air Arm had operated before, being faster than the Sea Hurricane, although less manoeuvrable and more difficult to repair, and it had folding wings. The modifications necessary for carrier operation meant that it was slightly heavier than the Spitfire, from which it was derived, and so slightly slower. Lieutenant Commander George Baldwin was one of the fighter pilots involved and was a former naval test pilot himself, having flown with the Naval Air Fighting Unit at RNAS Yeovilton. He visited the Royal Air Force to discover the latest in fighter tactics and up-to-date intelligence on German aircraft. The Royal Air

Force personnel were helpful, but this couldn't disguise bad news. The latest versions of the Messerschmitt Bf109 and the new Focke-Wulf Fw190 were indeed formidable opponents, with the latter aircraft also having the manoeuvrability that the Bf109 lacked. Anxious to squeeze the last ounce of performance out of the aircraft, a programme of 'local modifications' was put in hand. The exhaust manifolds were removed and replaced with exhaust stubs to reduce drag and increase the thrust from the exhaust. The knobs for catapult (known at the time as 'accelerators') operation from carriers were also removed, further reducing drag. Good quality furniture polish was somehow obtained, despite wartime rationing and restrictions on production of quality materials, and everyone, pilots included, spent hours polishing the leading edges of the wings to make the aircraft more slippery. Introduced between May and June 1943, in time for the invasion of Sicily, these changes gave the aircraft another 15 knots maximum speed. The Seafire rarely needed catapult assistance during take-off, but at Salerno the question was academic for most of the Seafire pilots as the escort carriers lacked catapults or accelerators, despite having a much lower maximum speed than the purpose-built carriers, known as fleet carriers in Royal Navy parlance. The Seafire suffered from two shortcomings. The first was that, in common with many British fighters early in the war, it was short on range. The second was its tendency to pitch forward on landing, at best damaging the propeller, at worst the aircraft could be damaged beyond repair.

The British carriers made a feint towards Taranto after leaving Malta, although the assault on Taranto was covered by six battleships from Force H and the Mediterranean Fleet, and by aircraft from Malta. The announcement of the armistice saw the Italian Navy leave its ports of La Spezia, Genoa, Castellamare and Taranto and steam towards Malta, being escorted by four of the Royal Navy's Mediterranean battleships, leaving the other two to accompany *Illustrious* and *Formidable* to Salerno.

The aircrew aboard the carriers of Force V were awakened at 04:30 on the morning of 9 September. Several of those present recalled not having had much sleep and few had any appetite for the breakfast of eggs and bacon put before them in the wardroom. Amongst the first into the air before dawn were eight Seafires drawn from *Unicorn*'s 809 and 887 Naval Air Squadrons, with four aircraft providing high cover and another four low cover, looking out for enemy dive-bombers and torpedo-bombers respectively. The practice was for aircraft to carry extra fuel in drop tanks, extending their patrol time, and to use this first as the tanks would have to be dropped to reduce drag before engaging in aerial combat. That first day, there was little sign of the Luftwaffe, but the troops landing encountered fierce resistance. In the days following the invasion, a strong counter-attack was mounted by mainly German forces accompanied by heavy aerial attack by the Luftwaffe, so that the entire operation soon appeared to be in difficulty.

The expectation was that the airfield at Montecorvino, just inland from the invasion beaches, would be captured soon after the landings, but determined resistance by Axis forces meant that this did not happen.

Life was difficult aboard the carriers, with Force V given a 'box' offshore in which to operate, flying off and recovering their aircraft. In practice, this box was far too small for the ships, giving the carrier commanders great difficulties as they charged from one end to the other, but the situation was even worse for those in the air, with large numbers of aircraft circling within a confined space, the danger of a mid-air collision was very real as they waited to land on ships steaming close to one another. At times a light haze added to the difficulties. As luck would have it, the whole operation took place in conditions of complete calm, with little wind – never more than 3 knots – and the Seafire needed 25 knots of wind over the deck for a safe take-off or landing, but the escort carriers could only manage 17 knots. Arrester wires had to be kept even tighter than usual, as were the crash barriers two-thirds of the way along the flight decks.

'Judgement of speed over the water, and height above the water, on the approach to land was extremely difficult,' recalled Lieutenant Commander George Baldwin, a Naval Air Wing Commander and responsible for the four squadrons embarked in the four British escort carriers.[1]

Looking at ways around the problems, Captain Henry McWilliams, commanding officer of the escort carrier HMS *Hunter*, asked Rear Admiral Vian for permission to saw nine inches off the wooden propeller blades of the Seafires. Vian wisely decided that the personnel aboard the carriers knew more about the problem than he did, and gave his permission. The modification was relatively easy for the ships' carpenters to do and had little effect on the performance of the aircraft, while propeller damage during landing was much reduced. After initial trials, the entire stock of replacement propellers aboard the carriers was also treated in the same way.

In other ways too, it often seemed to be a case of learning through trial and error. The casualty rate among the Seafire pilots seemed to be unduly high in the air, not just in landing, as many seemed to be unable to bale out quickly enough. Learning the hard way, it was soon discovered that the Royal Air Force-recommended method of escaping from a Spitfire, rolling the aircraft and opening the canopy before undoing their seat belts and 'ejecting' (in other words, falling out) from the aircraft, didn't work. Possibly this was due to the higher weight of the Seafire. Eventually pilots were advised to jump over the side of the aircraft, and the survival rate amongst those shot down improved immediately.

Turning their attention to the carriers, the Luftwaffe mounted intensive attacks during 11 September, forcing the carriers to operate at full speed even when not flying-off or landing aircraft, and fuel consumption increased considerably. For the first time, the Germans used glider-bombs, saving their aircraft from the intense AA fire put up by the fleet offshore. That evening, Vian was forced to signal Vice Admiral Henry Kent Hewitt in overall command of the operation: 'My bolt will be shot this evening, probably earlier.'

Hewitt had just been briefed by Lieutenant General Mark Clark on the situation ashore, and guessed that more air attacks were imminent. He signalled back, 'Air conditions here critical. Can your carrier force remain on station to provide earlier morning coverage tomorrow?'

'Will stay here if we have to row back to Sicily,' Vian confirmed.

Hewitt's guess proved to be right. He wasn't surprised to learn that the carriers were low on fuel, but he didn't realize that they were already on their emergency supplies. The reason for the difficulty was not so much the German attacks forcing the carriers to operate at maximum speed throughout the day, but that the planners had assumed that the Fleet Air Arm would be needed for two days, or three days at worst if the invasion met stiff resistance. After that, it was expected that airfields ashore would have been taken and would be available. As so often happens in warfare, everything was not going to plan. The airfields were not available that would allow the Royal Air Force and United States Army Air Force to bring aircraft forward from their bases in Sicily.

In the end, the carriers remained on station until 14 September, by which time the 180 Seafires had been reduced to just thirty, more by accident than the efforts of the Luftwaffe. One consequence of this was that many senior officers blamed the Seafire for the losses, rather than a combination of factors that had to include the difficulty in operating high performance aircraft off escort carriers with their short decks, lack of accelerators and low speed, in light wind conditions. The aircraft had its weaknesses, and as one naval officer put it, '. . . was too gentle for the rough house of naval flying', but it had its strengths, as Baldwin had discovered earlier during Operation Torch. It was also true that the naval air squadrons had carried out far more than the planned number of sorties, despite the high accident rate. A small number of aircraft did manage to get ashore as early as 12 September, to the airfield at Paestum, which was little more than a landing strip cut out of tomato fields. Conditions ashore were little better than on the carriers for the naval fliers. 'Every time an aircraft took off the air was full of dust and flying stones,' recalled Lieutenant Commander (later Captain) John Cockburn, RN. 'We had no tools, not even a screw driver, and we had to use flints to remove the cowlings and service our aircraft, refuelling them from some petrol drums we found in the corner of a field and transported in a lorry borrowed from the Americans.'[2]

Many of the pilots flying the Seafire must have led charmed lives, although no doubt this wasn't apparent to those involved at the time. One naval pilot, Peter 'Sheepy' Lamb, later a lieutenant commander, crashed no less than seven Seafires between March and October 1944.

Nevertheless, despite the huge cost in aircraft, one cannot help but wonder whether the absence of close air support for the landings at Anzio, further up the coast of Italy, in January 1944, contributed to the near failure of this campaign. There were problems enough with the commanders ashore, and especially the

American General Lucas who concentrated on securing the beach-head rather than thrusting towards Rome, which prompted Britain's wartime Prime Minister Winston Churchill to say that: 'We thought that we had landed a wild cat, but instead we have stranded a vast whale with its tail flopping about in the water.' At the Admiralty in London, Cunningham, the First Sea Lord, maintained that Churchill could '. . . rest assured that no effort will be spared by the navies to provide the sinews of victory.' Yet, the Germans were able to fight a highly mobile and flexible defence and counter-attack, and deploy their heaviest artillery. Cunningham in his memoirs remarked that the prolonged assault on Anzio and the delay in linking up with other forces caused a heavy demand for shipping to maintain effectively a shuttle service of supplies from Naples, and at a time when the Allies were attempting to concentrate shipping for the Normandy landings, but escort carriers were not needed for Normandy as it was within reach of good air bases in the south-east of England.

Landing in the South of France

By August 1944, the entire strategic situation in Europe had been transformed. Not only had German resistance been broken and Rome liberated, but Allied forces had landed in Normandy in June. This had been another major operation without carrier air cover, but on this occasion the reasons had been simple, it wasn't necessary. The Normandy beachheads were within range of airfields in the south of England and the sheer size of the invasion force and the constant stream of vessels across the English Channel meant that there would have been no room for carriers to operate their aircraft. A number of Fleet Air Arm aircraft had flown from shore bases in the south of England in support of the landings and the bridgehead, while naval aircraft also flew reconnaissance sorties and operated in the spotter role for the heavy guns of the battleships and cruisers covering the landings. The Italian campaign was maintained throughout this period because it forced the Germans to divert ground and air forces from the Normandy campaign.

Landings in the south of France were an easier option than landing in Normandy, although logistically it would have been difficult to have put the same quantities of men and *matériel* into such an operation as had been achieved in the Normandy landings, which had even included the construction of two ports to keep the invaders supplied. Serious consideration had been given to an invasion of the south of France as early as August 1943, but the British had objected, declaring that it would divert resources from the advance through Italy, which they believed would lead to an invasion of Germany through Austria – a highly optimistic assumption given the intervening terrain! The south of France had then slipped down the Allied order of priorities as attention focused on the invasion of Normandy, through which France and the Low Countries could be liberated, and meanwhile further landings in Italy at Anzio had proved necessary. The original name for the invasion was Operation Anvil, but this was later changed to Dragoon.

The south of France was seen as being easier than Normandy as the Germans had not taken Vichy territory until late 1942, and not only did they not have the time to build anything on the scale of the famous 'Atlantic Wall' fortifications along the English Channel coastline, but the resources were also becoming increasingly scarce. By this stage in the war as well, interference from enemy naval forces could also be discounted. As a consequence, the fast armoured carriers of the Royal Navy were sent to the Pacific to join the US Navy in taking the war ever closer to Japan. The entire air defence and ground attack needs of the landing force were entrusted to the two navies using nine escort carriers, with the five British ships, *Attacker*, *Emperor*, *Khedive*, *Searcher* and *Stalker* carrying Supermarine Seafire L2Cs again, and the four American ships, including the USS *Kasaan Bay*, carrying the new Grumman Hellcat, a true carrier fighter aircraft. Heavy fire support was provided by three US battleships plus one each from France and the UK, while the US Navy also provided three heavy cruisers.

The overall invasion fleet was under the command again of Vice Admiral Henry Hewitt who was to land Lieutenant General A. M. Patch's US Seventh Army and General de Lattre de Tassingny's II Free French Corps along the French Riviera between Baie de Cavalaire and Calanque d'Antheor. Rear Admiral Tom Troubridge commanded the British carriers and Rear Admiral Durgin the US ships.

More than 56,000 troops were landed on the first day, 15 August, and by 28 August, the key naval base of Toulon had been surrendered as well as the major port of Marseilles. The most notable feature of these landings was the limited effort from the Luftwaffe, leaving the naval airmen to provide support for the ground forces. One pilot recalled having a good relationship with the US Army commanders who made good use of naval aerial reconnaissance.

The lessons of the Salerno landings had been learnt, with more aircraft carriers and adequate room to manoeuvre, while the carriers were able to retire to Corsica for replenishment and new aircraft, so there was none of the fuel shortages that had so nearly placed the Salerno operation in jeopardy. It was also fortunate that the weather conditions were ideal for carrier operations with a breeze and gentle swell offshore.

For many of the American carrier pilots, it was their first experience of operational flying, and much attention was paid to minimizing their casualties during the vital first sorties. George Baldwin again:

> We were very worried about the Americans, they were . . . unblooded. They had come straight from the United States and never seen any kind of action before. So they had been given a very considerable briefing by some of our air staff on the sort of things they needed to know about the German opposition . . . type of anti-aircraft fire and what not to do. . . The poor chaps, they flew a flight of four aircraft over Marseilles the first morning in formation in a straight line and the first salvo from the 88-mm guns knocked two of the four aircraft out of the sky. Sad loss . . .[3]

The Americans had been warned that aircraft should never fly in formation or in a straight line, but instead be well spaced to allow weaving and only to fly between 9,000 and 11,000 feet when climbing since the German 88-mm AA guns were very accurate between these heights. Sound advice, but it had either not been passed down to the squadrons or had been ignored.

The landings in the south of France were successful, putting additional pressure on German forces and providing yet another front on which German troops had to fight. They were followed soon afterwards in September and October by British naval forces, using nothing heavier than cruisers and escort carriers, cutting the German evacuation routes across the Aegean from Greece and destroying the remaining German naval units in the Aegean.

Attacking the German Convoys

Far more successful were the attacks on German coastal convoys sneaking down the coast of Norway, often with vital iron ore from Sweden. These had been attacked by the Royal Air Force, and daylight raids by de Havilland Mosquitoes had been so successful that the Germans had taken to moving their ships only at night. As a result, within the tight confines of the Norwegian fjords only Stringbags, with their tight turning circle, could operate safely and effectively. This was as true in 1945 as it had been in 1939 and 1940.

Typical of such attacks on German coastal convoys was that mounted on the night of 28–29 January 1945 by Swordfish of 835 Squadron aboard *Nairana* and 813 Squadron aboard *Campania*, with the carriers escorted by a cruiser, HMS *Berwick*, two destroyers and four smaller vessels. During 27 and 28 January, the need for constant anti-submarine patrols saw one of 835's and two of 813's Swordfish damaged in landing accidents, reducing the number of aircraft available for that night's operation to twenty-five. No combat air patrols were flown by the fighters, but two Wildcats were kept ranged on deck on standby in case of German aerial activity, although by this late stage in the war, a growing shortage of fuel was keeping Luftwaffe operations to the bare minimum.

The aircraft were to be launched from the carriers while seventy miles off the coast of Norway, with the target for the night being shipping moving through Rovde Fjord, not in fact an inlet but a narrow coastal channel, no more than a mile or two wide, with mountains on either side rising precipitously to 3,000 feet. The Swordfish of 835 were to hunt for shipping over a distance of forty miles, with those of 813 doing the same in a sector to the north. Both carriers were to send their aircraft in two waves, with the first wave consisting of seven aircraft from *Nairana* and six from

Campania. Navigation on such an operation was aided by the use of ASV, with the small island of Riste used as a navigational point for 835's aircraft. The first strike was planned to take-off at 20:00 and the second at 20:40 consisting of six aircraft from each ship. In 835 Squadron, one aircraft in each strike was armed with six bombs; the remainder had eight armour-piercing rockets. The lack of room to manoeuvre into the ideal position for an attack with torpedoes meant that rocket projectiles were far more likely to be successful, and would inflict considerable damage on the thin plating of unarmoured merchant vessels.

Taking off from two carriers at once meant that the squadron commanders had to be careful that their aircraft did not get mixed up while formating after take-off or, worse still, collide. As a result, 835's aircraft took-off from *Nairana* and then circled to port, while those of 813 from *Campania* circled to starboard. Within five minutes the two strikes were in echelon formation, and heading towards the target area at a steady 80 knots.

Flying on a clear moonlit night, the pilots could see the Norwegian mountains from a distance of thirty miles, and Riste became visible to the naked eye within minutes of it being identified by the observers on the radar screens. No. 835, led by the now Lieutenant Commander John Godley, was ordered to over fly Riste at 1,200 feet rather than passing it at sea level, doubtless because British intelligence believed that the island was only populated by a few farmers. They were in for a rude awakening. As the aircraft approached the island at a highly vulnerable altitude and clearly visible on the moonlit night, two batteries of Bofors guns opened up. Fortunately, the gunners were used to the 300-plus knots of Mosquitoes and not the 80 knots of the Swordfish, and their first bursts were deflected to a point some fifty yards ahead of the aircraft, giving Godley the opportunity to put his aircraft, followed by the rest of his formation, into a steep twisting dive to sea level. The Bofors gunners could not follow the twisting turns, and once at sea level could not depress their weapons sufficiently to hit the Swordfish.

The damage was done, however, with the AA batteries on either side of the fjord alerted. John Godley could see those on the mainland and those on the nearest offshore island already firing, although no aircraft was close. Unfortunately, one of his least experienced pilots accidentally switched on his navigation lights, and despite repeated calls on the radio – another innovation with the Swordfish III – did not switch them off until signalled to do so by Aldis lamp! The German AA gunners by this time had a clear idea of the exact position of the Swordfish, but curiously, they stopped firing. Flying low so that any AA fire was more likely to hit the AA batteries on the other side of the fjord than the aircraft, Godley guessed that the Germans had decided that the formation of biplanes with fixed undercarriages and with one of them careless enough to switch on his navigation lights could only have been one of their own training formations.

As the aircraft roared up the fjord just above wave height, the noise prompted the locals to switch on their lights and open their front doors, as if to show them the way and, as likely as not, ensure that no aircraft crashed into the sides of the fjord. Godley again:

> The whole country deep in snow, the white mountains bathed in moonlight rising high above us on either side. Till at last we sight a target. A merchantman sailing towards us on her own. I lead the flight over her, hesitate, decide to fly the last ten miles of our patrol in search of a larger vessel. But the rest of the fjord is empty. Turning back, climbing to 1,500 feet, the perfect height for rockets . . . My aim as I banked to dive, absolutely calmly, at the correct angle of twenty degrees towards this doomed vessel, was to strike her with my rockets below the water level. Flak may have been coming up but I simply wasn't aware of it, I was concentrating solely on my aim. I'd had so much practice and the conditions were so perfect that I expected to be accurate within a very few feet. And I was. Firing my eight rockets in a ripple of four pairs at a range closing from 2,000 to 1,500 feet. Seeing them all striking the water as planned, a yard or two short of the merchantman amidships.[4]

Godley broke off to starboard and watched the others follow him, seeing two aircraft score hits even though his own rockets had probably been enough as the ship was dead in the water and on fire. Sending the four remaining aircraft to seek targets ashore rather than waste their rockets, he watched as the merchantman lowered her lifeboats and then made a further sweep of the search area, only to find two more merchantmen entering Rovde Fjord. He called his second strike, led by his senior pilot, Lieutenant Geoffrey Summers, and directed them towards the merchantmen, three aircraft to each ship. The first ship was hit by at least six rockets, but the inexperienced pilots of the other sub-flight meant that two aircraft fired their rockets badly off the target, but the more experienced pilot with the six bombs scored a direct hit and two near misses. The first ship was beached by her crew before she could sink, although she was on fire, but the second ship settled rapidly.

Godley then decided to return to his ship, having to find *Nairana* in the dark, since he had been in the air for more than three hours already and the normal endurance with a full war load for the Swordfish was only supposed to be four and a half hours. He approached the carrier shortly before midnight, finding that all of the other aircraft in his strike had returned safely, having been told to make their way back independently. Looking at his fuel gauge, he was surprised to find that he still had nearly forty gallons of fuel left, sufficient for more than an hour. Reassured by this, Godley allowed some of the pilots of the second strike, who believed that their aircraft had been hit by flak or had developed engine trouble, to land ahead of him, so that he was almost the last to land at 00:17.

The carriers and their escorts then headed for home, since a German counter-attack was expected because of the extensive use made of radio during the attack and as the aircraft returned to the ships, but none developed.

Post attack, John Godley went to see what damage there was to the aircraft, but none of them had so much as a single scratch. Better still the aircraft damaged in the pre-raid landing incident had been repaired, so the squadron was back up to full strength. Nevertheless, a shock was in store for him. Asked by his fitter how much fuel he had on landing, he replied that he had more than thirty gallons, only to be told that he had had just three or four, enough for six minutes in the air at most! His fitter couldn't believe that the aircraft had been so meagre in her fuel consumption and had checked fuel levels with a dipstick – the fuel gauge had been faulty.

Nairana's aircraft did at least have the satisfaction of having sunk two and crippled a third enemy merchant ship, but those from *Campania* had carried out just one attack and had no idea of whether or not it had been successful 'in the absence of a flare-dropping aircraft'. Moonlight was clearly not enough!

Amongst the escort carriers, during the various Norwegian campaigns, ships involved included *Campania*, *Emperor*, *Fencer*, *Nairana*, *Pursuer*, *Queen* and *Trumpeter*, so obviously the American welded hulls stood up much better to Arctic conditions than the Admiralty expected! By contrast to these demanding conditions, *Fencer* had earlier escorted the force sent to install the new Royal Air Force Coastal Command base on the island of Terceira in the Azores, flying her Seafire fighters ashore to operate from the base until the first maritime-reconnaissance B-17 Flying Fortress bombers arrived.

The Offensive against the *Tirpitz*

Having sunk the German battleship *Bismarck*, attention invariably had to turn to the fate of her sister ship, the *Tirpitz*. The pride of the German fleet had been lost in May 1941 and the Germans were understandably reluctant to see *Tirpitz* share the same fate. They didn't need to risk the ship. The mere presence of the ship in a Norwegian fjord was enough to keep the British on their toes, and the mistaken belief that she was at sea caused the Admiralty to order that convoy PQ17 to Russia should scatter, with disastrous consequences. The ship also caused the Royal Navy and Royal Air Force to expend a considerable effort on attempts to sink her, with the Fleet Air Arm mounting no less than nine attacks on the ship and the Royal Air Force seven raids. This was difficult given the strong natural defences of her hiding place, but on 22 September 1943 an attack by British midget submarines damaged the *Tirpitz* so badly while she lay in the Altenfjord, that she was out of action for six months.

Beyond the reach of the heavy guns of the fleet and situated where normal submarines could not get to her, attack from the air seemed to be the only course. The German battleship was in the Kaa Fjord when the next attack was mounted. Warned by Ultra intelligence that the ship's sailing had been brought forward by twenty-four hours, on 3 April 1944, the Fleet Air Arm launched a major attempt, Operation Tungsten, to sink the ship using no less than five aircraft carriers, including HMS *Victorious*, a sister ship of *Illustrious*, and the elderly *Furious*, as well as the three escort carriers, *Emperor*, *Pursuer* and *Searcher*. The larger carriers carried Fairey Barracudas for dive-bombing and torpedo-dropping, while the escorts carried a mixture of Grumman Wildcats and Hellcats and Vought Corsairs to provide fighter cover. Both *Searcher* and *Emperor* carried twenty-four aircraft each, while *Pursuer* carried eighteen. A more effective aircraft than the Albacore, the Barracuda was another attempt to replace the Swordfish, and around 2,600 were built, even though it was described by some as a 'maintenance nightmare', and also had the unfortunate reputation of occasionally diving into the ground.

Given the difficult location, the raid needed to be conducted in daylight, and a dawn raid was decided upon to give the attackers at least the cover of darkness while on their way to the target. The aircrew were woken at 01:30, having been briefed that this was to be a very dangerous operation and that heavy casualties must be expected.

The aircraft of the first of two strikes were flown off at 04:30, flying just above sea level to evade enemy radar, before climbing to 8,000 feet to cross the snow-covered mountains. They arrived over the ship at 05:30. John Herrald was a Royal New Zealand Navy Volunteer Reserve sub lieutenant flying a Barracuda with a good view of the action:

> As I looked at this hill, it fell below us slowly, and then with a sudden surge we were over the top. There below us lay the *Tirpitz* in the exact place we had been told to look for her. Suddenly the leader shouted over the intercom: 'Attention fighters! Anti-flak! Over, over!' and as he said that he was slowly doing a half-roll and going down to the target. We peeled off and dived down behind him. While we were going down on our attack, the fighter squadrons were strafing the anti-aircraft positions and ships. They supported us with everything they had got, no risk seemed too great for them to take.
>
> I had the nose of my aircraft pointing just below the

funnel of the *Tirpitz*. I could see the fighters raking her decks, and for a few seconds I lived in a world which just contained my aircraft and the *Tirpitz*. I kept her nose glued to that point of the ship. I gazed at my altimeter and saw that I had a thousand feet to go until I got to my bombing height. In the few seconds that followed I could see the details of the ship; the swastika painted on her funnel, the faces of the ack-ack crews glaring up at us, and, a great sight, the leader's bombs bursting on the turrets.[5]

He dropped his bombs as he pulled out of his dive and started to weave to avoid enemy flak as he climbed away.

A second wave of aircraft appeared an hour later, fully expecting a hot welcome from the Germans, but they could still see the ship through a smoke screen produced by canisters placed around the fjord, while the smoke made it difficult for the AA gunners to see the attacking aircraft. The attack succeeded in inflicting further damage on the warship, with a large oil leak as evidence, while she was out of action for another three months.

Captain H.J.K. Hilken was in command of the escort carrier HMS *Emperor*, whose Grumman Hellcats provided fighter cover for the attacking Barracudas:

Perfect weather, light breeze, calm sea. Numerous hits seen on *Tirpitz*. All our aircraft returned safely, but one (Hoare) had to ditch as his hook had been damaged by flak. Picked up safely by destroyer. Expected enemy air attack all day, but none came. Similar strikes ordered for tomorrow, but later cancelled.[6]

The raid had been just in time, for the first aircraft had crossed the mountains over the fjord to find the crew shortening cable as *Tirpitz* prepared to put to sea.

One 1840 Squadron fighter pilot, Lieutenant Commander Ron Richardson, was flying one of the Grumman Hellcats that had strafed the *Tirpitz* and on his climb away from the ship spotted a German radar station on a hill top. Out of ammunition, he dropped his arrester hook hoping to catch the wire strung between two masts, and as he did so, he was caught by German AA fire and killed.

Despite the difficult location, the Barracudas managed no less than fifteen bomb hits with 500-lb and 1,600-lb bombs, and with the fighters strafing the superstructure and upper deck, accounted for 122 of her crew killed and another 316 wounded, including her commanding officer. Three Barracudas and one Hellcat were shot down and, as already mentioned, a fighter, damaged by German AA fire, had to ditch. As they left, the battleship was sitting with her stern on the bottom of the fjord and had been blown from her moorings, possibly by the effect of near misses.

A further attack on the *Tirpitz* followed in August 1944. On this occasion, a substantial force was deployed including three large fleet carriers, but the force was augmented by HMS *Nabob*. *Nabob* and *Puncher* were two escort carriers assigned to be manned by the Royal Canadian Navy, although the men of the embarked squadrons were Royal Navy and officially the ships remained on loan to the Royal Navy as the Admiralty didn't want to see American largesse handed on to another navy, no matter how closely allied, in case questions were asked. Had the ship been assigned directly to the Royal Canadian Navy, they would have used her as an escort carrier or possibly for anti-submarine sweeps in the North Atlantic, but the Royal Navy had decided that both *Nabob* and *Puncher* would be used in the attack role, and so the fitting out of the ships and their subsequent operations largely reflected this. Canadian interest in having carriers was due partly to national pride, a case of not wanting to end the war as a small ship navy, although this was hard to overcome as the Royal Canadian Navy operated a massive force of corvettes in addition to destroyers and frigates.

Mixed crewing was not an unmitigated success, and on one occasion the acrimony was such that a mutiny was only avoided by the ship having to go immediately to action stations. The perception is that the Royal Navy was still traditional and the Canadians were more relaxed, but as in any comparison of the Royal Navy and the US Navy, this wasn't always the case. Bill Drake was an artificer who volunteered for a secondment post-war with the Royal Canadian Navy aboard the light fleet carrier HMCS *Magnificent*:

The Royal Canadian Navy was not immune from Royal Navy 'bull'. Cdr Debbie Piers, the Executive Officer, introduced morning PT and evening quarters, the latter routine normally associated with *Nelson* and sailing ships. However the spirited Canadians had other ideas, and the Commander's prized Dartmouth telescope disappeared from his cabin. All leave was stopped and a search was carried out; the telescope was not found, and was said to have been seen floating away in the Solent.[7]

After her arrival in the UK, *Nabob* was used for a number of strikes against German coastal shipping off Norway, before taking part in Operation Goodwood, where she accompanied three fleet carriers and a battleship, as well as three cruisers and escorting destroyers for one of the nine Fleet Air Arm attacks on the *Tirpitz*.

On this operation, *Nabob* and the rest of the strike force steamed north of the Artic Circle through the summer's constant daylight into the Barent's Sea. *Nabob*'s four Grumman Wildcats flew combat air patrols while her Grumman Avengers flew anti-submarine patrols, recognizing that the threat from the U-boats remained high even this late in the war. Despite it being high summer, with daylight for most of the twenty-four hours, bad weather affected the operation. Even so, on 22 August 1944, once again three squadrons of Barracudas from the fleet carriers managed to get their bombs onto the *Tirpitz*, but at a cost of eleven of the ungainly aircraft.

It was likely that a second strike would be called for, and *Nabob* moved to the west so that she could re-fuel the destroyers, whose primary role was the maintenance of an anti-submarine screen around the strike force.

In clear, calm weather, *Nabob* laid out her fuelling hose, but without as much as a hint of a contact from destroyer Asdic (today more usually known as sonar) or a sighting from the encircling Avengers, *U-354* sent a torpedo into the carrier. None of the escorts got a sniff of a submarine. The torpedo had ripped through the flimsy unarmoured merchantman hull, tearing a hole fifty feet wide below the waterline on the starboard side towards the stern and killing twenty-one members of her crew. Within minutes, her stern began to settle, sinking fifteen feet, while her power supply failed. In the engine room, the cooling fans stopped and the temperature soared to 150 degrees F, forcing the duty engineer to shut down the engines. She was now dead in the water, wallowing in the Atlantic swell, and those aboard feared the worst, and boats and Carey floats were slipped ready for the order to abandon ship. Risking their lives, damage control parties went down into the bowels of the ship, risking being cut off by the rising waters, but most of all, risking being caught below the waterline if another torpedo hit the ship. There was also the chance of bulkheads giving way and the ship rolling over and sinking within minutes.

While this was happening, another torpedo was put into the destroyer HMS *Bickerton*, leader of the destroyer screen.

Back aboard the stricken *Nabob*, working in the dark, the damage control parties pressed on, managing to start emergency diesel generators and link these to auxiliary switchboards so that the ship once again had light and cooling fans and, most important, pumping mains could be patched and portable pumps dragged and wrestled into place. As the main working spaces were pumped clear, it was evident that the engine room bulkheads were under considerable pressure, bulging inward with the water that had found its way into the ship. As the ship wallowed, the bulkheads creaked and those attempting to save the ship were worried that they would burst, bringing their efforts to nought – not that they would have long to worry about it. The chief shipwright, who before the war had worked salvaging ships off St John's on Canada's Atlantic coast, calmly supervised a timber-shoring effort, reinforcing the bulkheads at the points of greatest strain.

Eventually with power restored and steam returning to the turbines, reports of U-boats reached Captain Lay on the bridge. Power restored, fans running again, steam on the turbines, the carrier began to creep forward, leaving her floats and the ship's boats behind, so that any further attack, or any problems as the stricken vessel encountered foul weather, would find her ship's company without any means of saving themselves in the chill Arctic waters. As a precautionary measure, the men injured by the blast of the torpedo and another 200 were transferred to a destroyer. Those left behind continued with the damage control work, which apart from pumping and shoring also meant ditching heavy equipment overboard or moving it forward to improve the vessel's sternward trim. The speed rose steadily to 10 knots.

Concerns about a further U-boat attack were well founded. Early in the morning of 23 August, first an HF/DF bearing and then a surface contact, warned that a U-boat was approaching. Despite the slope on the flight deck and the low speed, two Avengers catapulted off, managing to clamber into the air where they spent the next three and a half hours keeping the U-boat submerged. This was enough for the carrier to steam to a safe distance, but it left the Avenger pilots with the tricky task of landing on to the slow moving ship, landing 'uphill'. The first aircraft landed successfully, but the second crashed and went over the barrier to wreck six others parked forward. Some of the aircraft were armed, ready for a patrol, and live depth charges rolled around the flight deck, threatening to cause further damage or injure the deck handling parties, or, worse still, disappear over the side where they would soon reach their pre-set detonation depth and would explode, fatally damaging the ship.

The Canadian destroyer *Algonquin* took more men onboard before *Nabob* steamed into a fierce gale that kept U-boats submerged, but pounded her damaged sides for eleven hours. Fortunately, down below the wooden posts and boards supporting the engine room bulkheads held firm. It took another four days for the ship to cover the 1,100 miles to Scapa Flow, but she managed to enter under her own steam.

It was not until she eventually continued to Rosyth after further emergency repairs that an attempt could be made to recover the bodies of fourteen of those killed in the torpedo attack while the ship was safe in dry dock. They had been deep down in the bowels of the ship for a month. True to form, the dockyard workers or 'mateys' refused to help, leaving it to volunteers amongst the ship's officers. The men fortified themselves with large tots of neat rum, before manhandling the rotting remains of the victims up through the ship deck by deck.

This was a fine achievement, saving a stricken ship with a crew, most of whom were reservists and even fewer of them had 'big ship' experience. Sound seamanship and excellent damage control had saved the ship, while the skill and dedication of the naval airmen who had continued to use her sloping flight deck for anti-submarine patrols had prevented her from becoming a total loss from a possible second torpedo. Yet, despite this, the ship was judged to be beyond economic repair, especially given the heavy pressure on ship repair facilities in the United Kingdom and the, by this time unceasing, stream of new ships across the Atlantic. Nevertheless, while *Nabob*'s wartime career was over, post-war she was considered worthy of repatriation to the United States, where she was converted into a merchantman, the fate for which she was originally intended, and remained trading on the seas until the late 1960s.

The Fleet Air Arm had done well to damage the *Tirpitz* for her position made it difficult to get low enough to launch a torpedo attack while the size of bombs used could only bounce off her armour plating. It was not until the advent of very heavy bombs that could be dropped alongside the ship that air attack presented a real threat. On 15 September 1944, Avro Lancaster heavy bombers from the Royal Air Force's famous 617 'Dam Busters' Squadron used 12,000-lb 'Tallboy' bombs, but again only caused damage, although this time it was serious enough for the ship to be moved south to Tromso for repairs. Here she was a far easier target, and on 12 November, operating without fighter protection, 617's Lancasters found her again, without defending fighters, and this time their Tallboy bombs scored three direct hits, causing her to capsize. The *Tirpitz* no longer presented a threat, but one Royal Navy officer had the bad grace to claim that she had still not been sunk as her hull was out of the water.

Notes
1. Imperial War Museum Sound Archive Accession No.12038/3–6
2. Daily Telegraph, 27 August 1999.
3. Imperial War Museum Sound Archive Accession No.12038/3–6
4. Kilbracken, op. cit.
5. Imperial War Museum Sound Archive Accession No.2508/D/B
6. Thompson, Julian, *Imperial War Museum Book of the War at Sea, 1939–45: The Royal Navy in the Second World War*, IWM/Sidgwick & Jackson, London, 1996.
7. Drake, op. cit.

IX

TAKING THE WAR
TO THE ENEMY
II – The Far East

The landings in North Africa marked the end of German and Italian ambitions in that continent, turned the balance of power in the Mediterranean and considerably eased the plight of Malta. They laid the foundations for the next step in the war, taking ground forces into Axis territory for the first time. These plans were not without controversy – the American Admiral Ernest King wanted specific tasks to be allocated to both the British and the Free French, with the British Eastern Fleet at the time serving little useful purpose when he felt that it could be used to sever Japanese shipping links with Rangoon. At the Casablanca Conference in January 1943, King explained that according to his estimates, just 15 per cent of the total Allied effort was being devoted to the war against the Japanese in the Pacific, and that this would not be enough to stop them from consolidating their gains. His view was opposed by General Sir Alan Brooke, Chief of the Imperial General Staff, who felt that the Japanese were by this time on the defensive in the Pacific. The First Sea Lord, Admiral Sir Dudley Pound, felt that the British could not send naval units eastwards without strong carrier air support.

King's view did not mean that he opposed the priority being given to Germany. He realized that German defeat was the key to releasing further men and *matériel* for the war against Japan. It was also possible to devote greater resources towards defeating Germany as German targets were within reach of Allied bombers, and by this time Allied troops were able to engage with German forces on the ground in Europe. Japan, by contrast, was at first a target for naval warfare only, until bases within reach of the Japanese home islands could be secured for the United States Army Air Force's bombers. Early on, the United States Army Air Force, operating from bases in India, had been limited to striking at Japanese forces in Burma. The Pacific war was for some time a war for naval air power, submarines and amphibious forces.

Even so, after their great success in the Battle of Midway, the Americans were in the position to take the initiative in the Pacific. It was American commanders who could decide where and when to strike, now on the offensive while Japanese forces were forced to be increasingly on the defensive. The construction by the Japanese of a naval base and airfield on the island of Guadalcanal, part of the Solomon Islands, posed a threat to sea communications between the United States and Australia. The Americans wanted to secure the sea lanes, having realized early on that isolating Australia from the United States would be a logical strategic move.

The still new Commander-in-Chief US Navy, Fleet Admiral Ernest King, described this phase of the war as 'Offensive-Defensive', the earlier stage having been 'Defensive-Offensive'. This was a realistic assessment. In the earlier stage that had really ended at Midway, the Allies, meaning primarily the Americans with Australian and British help, were mainly concerned with stopping Japanese expansion, and took the war to the enemy whenever they could and whenever their resources allowed. Midway had started as a defensive battle, as had the Coral Sea before it. Now, the Allies were increasingly well placed to attack the Japanese, but could still not neglect defensive measures. Officially, however, that is to King and to his Army counterpart, General George Marshall, the offensive-defensive started with the landing on the Solomon Islands on 7 August 1942. King's strategy was clear. Priority was to be given to holding Hawaii, followed by maintaining communications with Australia, the very line of communication that many Japanese strategists wanted to see broken. This line secured, King advocated a step-by-step general advance through the New Hebrides, Solomons and the Bismarck Archipelago. In fact, both aspects of the strategy were interdependent since Japanese forces would be drawn away from their attempts to isolate Australia from the

United States to ward off the American advance. This step-by-step approach, creating a number of strong points along the way, also recognized that it was the only way of bringing substantial forces within reach of the Japanese home islands. King's approach was cautious and never under-estimated the enemy. There were to be no short cuts.

There was extensive use of United States Marine Corps aircraft at Guadalcanal, where a third of the ground attack aircraft were flown by Marine pilots. It was all the more surprising that following the capture of Guadalcanal early in 1943, Admiral Chester Nimitz, the commander of US forces in the Pacific decided to omit carrier training from the syllabus for USMC pilots, especially as the new escort carriers were starting to become available and could have been designed 'Marine carriers'. Doubtless two considerations were foremost in his mind. The first was the need to get as many pilots through training as possible, and naturally the carrier element of the syllabus prolonged training. The second was that as US forces advanced across the Pacific, more land bases became available. Nevertheless, the result was that for most of 1943 and into the following year, an increasing number of USMC pilots suffered from relative inactivity, denied what had become their natural role supporting amphibious forces as they stormed ashore, and it was not until late in 1944 when the marines returned to carrier aviation that this was remedied. In fact, logic really dictated that the 'beach storming' tradition of the USMC was best served by having Marine air squadrons aboard escort carriers providing close air support for their comrades on the beaches, but it was not until towards the end of the war, shortly before the fall of Okinawa in May 1945 that the first 'Marine carrier' arrived, USS *Block Island*, CVE-106, with eight Vought Corsairs, ten Grumman Hellcats and twelve Grumman Avenger bombers, and operated alongside British carriers in close support operations. This first escort dedicated to Marine aviation was soon joined by the USS *Gilbert Islands*, and a little later by the *Cape Gloucester* and *Vella Gulf*. These were all Commencement Bay-class escort carriers, the largest to enter service with the US Navy and incorporating many more of the US Navy's requirements than the earlier ships.

Pressing towards Rabaul

Although Japan had occupied two of the Aleutian islands close to Alaska, that isolated state on the mainland of North America, the main strategy was based on advances in Micronesia, which was initially to smash through the Bismarck Archipelago and capture the major Japanese base at Rabaul. A step-by-step approach was put in hand; anything else would have been risky and foolhardy. On 21 February 1943, the first step was taken when the US 43rd Infantry Division landed on the Russell Islands, finding that these were unoccupied. Landing on an enemy shore has never been an easy business, and certainly not safe, but a major step forward came on 30 June 1943 with the American landings on Rendova Island, uncomfortably close to the Japanese air station on New Georgia. For the first time, purpose-designed landing craft were used, with three basic types introduced that made seaborne assaults much easier and faster. Rear Admiral R.K. Turner's landing fleet at Rendova included Landing Ship Tanks, or LSTs, each capable of carrying twenty tanks to the shore; Landing Craft Tank, LCT, each of which could carry three tanks; and Landing Craft Infantry, LCI, capable of carrying 400 men. Protecting this force were two aircraft carriers and three escort carriers, five battleships and supporting cruisers and destroyers, all in Task Force 31. A number of minor naval engagements took place as the landings and the re-supply operations proceeded.

In preparing for the assault on the Gilbert Islands, the Americans not only had their two new classes of aircraft carrier, but they also had the escort carriers. Still known officially to the British as 'auxiliary aircraft carriers', by this time it was becoming clear that the British had a point as the Battle of the Atlantic had been virtually won by late 1943, and the so-called escort carriers, that had done so much in this and on the Arctic convoys, were now free for other tasks, acting as aircraft transports, maintenance carriers or providing additional flight decks, usually in support of forces ashore, as at Salerno, since their low speed made them unsuitable for fleet actions.

American tactics at this stage were also well-defined. Before mounting any landings, considerable effort would be devoted to 'softening up' the target area using carrier-borne aircraft and the heavy guns of the battleships and heavy cruisers. This has become the standard since for any invasion, or indeed even any major assault across a front line. While such efforts obviously alert the enemy to the forthcoming attack, it not only wears him down, it also means that coastal artillery and fortifications, airfields, barracks and communications are all battered, hopefully reducing loss of life in the invasion force and enhancing the chances of success.

For the landings on the Gilbert Islands, Admiral Spruance had six large aircraft carriers, five light carriers, five battleships and six cruisers, as well as twenty-one destroyers. The landings in the Gilbert Islands were preceded by a series of attacks by the 700 carrier aircraft of the Fifth Fleet, starting on 19 November. The main targets were all Japanese airfields within range of Makin and Tarawa, the two islands selected for the initial landings. It took just three days to put most of the aircraft, mainly belonging to the Japanese Navy Air Force, on the Gilbert Islands and the eastern Marshall Islands nearby, out of action. On 20 November, the landing fleet put ashore the US 2nd Marine Division and part of the US Army's 27th Infantry Division, with some 7,000 men landed on Makin and another 18,000 on Tarawa, which had the main Japanese garrison of 5,000 troops. Makin was taken on the first day, despite fierce resistance by the Japanese garrison of 800 men. On Tarawa, despite the intensive softening up raids that continued, a third of the Marines making the initial assault were hit by enemy fire, and it took three days to suppress Japanese resistance which culminated in mass suicide attacks by infantry on the night of 22–23 November.

The landings were not without cost for the US Navy, which saw the USS *Independence* crippled by a torpedo dropped by one of the few Japanese aircraft to become airborne on 20 November, putting the carrier out of service for six months. The contrast between the light carriers and the escort carriers was highlighted once again when, on 24 November, the USS *Liscombe Bay*, an escort carrier that had only been in service for a few weeks, was torpedoed by the submarine *I-175*, and sank shortly afterwards. Nevertheless, by 26 November, the US forces had overcome the fierce Japanese resistance and had occupied the Gilbert Islands.

Further operations in the area continued into 1944, culminating in the landings in the Marianas starting with the island of Saipan on 15 June 1944. Here, Task Force 52 under Vice Admiral Turner USN included eight escort carriers with 170 aircraft for operations, plus some reserve aircraft for TF58, the strike carrier force. This was the action that developed into the 'Marianas Turkey Shoot' and saw massive losses in Japanese aircraft. An unusual feature of the operation was that seventy-three United States Army Air Force aircraft were catapulted off the decks of the escort carriers in late June to fly to shore bases to provide close air support for forces ashore in Saipan and Tinian. The escort carriers were also home to USMC Stinson OY observation aircraft, largely flown by personnel who were not regular USMC aircrew but had private flying experience before the war, while the aircraft had been provided by the United States Army.

Later, good use seems to have been made of the 'Marine carriers', as in May 1945, two were detached from the forces surrounding Okinawa with the USS *Suwannee* to cover landings in Borneo by Australian forces. Quite clearly, the Royal Australian Navy could have done with an escort carrier or two on its strength, but unlike the Royal Canadian Navy, convoy protection was not such a major issue and it was this, rather than the strike role, that had first awakened Canadian interest. This operation marked the operational debut of the Curtiss SC-1 Seahawk.

Leyte Gulf

By late 1944, the United States had more than regained the upper hand in the war against Japan, having taken the Marianas in June 1944 and brought the United States Army Air Force bases within reach of Japan. The air raids on Japan started that autumn. The next priority was to re-take the Philippines, which would not only fulfil General MacArthur's promise to return, but also effectively enable the US Navy to cut the vital shipping route from the East Indies and Malaya to Japan, carrying much-needed oil and rubber without which the war effort would be crippled. Already minelaying operations and submarine warfare had had a tremendous impact, so that between March 1944 and August

1945, the volume of shipping through the Shimonoseki Straits fell from more than half a million tons to just 5,000 tons. By August 1945, the daily ration could provide just 1,400 calories, and many believe that had the war continued for another year, as many as 8 million Japanese could have died from malnutrition.

The invasion started on 20 October 1944 with Vice Admiral Kinkaid's Seventh Fleet of 300 landing ships and transports landing Lieutenant General Krueger's Sixth Army at Tacloban on Leyte, one of the smaller islands in the Philippines. As on previous landings, heavy fire support was given by six battleships and nine heavy and light cruisers, supported by fifty-one destroyers and with no less than eighteen escort carriers with aircraft to provide close air support and fighter protection, all under the command of Rear Admiral Oldendorf.

The eighteen escort carriers were commanded by Rear Admiral Sprague, and were divided into three groups known as 'Taffy One, led by Sprague himself, with subordinate commanders leading 'Taffy Two' and 'Taffy Three'. Japanese airfields on Luzon and in the central Philippines were kept under constant attack by aircraft from Vice Admiral Halsey's Third Fleet, with Mitscher in command of TF38 with its four carrier groups with eight fleet carriers and another eight light carriers, supported by six battleships, fifteen cruisers and sixty destroyers. Halsey's other task was to protect the escort carriers by effectively closing the San Bernadino Strait to the Japanese.

Japanese desperation now reached its peak with a defiant plan calling for four aircraft carriers, the recently repaired *Zuikaku* and the light carriers *Zuiho*, *Chitose* and *Chiyoda*, with just 116 aircraft, still commanded by Vice Admiral Ozawa, and a total force of nine battleships, nineteen cruisers and thirty-five destroyers. The primary objective was to finally bring the Japanese battleships, which had enjoyed a quiet war as fleet clashes had become the preserve of carrier-borne aircraft, into action.

The American invasion force was to be attacked from the west by Vice Admiral Kurita's First Striking Force with five battleships. Belatedly, the Japanese had come to realize that they could no longer look for and expect to win any air-to-air combat, and that a classic ship-to-ship naval engagement was not to be expected, but that the only hope of success lay in attacking American troop

145

transports before they reached the landing areas, while they were still at sea and where the loss of life would be greatest. This was a major weakness of the Japanese plan – the landings had been made before the Imperial Japanese Navy appeared on the scene – and was doubtless due to faulty intelligence and reconnaissance as much as poor planning. The failings are all the more difficult to understand because the Japanese had expected any American invasion to be through Leyte. Nevertheless, they still posed a very real threat to the escort carriers engaged in providing vital close air support for the troops fighting ashore.

The action that the Japanese were anticipating was known to them as the Second Battle of the Philippine Sea, and to the Americans as the Battle of Leyte Gulf. At the outset, Kurita was pessimistic:

> . . . the enemy transports would have to be destroyed completely. My opinion at the time was that, in view of the difference in strength of the opposing forces, our chance for a victory after the sorties would be about fifty-fifty. I had also thought that the aerial support would fall short of our expectations.

The Japanese effort got off to a bad start when, on 23 October 1944, two American submarines, *Dace* and *Darter* discovered the First Striking Force and torpedoed three heavy cruisers including Kurita's flagship *Atago*, which sank almost immediately as did the *Maya*. Kurita's orders were to be off Leyte on 25 October, but fighting had started the previous day when aircraft based on Leyte attacked the most northerly of the American carrier groups in the Battle of the Sibuyan Sea. This attack was intended to involve Ozawa's carrier-borne aircraft, so that the US Third Fleet would be drawn away and leave Kurita with a clear run at the transports, but the aircraft failed to find the American ships and, running short of fuel, attempted to fly to bases on Luzon and many of them were intercepted by American fighters on the way.

At 06:45 on 25 October, American reconnaissance aircraft discovered Kurita's battle fleet east of Samar, a large island to the north-east of Leyte. Just thirteen minutes later, the Battle of

Samar began, with Kurita's Centre Force battleships discovering and starting to shell Sprague's 'Taffy One' group of escort carriers, the most northerly of the force. The escort carriers, with only AA armament, were unable to respond, so Sprague ordered all of the aircraft to be flown off and withdrew his ships to the south. A number of the escort carriers were able to put up smoke, while the remainder attempted to improvise a smoke-screen by changing the fuel-air mixture for their boiler fires, but this was a dated tactic as the Japanese flagship *Yamato* now had radar, as did some of the other ships. In desperation, the Americans mounted another destroyer torpedo attack, damaging the cruiser *Kumano* and causing her to withdraw, but at the cost of three US destroyers.

Life aboard the escort carriers supporting the landings became very exciting as the Japanese attacked. George Smith was a maintainer aboard one of the ships under attack:

> That morning I had a duty on the flight deck . . . someone yelled at me and said you'd better get your helmet on and your Mae West – your life belt – because here comes the Japs and about that time I heard an explosion on the fantail. First I thought it was one of our own planes exploding back there and I looked up and saw all this tin foil falling, this tin foil to jam our radar and of course GQ (General Quarters) and everybody manned GQ stations and then they started shooting . . . trying to get our range, our skipper turned the ship . . . zigzagged it, as we were trying to escape from the Japanese . . . Then we started laying down smoke . . . trying to blind the Japanese . . . and they pulled pretty fast on us, they caught one of our carriers back there and they sank it . . . they got so close we could even see the Japanese flags flying . . . of course we were opening up with everything we had . . . this was running battle of about two hours . . . we were going between these two islands and the Japanese decided that it was leading to a trap . . . so they broke off the engagement.[1]

The escort carriers were like sitting ducks and this was the best opportunity the Japanese ever had of destroying part of the

American carrier fleet. Aboard the ships, those without any role were left trying to take what shelter they could. The aircraft that had been flown off attempted to attack the Japanese ships, but this had little effect as they were either loaded with fragmentation bombs for use against Japanese ground troops or simply had their guns, with which they attempted to strafe the warships hoping to catch crew members in exposed positions such as the flying bridges. Inevitably, there were some without any ammunition who could only hope to distract the Japanese, and many were short of fuel having been scrambled with whatever was in their tanks, often just the remains of the previous day's final sortie. Some of the aircraft did run out of fuel and their pilots ditched close to the fleeing carriers, hoping to be picked up, but no one dared stop.

Meanwhile, Rear Admiral Clifton 'Ziggy' Spragues had sent three destroyers and four destroyer escorts to launch a torpedo attack on the Japanese battleships, but three of these ships were sunk in what had to be an unequal contest, similar in some ways to the desperate attempt by the British destroyers *Ardent* and *Acasta* to save the carrier HMS *Glorious* from destruction by the German battlecruisers *Scharnhorst* and *Gneisenau* off Norway in 1940. Nevertheless, three Japanese heavy cruisers were bombed and torpedoed, and later sank from the damaged caused.

The escort carrier sunk by Japanese shellfire from the cruisers *Chokai*, *Haguro* and *Noshiro*, was the USS *Gambier Bay*, CVE-73, which had served in the Pacific for eight months in a variety of roles, including that of aircraft transport, but another three, *Fanshaw Bay*, *Kalinin Bay* and *White Plains*, were damaged by Japanese gunnery. Then it all ended as the Japanese broke off the one-sided engagement and turned away.

Kurita was convinced that he was heading into a trap but, once again, Japanese naval intelligence was lacking, as instead of escort carriers, he was convinced that he was attacking standard fleet carriers which, with their much higher speed, would take some time to overtake. This conclusion was strange indeed, since it meant that Kurita, an experienced senior naval officer, thought that the escort carriers were withdrawing at 30 knots or more, double their maximum speed! A second group of escort carriers ahead of him was also mistaken for further fleet carriers. Expecting further American carriers to approach from the north – Halsey's Third Fleet – he decided that it was safer to do battle in the open sea rather than in the confined waters of Leyte Gulf.

Taffy Two, the second group of six escort carriers, was next to receive the unwanted attentions of the Japanese, as the first properly planned kamikaze attacks started. Four aircraft from shore bases dived on to the Second Escort Carrier Group, hitting both *Suwannee* and *Santee*, with the second ship also being hit by a torpedo from a Japanese submarine. As Kurita returned to the east of Samar, there were further kamikaze attacks, where the escort carrier *St Lo* had the unwanted distinction of being the first victim of the Japanese suicide pilots when she was struck by a Mitsubishi Zero fighter which burst into the hangar deck and whose burning fuel set off explosions and fires, causing the carrier to sink within half an hour. Other kamikaze attacks were responsible for damaging both *Kalinin Bay*, which was also struck by shells from Japanese warships, and *Kitkun Bay* in Taffy One. Kurita was unaware of the kamikaze attacks, and certainly knew nothing about their successes. This was the man who had signalled to his ships the previous day: 'Braving any loss and damage we may suffer, the First Striking Force will break into Leyte Gulf and fight to the last man.' Yet, at noon, he ordered a withdrawal, having failed completely in his mission to destroy the American transports, scuttling three of his heavy cruisers, while another two, although badly damaged, were considered to be capable of returning safely to Japan.

It was not until later that the Americans realized that they were the targets for suicide attacks. The first few aircraft were seen either as having crashed out of control or having been deliberately flown into the ships by pilots who were frustrated after their aircraft had been badly damaged. After all, in the days before ejection seats, escape from a fast low flying aircraft was well nigh impossible.

George Smith was close, too close, to the kamikaze attack:

We thought they was (sic) dropping bombs on us because one of the carriers off the port side took a direct hit from a kamikaze. They hit this carrier just dead centre and as we went by men were abandoning ship . . . and as we got beyond it the whole ship just seemed to explode . . . there was nothing there. And about that time on our ship a kamikaze came in on us . . . just like regular landing I guess he was trying to sneak in on us like one of our own planes . . . And he started to drop in and of course the skipper seen what was going on so he turned the ship hard port . . . the men on the starboard side were banged against there, they swung our guns round and shot across the flight deck hitting the kamikaze and the kamikaze he winged over and dropped on the other side . . . into the water and exploded.[2]

The senior officers in both navies were confused and unaware of the true situation. Both Nimitz and Kinkaid believed that Halsey was working to plan and safeguarding the San Bernardino Strait, and then had to send signals demanding to know his true position once they realized that he had left the Strait open to the Japanese. Halsey was then ordered to return south. Had he sent part of his force northwards, Halsey could have covered the Strait with his remaining force.

On 26 October, there were further kamikaze attacks. The USS *St Lo*, CVE-63, Captain F.J. McKenna, was so badly damaged that she soon sank, while four others were also damaged, although less seriously. Nevertheless, later that day aircraft from Taffy 2 attacked a Japanese force withdrawing through the Visayan Sea after landing reinforcements on Leyte and sinking the light cruiser *Kinu* and the destroyer *Uranami*.

Overall, the Americans had lost a light carrier and two escort carriers as well as three destroyers. The Japanese had lost 150 aircraft, both shore-based and carrier-borne, compared with 100 US aircraft. Some 10,000 Japanese had lost their lives compared with 1,500 Americans.

Obviously, this was another American victory and yet another Japanese defeat. Kurita had failed to make the most of his opportunities, but Ozawa's strategy had worked, drawing Halsey northward and giving Kurita an opportunity, except, of course, that Ozawa did not have sufficient aircraft even at the outset to ward off a determined American attack.

The kamikaze attacks continued until 5 November, with six carriers damaged, including the *Suwannee*, CVE-27, as well as a light cruiser and several destroyers, one of which was sunk. Nevertheless, the Japanese had been beaten back to within reach of their own home islands as, by 24 November, United States Army Air Force B-29 Superfortress bombers were able to make their first attack on Tokyo using airfields in the Marianas.

While poor weather was a constant danger on the convoy routes to the Arctic, the Pacific was not always as calm as the name suggests. This was brought home to the US Navy on 18 December 1944, when Admiral Halsey's Fifth Fleet was caught in a typhoon off the Philippines, with the loss of three destroyers and damage to eight small carriers, with 765 men drowned. Halsey was later blamed by a court of inquiry for not getting out of the typhoon's path.

The escort carriers were very much in the front line as the war moved closer to Japan, as 1945 started off with the advance to the Lingayen Gulf between 2 and 6 January, with Task Group 77.2 under Vice Admiral Jesse B. Oldendorf including twelve CVEs. Once again kamikaze attacks were inflicted upon the fleet, with the loss of the USS *Ommaney Bay*, CVE-79, and a destroyer. Meanwhile, Admiral Thomas C. Kinkaid's Seventh Fleet attack force, TF 77, followed TF 77.2, and while the kamikaze vented most of their fury on the latter, both the USS *Kadasham Bay* and *Kitkun Bay*, were put out of action in attacks. On 16 February, the pre-invasion bombardment of Iwo Jima began with the Fifth Fleet's battleships joined by a number of escort carriers. After the invasion started on 19 February, on 21 February, at dusk, the *Bismarck Sea*, CVE 95, Captain J.L. Pratt, was struck by a kamikaze off Iwo Jima, and sank three hours later with the loss of 218 of her 943 officers and men. In attacks by kamikaze on 3 and 4 May 1945, the *Sangamon*, CVE-26 was among the ships sunk.

Royal Navy returns to the East

The American successes in the Pacific War had been just that, with the deployed forces overwhelmingly United States in origin, although Australian and New Zealand forces were also involved, and there were a number of Royal Navy units, usually cruisers and destroyers. Now with the war in the Mediterranean going the way of the Allies and with a growing number of land bases in Italy, and the Battle of the Atlantic over, with the German submarine menace neutralized and the remaining major surface units stuck in port, the Royal Navy could send its major fleet units to the East. The operations of the Eastern Fleet had in any case been restricted following the Japanese attacks against Ceylon because of the lack of carrier air cover, and even had carriers been freed from European waters earlier, there would still have been the question of suitable fighters and, even, suitable bombers, as the Fairey Barracuda was to prove ill-suited to operations in the tropics and was soon withdrawn and replaced by Grumman Avengers.

As with the US Navy, the war in the Pacific saw the most exciting and decisive roles assigned to the fast fleet carriers, ably supported by light carriers of the American Independence-class. The British equivalent, the Colossus-class, was larger and designed as a carrier from the keel upwards, but slower than the Independence-class ships. Most important of all, it was not available until the final few months of the war and took no part in the fighting.

Nevertheless, a small number of the Royal Navy's escort carriers found their way to the Pacific, predominantly acting as aircraft transports and as maintenance and repair ships, but first a number were also deployed to the Indian Ocean to provide trade protection. One of these was HMS *Ameer*, maintaining anti-submarine patrols in the Indian Ocean, through which convoys from the United States passed on their way to the Gulf, then usually known as the Persian Gulf, through which the bulk of supplies for the Soviet Union passed with transhipment to land transport at an Iranian port.

Ameer was also present when Ramtree Island off the coast of Burma was attacked by the Royal Navy and Royal Indian Navy in January 1945, a few months before combined amphibious and overland assaults saw the fall of Rangoon. The landing beaches were within the field of fire of Japanese artillery hidden in caves, but these were silenced by the guns of the battleship *Queen Elizabeth* and cruiser *Phoebe*, supported by *Ameer*'s twenty-four Grumman Hellcat fighters of No. 815 Squadron, allowing the island to be taken as a springboard for the capture of Rangoon in May.

152

Another operation was in the Netherlands East Indies in April 1945. Operation Sunfish on 11 April 1945, saw Force 63 led by the battleships *Queen Elizabeth* and the French *Richelieu*, with the cruisers *London* and *Cumberland*, the latter leading the 26th Destroyer Flotilla, and including the escort carriers *Emperor* and *Khedive*, attack Sabang and Oleheh. On 16 April the same force turned their attentions to Emmahaven and Padang. The two escort carriers shared No. 808 Squadron with its twenty-four Grumman Hellcats. The squadron was officially embarked in *Khedive*, but six of its aircraft were detached to *Empress* for some of the operations.

C. S. 'Bill' Drake was one of the maintainers with No. 896 Naval Air Squadron that had embarked in HMS *Ameer* for the passage from South Africa to Colombo in Ceylon, now Sri Lanka, where they arrived on 8 May 1945. This was VE day in Europe, but there was little cause for celebration in the Far East, where American, Australian, British and New Zealand forces were gradually easing closer to Japan in the face of heavy resistance, and fiercer resistance still was expected if, as everyone believed likely at the time, the Japanese home islands had to be invaded.

Neither the squadron nor the carrier was new to warfare. No. 896 had operated from *Victorious* and from the escort carrier *Pursuer* against the German battleship *Tirpitz*, that had spent almost its entire career tucked away safely in Norwegian fjords, menacing Allied convoys to the Soviet Union. *Ameer* had been engaged in trade protection duties in the Indian Ocean with No. 845 Squadron embarked with its Grumman Wildcat fighters and Avenger bombers, before moving to a more combative role with No. 804 squadron, whose Grumman Hellcats had covered landings on both Ramree Island in Operation Matador and Cheduba Island in Operation Sankey. Then 804's Hellcats had provided fighter cover for 888 Squadron on Operation Stacey as it conducted photographic reconnaissance over the Kra Isthmus, Penang and north Sumatra. At the time, this was seen as steady progress towards the eventual liberation of Singapore, with no one in South East Asia Command aware that Japanese surrender would be first forced by the use of nuclear weapons.

Later, 804 Squadron was to have its aircraft assigned to other escort carriers, including *Empress* and *Shah* for raids on the Andaman Islands and the coast of Burma, before returning to

Ameer in June for attacks on Sumatra and Phuket in Thailand. No. 896, meanwhile, transferred to *Empress* to cover minesweeping off Phuket.

When Rangoon was eventually liberated in May, No. 807 Squadron embarked in *Hunter* provided fighter cover and afterwards provided air cover for anti-shipping strikes. No. 809 Squadron aboard *Stalker* undertook similar duties.

Sink the *Haguro*

By spring 1945, the British were re-establishing themselves in Burma. Supported by the British Eastern Fleet they eventually retook Rangoon from the Japanese, who were anxious to keep hold of the oilfields in Burma. The landings near Rangoon, Operation Dukedom, were covered by escort carriers including *Emperor*, although *Shah* would also have been involved had not a fault appeared with her catapult. The fleet was in Trincomalee on 9 May when Ultra intelligence discovered that a Japanese Nachi-class cruiser was to leave Singapore the following day to evacuate the garrison in the Andaman Islands. Almost immediately, the fleet sailed hoping to intercept the Japanese. Japanese reconnaissance, not always reliable, on this occasion did succeed in warning the cruiser *Haguro* and her destroyer escort, *Kamikaze*, that the Royal Navy was at sea, and the two ships returned to Singapore.

Ultra was able to warn that the two ships had sailed again on 14 May, and also confirmed that the Japanese supply vessel *Kurishoyo Maru*, escorted by a submarine chaser, had successfully carried out an evacuation of the Nicobar Islands and was on her way to Singapore. The following day, the escort carrier HMS *Emperor* launched a strike of four Grumman Avengers from 851 Naval Air Squadron, commanded by Lieutenant Commander (A) Michael Fuller, RNVR. The four aircraft were armed with bombs, and attacked the two ships, but one aircraft was shot down by heavy AA fire, although its crew were able to take to their dinghy. A second strike, again of four aircraft, was then launched from *Emperor*, led by Fuller, but one aircraft was forced to return with engine trouble. Two of the remaining aircraft then sighted five destroyers, and spent thirty-five minutes trying to identify them – and eventually decided what they were, which was fortunate since it was the 26th Destroyer Flotilla at sea in an attempt to intercept the *Haguro*. By this time, the two aircraft were short of fuel and had to return. This left Fuller on his own, with orders to search for the dinghy carrying the aircrew down on the first strike. He jettisoned his bombs to increase range, but failed to find the dinghy as he had been given the wrong search coordinates; instead he found *Kurishoyo* and the submarine chaser, and started to fly around them while fixing their position. At this point, Fuller noticed two more ships some fifteen miles to the south of his position, heading north, and keeping out of AA range, and succeeded in identifying them as a Nachi-class cruiser and a Minikaze-class destroyer before they changed course to the south-west having spotted his aircraft.

'She was very large and very black against a very dark monsoon cloud,' Fuller recalled later. 'An enormously impressive sight, just as a warship ought to look.'[3]

He was convinced that the Japanese were trying to remain unobtrusive, wanting to keep out of sight. Not being inclined to oblige them, he signalled the rest of the British fleet at 11:50: 'One cruiser, one destroyer sighted. Course 240. Speed 10 knots.' He maintained this flow of information for an hour before climbing directly over the *Haguro* at 12:50 to make a final signal, giving the direction finders with the fleet the chance of making an exact fix, before returning to the carrier to land with just ten minutes' fuel left.

Haguro was still some considerable distance from the *Emperor*, but the carrier launched three more Avengers which found the cruiser and dive-bombed her. They achieved one direct hit and another near miss. Their return flight of 530 miles was the longest attacking flight from any British carrier during the war, and the one and only occasion that a major enemy warship at sea was dive-bombed by British naval aircraft. The attack left *Haguro* only slightly damaged, and heading for Singapore, but after dark she was finally cornered by the 26th Destroyer Flotilla and sunk by gunfire and torpedoes in the entrance to the Malacca Straits early on 16 May.

Aboard the Escort Carriers

Bill Drake recalls that the steel deck of the hangar curved upwards fore and aft, making handling of aircraft very difficult in heavy weather. At least the ships of what has been variously known as the Ameer-class or Ruler-class, had lifts at each end of the hangar, providing not only some safeguard in case one broke down, but also reducing the number of aircraft movements. *Ameer* could carry twenty-four Hellcats, while a Supermarine Walrus was deployed from No. 1700 Squadron ashore at Trincomalee, or 'Trinco', in Ceylon for the vital task of search and rescue, with other aircraft from the squadron also embarked in *Attacker*, *Emperor*, *Hunter*, *Khedive*, *Shah* and *Stalker*.

The Hellcat was as close to the perfect carrier-borne fighter aircraft as anything seems to have been during the Second World War. It was sturdy, unlike the Seafire, and lacked the natural inclination to bounce and topple forwards onto its nose that seemed to afflict not just the Seafire but also the otherwise highly regarded Vought Corsair. The designer clearly knew about life aboard a carrier. The wings were folded manually, swivelling and rotating backwards to lie alongside the aircraft fuselage, leaving enough headroom on the eighteen foot high hangar deck for spares to be stored – useful for large spares such as replacement mainplanes. Better still, the designer obviously knew that in the tight confines of a carrier's hangar, everything ought to be idiot-proof, so once folded, the guns in the wings pointed safely downward, sparing carriers carrying these aircraft the type of accident that so afflicted the fast, armoured carrier *Formidable* on 18 May 1945, when an armourer working on a Corsair in the hangar failed to notice that the guns were still armed. Unintentionally, he fired the Corsair's guns into a parked Avenger, which blew up and set off a fierce fire that eventually accounted for thirty aircraft.

Bill recalls that *Ameer* had a single hydraulic catapult, still known to the Royal Navy as an 'accelerator' forward, and that this used the new US Navy wire strop method so that heavier aircraft could be launched in the light winds that were usual in the Indian Ocean, and of course, that had been the lot of the escort carriers at Salerno. One catapult was better than none, and while it could ensure that, when steaming at 18.5 knots, an aircraft could leave the deck at 74 knots, if the catapult failed, the ship was still useless in light winds. Then again, similar weaknesses were to occur with the Colossus-class, still with a single catapult, although eventually these were steam operated, and with a maximum speed of just 24 knots.

The gentle breezes of the Indian Ocean were to prove too much for one British naval aeroplane, the Fairey Barracuda. No. 815 squadron sailed from Belfast with twelve Barracuda IIIs aboard the escort carrier *Smiter*. In late spring 1945, they sailed to Cochin in India via the Mediterranean and the Suez Canal. In the gentle breezes of the Indian Ocean, even with rocket-assisted take-off gear or RATOG, the Barracuda could only just clear the flight deck without a bomb load. 'We were only just clearing the ship's bows with rocket-assisted take-off gear without a bomb load,' recalls Lionel 'Lee' Ward, who was a Royal Naval Volunteer Reserve Lieutenant. 'Sinking down to the water, we created a slipstream wash in the sea before gaining enough lift. The Barracuda III plus bomb load off an escort carrier was a hopeless conception. Thank God the Americans dropped the atomic bomb which saved us from extinction.'[4]

The aircraft would have been a disaster if a bomb load had been attempted. In the end, the aircraft were left ashore at the Royal Naval Air Station at Katukurunda in Ceylon, and 815 squadron's personnel were taken back to UK aboard *Fencer*, another escort carrier, at the end of August after the Japanese surrender.

No. 884 Squadron was deployed ashore in Ceylon for a period, and while the original intention had been for the squadron to embark in a sister ship of *Ameer*, HMS *Empress*, it was decided that rather than wait for her arrival, the squadron should re-embark aboard *Ameer* for Operation Collie. This operation was intended to mount attacks on Japanese forces in the Nicobar Islands, Indian territory but slightly more than 300 miles off the coast of what is now Malaysia. Another objective was to provide air cover for minesweeping operations in the area, clearly with an invasion in mind. The task force for Operation Collie included the two Ruler-class carriers *Ameer* and *Empress*, the cruiser *Nigeria*, flagship for Rear Admiral Patterson, and the 6th Minesweeping Flotilla. Unlike the Corsair, the Hellcat was only rarely used as a fighter-bomber, and these may have given rise to some problems, not least because of the inexperience of the pilots.

Bill Drake again:

> Our aircraft were loaded with a single 500lb bomb under the port wing and this may have affected the handling, because one of the first to launch veered to port, hit the sea and the pilot was killed. Shortly afterwards a second plane did the same thing but the pilot regained control and landed on after the mission trailing a length of wire cable that he had picked up from the catwalk as he went over the deck edge. Our C.O., Lt-Cdr Norris was shot down and killed during the attack on Nancowry harbour when he made a second strike when the defenders were already alert . . . During the same attack a second pilot was also shot down, but managed to ditch his aircraft offshore and was picked up by the *Eskimo* (a destroyer). On 8 July, Sub-Lt Gregory was also shot down and was recovered from the sea by *Emperor*'s A.S.R. Walrus. Our own Walrus did not get airborne as the tail wheel strut collapsed while it was being ranged in the hangar. No less than fifteen Hellcats had protected the Walrus during the rescue. The flight deck party were rather redundant when the Walrus landed, as it flew so slowly that it seemed unlikely to overtake the ship. Take-off was equally straight-forward, and with just a few knots of wind over the deck the Walrus lifted off almost at once.[5]

The loss of a senior officer taking a second run over a target at this late stage in the war was strange, since it was strongly discouraged by the Fleet Air Arm. Not only were the defenders on the alert, the anti-aircraft gunners had also 'got their eye in', meaning that they were able to judge the speed and direction of any attack. While the use of fifteen fighters to protect the Walrus might seem excessive, this aircraft was highly vulnerable. It was slow, like the Swordfish, but with none of that aircraft's manoeuvrability.

Operating any aircraft from the confines of a carrier flight deck, which never, ever seems to be big enough, has always been a difficult and demanding task, with many dangers for the unwary. The Hellcats tried to use free take-off whenever possible, thus speeding up the rate at which aircraft were flown off and reducing the time and fuel lost while getting into formation at the start of a mission. As always with a free take-off, aircraft were ranged as far aft as possible, waiting for engines to be started and wings spread. At this stage, problems sometimes arose, and the flight deck crew had to be on hand to sort these out if at all possible.

Aircraft were armed before being ranged on deck. In the Royal Navy, 3-inch rocket projectiles were always loaded by the electricians. There were strict safety procedures, with insulation checks and testing of all circuits using test lamps, which were left connected to ensure that there was no power present when the rockets were finally connected. Connections were made working from inboard to outboard in case of accidental ignition of a rocket. The artificers, as the Royal Navy calls its skilled tradesmen, on *Ameer* must have been conscientious, since there were no accidents, although on occasion aircraft returning from a mission with unfired rockets lost these as they hooked on, and it was not uncommon for a rocket to skid across the flight deck, doubtless giving a few nasty moments for those waiting to catch the aircraft after it had taxied across the barrier and fold the wings prior to placing it on a lift to 'strike down' into the hangar deck.

The availability of spare mainplanes was also put to good use. Towards the end of Operation Collie, one of *Ameer*'s Hellcats sustained serious flak damage to a wing, and it was decided that this should be changed rather than repaired. The spare mainplane was found to be to a different modification from the original, but even so, it was replaced overnight and the aircraft was in the air next day as part of the task force's combat air patrol, or CAP. The aircraft concerned must have been fated, however, as it then suffered an engine failure and the pilot had to ditch, but was rescued and returned to the ship unharmed.

The task force returned to Trincomalee on 13 July. *Ameer*'s Hellcats had flown eighty-two sorties and accumulated 142 flying hours, but two pilots had been killed, one in an accident taking-off and one in action, and six aircraft had been lost, three of them to enemy action. This was not a bad ratio, as experience at Salerno had shown, and while the Hellcat was a better carrier-borne fighter than the Seafire, it was also a much heavier aircraft.

Back in 'Trinco', 884 Squadron replaced its aircraft and a new commanding officer took over from the senior pilot, who had assumed command on the death of the previous CO. The squadron was transferred to HMS *Empress*, and on 19 July the ship left on Operation Livery to attack Phuket Island, off the coast of Malaya, and to attack targets in the north of Malaya and southern Siam, now Thailand. As on the previous operation, the carrier aircraft were to provide cover for minesweeping, on this occasion in the entrance to the Straits of Malacca, the main route for shipping between the Indian and Pacific oceans, running between the coast of Malaysia and what was then the Netherlands East Indies, now Indonesia. That the minesweeping was necessary was soon proven when the minesweeper *Squirrel* hit a mine and had to be sunk by gunfire from other warships, and even aboard *Empress*, at some distance from the minesweeping, those aboard were treated to the sight of a mine floating past, which became the target for small-arms fire before it could be hit by any of the ships. No. 884 also enjoyed a better operation, losing just one pilot when his aircraft was shot down over Dhung Song in Thailand. Over three days, 884 conducted eighty-six sorties.

This was the British escort carriers' first experience of Japanese aerial attack. Three planes attacked a cruiser, but two were shot down and the other made its escape, while a 'Sonia' Japanese Army Air Force single-engined light bomber attempted to make a kamikaze attack on *Ameer* but, to the delight of her gunnery officer, her AA gunners were able to shoot the attacker down so that it crashed harmlessly into the sea. The success of the AA gunners aboard the cruiser was even more noteworthy, as they were so afflicted with dysentery that they had to have buckets in their turrets.

Japanese propaganda maintained that they had repelled an invasion!

The American cynics who described the escort carriers as 'combustible, vulnerable, expendable', may well have experienced some of the casual attitudes to safety on some of the British ships, including both *Ameer* and *Empress*. Aboard these ships, crew members do not recall being trained in damage control. Personnel safety also seems to have suffered from a relaxed attitude, with no protective clothing or anti-flash gear. The only safety measure taken was to have an inflatable lifebelt and red light tied to the waist.

Inevitably, the place for accidents was on the flight deck, something doubtless made more likely by the low speed and relatively short flight deck of the escort carrier. Aboard *Empress* on one occasion four replacement Hellcats were flown out to the ship from Trincomalee. The first one to attempt to land on was 'waved off' by the batsman, and the remaining three aircraft were landed on safely and moved forward over the barrier. The first aircraft then attempted a second landing, but came in too high and seemed to ignore the batsman's signals. The young midshipman pilot cut his engine while the aircraft was too high to catch any of the arrester wires, and too high for the barrier, which he glided over to land on top of the other three aircraft. All four aircraft, or at least their remains, were returned ashore, and the errant pilot, who had miraculously escaped serious injury, followed. Some believe that the reason for the failure was that the pilot had been trained in the United States, and some of the US Navy deck landing signals were exactly the opposite of those used by the Royal Navy, but by this time the British had standardized on the US signals. In any case, after completing their basic training with the US Navy, pilots for the Fleet Air Arm were given the final stages of their training by the Royal Navy, which included 'converting' to British practice and terminology.

No. 884 squadron's diary showed that the escort carriers suffered 91.06 per cent of aircraft accidents during deck landing in July 1945, with 5.36 per cent in-flight, and a surprisingly low 1.79 per cent on taking-off. There were also 1.70 per cent described as 'miscellaneous' accidents, which could have been deck or hangar handling problems. The in-flight accidents were likely to have been mainly due to engine failure.

Further investigation suggests that on the ten escort carriers, practice really did make perfect. On *Ameer*, with a total of 211 deck landings and nine accidents, only 4.3 per cent of deck landings resulted in an accident, while *Emperor*, 94 deck landings, suffered a 4 per cent accident rate. *Shah*, with 133 deck landings, and *Khedive*, with 132, did even better, with just 2.5 per cent of deck landings resulting in an accident. Best of all was *Empress*, with 153 deck landings and just 2 per cent ending in accident. *Pursuer*, with just seven deck landings, saw these account for 14 per cent of accidents, but that was just one crash landing. *Begum* with the relatively high figure of 101 deck landings saw these account for 12 per cent of accidents, but worst of all was *Attacker* with thirty-six deck landings with no less than 39 per cent ending in accident. Out of fifty-six accidents in July 1945, twenty-seven were suffered by Hellcats, twenty-five by Seafires, and there was one each for the Corsair, Swordfish and a Walrus.

No matter what safety precautions are designed into an aircraft, there is nothing that human ingenuity cannot achieve. On one occasion a Hellcat on the flight deck with wings folded, and so with its guns pointing down towards the deck, had its guns accidentally fired by an armourer. The half inch bullets went through the flight deck, which consisted of wooden decking over steel plate, through the steel hangar deck and ended up in the wardroom (officers' mess) below. Fortunately, there were no serious injuries, only scratches and grazes from fragments of cupro-nickel casing, but had the bullets found an aircraft in the hangar, fuelled and armed, it could have been a different story.

Bill Drake had been entering the hangar when the Hellcat's guns had been fired, but had an even closer shave on another occasion. Waiting for returning aircraft with other deck crew, so that after the aircraft had caught the wire and taxied forward over the barrier they could find out from the pilots if any defects needed attention, they saw a Hellcat approach too low and snap off its arrester hook on the round-down. Unable to arrest its progress, the aircraft raced towards the barrier and the waiting maintainers. Bill Drake recalled:

> At this point, evacuation seemed to be in order. I found unexpected agility by leaping clear over the assembled obstacles and into the starboard forward catwalk. At least that was the . . . idea . . . I landed well below the flight deck in a Bofors gun sponson without hitting anything on the way; it could so easily have been straight over the side![6]

Equally lucky was the Hellcat pilot, uninjured after the aircraft hit the barrier and ended up on its nose.

A further operation saw the British task force leave port on 9 August, heading once again for the Straits of Malacca, but they were back at Trincomalee just six days later on 15 August, VJ Day, without conducting any operations. Nevertheless, their work wasn't complete and 808 Squadron aboard HMS *Empress* was present when the Japanese forces in Malaya surrendered.

Notes
1. Imperial War Museum Sound Archive Accession No.3060/1
2. Ibid.
3. *Daily Telegraph*, 25 November 1997
4. Drake, op. cit.
5. Ibid.
6. Ibid.

X

THE JAPANESE AUXILIARY CARRIERS

The strategy of the Imperial Japanese Navy was centred on one policy; attack. The concept of escorting convoys waiting for attack was contrary to official philosophy, and even when, on one occasion, the First Fleet was asked to escort a convoy as it moved from one zone to another, its commanders arrogantly declared that the First Fleet could not have its freedom of movement restricted. Contrast this with the famous Malta convoy, Operation Pedestal of August 1942, when no less than four aircraft carriers were allocated, and these were not escort carriers but fleet carriers, two of them modern, fast armoured ships. The Japanese were equally oblivious to the need for escort vessels, and it was not until late in the war that a class of escort vessel started to enter service, but by this time it was too few ships, too late.

Japan was at least as heavily dependent upon imported food, fuel and raw materials as the United Kingdom, and possibly even more so, despite the seeming ability to survive and fight on meagre rations. The need for oil and rubber had been among the reasons for the frantic expansion across Asia to take the Netherlands East Indies and its oil, the British territory of Malaya, with its rubber and tin, and Burma with yet more oil. This was no small military achievement. Yet Singapore was as far from Japan as Southampton was from New York, more than 3,000 miles, and while much of the distance was within range of land-based aircraft, it also left the Japanese merchant shipping as dangerously exposed to American submarines as Allied merchant shipping had been to the German U-boats.

Yet even when the Japanese did concede that a convoy would

be necessary, the idea of a convoy would be a handful of merchant ships escorted by a destroyer or two. Strangely, the Germans and Italians also seemed incapable of grasping the degree of protection needed by a convoy, despite their success in creating havoc amongst Allied convoys. Across the Mediterranean in particular, from Italy to North Africa, convoys often consisted of small numbers of ships escorted by one or two warships. When British submarines posed a threat to an Italian convoy, the escorts did on at least one occasion include a cruiser, incapable of dealing with a submarine but presenting a welcome target! The small size of the Italian Mediterranean convoys could at least be excused on the grounds that the distance was short, and to wait for large convoys to gather could have interrupted supplies, while doubtless the waiting ships would have presented excellent targets for the British. Also, some of the ports in use at either end would have been incapable of turning a large number of ships around at once.

None of these excuses applied to the Japanese, as the distance was substantial. More significant, as former First World War allies of the British, they knew the dangers of submarine warfare and during the early post-war period had the benefit of a British naval mission to pass on wartime experience and the importance of naval aviation and submarine warfare.

In fact, the auxiliary carriers developed by Japan during the war years owed far more to the need to transport aircraft than to escort convoys, hence the use of the word 'auxiliary' rather than 'escort' for this chapter. As the Imperial Japanese Navy had aircraft carriers in plenty during the late 1930s as the intensity of the fighting in China grew, and these were used as transports on occasion, it is not surprising that the main driving force for the Japanese to convert merchant ships to carry aircraft was the Imperial Japanese Army, which needed to get its aircraft across the seas to combat zones.

We should not forget that Japan was a maritime nation and regarded itself as such. In common with the Germans, it felt that it needed *Lebensraum*, living room or space for an expanding population. With the exception of the United States, of the main combatants during the Second World War, none was self-sufficient in food, fuel or raw materials. Germany struck east looking for food and fuel. When German forces were pushed back by an increasingly confident and competent Red Army, Italy was first to suffer from the shortage of fuel as its German ally kept the available resources for its own needs.

The Japanese Auxiliaries

In common with the United States, the first Japanese aircraft carrier was the conversion of a non-combatant vessel. While the *Langley* had been a collier, *Hosho* was laid down as an oiler, but conversion started at an early stage during construction. The Imperial Japanese Navy benefited from its close liaison with the Royal Navy at the time. Nevertheless, the Japanese carriers developed a distinctive style of their own, usually failing to take advantage of the full length of the hull for the hangar and leaving the flight deck supported fore and aft on girders rather than plating up the hull to flight deck level.

The first Japanese escort carrier, or auxiliary carrier, was prompted by the need to provide aircraft transports for the Imperial Japanese Army, as the Japanese Army Air Force needed to bridge the long distances across the Pacific over which ferrying aircraft was seldom a practical option. This was so important that despite the growing shortage of merchant shipping, two passenger cargo liners were requisitioned, the *Akitsu Maru*, 9,186grt, and the similar but slightly larger *Nigitsu Maru*, 9,547grt, which together became known as the Akitsu Maru-class after conversion, giving a tonnage of 11,800 tons. Conversion was kept as simple as possible, with the superstructure left largely intact and the flight deck running up to the level of the boat deck, so that the boiler uptakes were simply redirected to the starboard side and a simple island was also provided for navigation. The space below the flight deck not taken up by the superstructure was left open and used for aircraft storage, with a simple lift at the after end of the flight deck to bring aircraft up. A pair of derricks, possibly belonging to the ships pre-conversion but moved aft and which would have made landing on impossible, was provided. Up to twenty aircraft could be carried, or small landing craft could be substituted for these. Anti-aircraft armament was limited to two 3-in guns, while another ten 3-in field guns were modified, possibly to provide some protection if threatened by an American warship.

Built by the Harima Shipyard, *Akitsu Maru* was commissioned on 30 January 1942, and the *Nigitsu Maru* followed in March 1943. Little further is known about the way in which these ships were used, other than that the *Nigitsu Maru* was torpedoed by the submarine USS *Hake* on 12 January 1944 while south of Okinawa, and her sister ship sank after being torpedoed by the submarine USS *Queenfish* off Kyushu on 15 November 1944.

Although the conversions seem more in line with those of the British and Dutch MAC-ships, it is clear that neither ship would have been able to operate as a convoy escort, partly because of the position of the derricks but in addition the height of the flight deck above the waterline on a narrow merchant hull could have given problems with stability in open waters.

Nevertheless, the Imperial Japanese Navy did convert a number of merchantmen as the desperate need for additional flight decks became clear, even before the losses of 1942. The first stage was the acquisition of three 17,100 ton passenger liners still under construction which had a maximum speed of around 21 knots; the *Kasuga Maru*, *Yawata Maru* and *Nitta Maru*. The *Kasuga Maru* was converted at the Sasebo Navy Yard and joined the fleet on 15 September 1941 as the class-leader *Taiyo*, the only one to enter service before Japan attacked the United States. The other two ships were both converted at the Kure Navy Yard, with *Yawata Maru* joining the fleet on 31 May 1942 as the *Unyo* and *Nitta Maru* on 25 November 1942 as the *Chuyo*. After conversion, all three resembled escort carriers, although at 17,830 tons they were larger and faster than their British and American equivalents. The boiler uptakes were re-routed to starboard with the usual Japanese downward pointing funnel, but no island was created leaving navigation from a wheelhouse at the forward end of the single 300 feet hangar built above the main deck and below the forward end of the flight deck. Although sponsons were provided on both sides for AA armament, the perceived need for additional armament at the bows and stern meant that the flight deck was foreshortened, and no arrester wires or catapults were fitted, which must have made life interesting for Japanese Navy Air Force pilots. Two lifts were provided at the hangar ends. AA armament seems to have been found at the back of the navy yard stores, consisting of redundant 4.7-in guns augmented by some 25-mm weapons, although on *Unyo* and *Chuyo* eight 5-in weapons were added later. Lacking an island, radar had to be mounted on the starboard deck edge, which must have limited its effectiveness considerably.

Despite their size, with their ability to accommodate up to twenty-seven aircraft, none of these ships was used on offensive operations or indeed as an escort carrier, all of them being used as aircraft transports and on training duties. The nearest they came to combat was when *Taiyo* accompanied the battleship *Yamato* during the campaign in the Eastern Solomons, but here too her role was that of support. All three met their ends in encounters with American submarines. Last to enter service, *Chuyo* was first to go, being torpedoed and sunk by the USS *Sailfish* off Yokosuka on 4 December 1943. *Taiyo* survived until 18 August 1944, when the *Rasher* found her off Luzon in the Philippines, and the following month *Unyo* was torpedoed and sunk by the *Barb* in the East China Sea off Hong Kong on 16 September, and far from the carrier acting as an escort, the tanker accompanying her was also sunk by the same submarine.

In late 1941, the passenger liner *Argentine Maru*, 12,755grt, was requisitioned by the Imperial Japanese Navy as a troopship, doubtless with the advance through south-east Asia and Indonesia in mind, but the following year other needs were more pressing and the decision was taken to convert her to an aircraft carrier. She joined the fleet as the *Kaiyo* on 23 November 1943, at just 16, 483 tons and her aircraft capacity was around twenty-four. Her original diesel engines were replaced by steam turbines, giving the relatively high speed for a conversion of 24 knots. Once again, there was no island and the trunking for the boiler uptakes was directed to a starboard side downward pointing smokestack. There was a simple box-like hangar with two lifts to the wooden flight deck, which seems to have had arrester wires but no catapult. Once again, radar was fitted to the edge of the flight deck. Her sister ship *Brazil Maru* was lost before she could be converted, but after serving as an aircraft transport and training carrier, *Kaiyo* was crippled by aircraft from HMS *Formidable*, *Indefatigable* and *Victorious* while off Kyushu on 24 July 1945.

War in Europe caught at least one major German merchant ship unawares and too far from home to be safely repatriated. This was the Norddeutscher Line *Scharnhorst*, an 18,184grt passenger liner, in port at Kobe in September 1939. Early in 1942, the ship was requisitioned by the Imperial Japanese navy as a troop transport, but as the losses of both carriers and carrier-qualified aircrew mounted that year, the decision was taken to convert her into an aircraft carrier. While the simplest form of conversion was sought, including retaining the original German steam turbines, the fact that this was a completed ship rather than a conversion partway through construction presented many problems, as did the pronounced sheer lines in her hull. The result was that the hangar deck was far higher than would have been ideal and naturally enough the flight deck was even higher, so that the ship became inherently unstable and large bulges had to be fitted to the hull. Otherwise similar to the naval conversions already mentioned, a flight control position was installed on the edge of the starboard flight deck with a lift mechanism so that it could be raised and lowered as required. The initial AA armament of eight 5-in and thirty 25-mm guns was raised to fifty 25-mm guns in mid-1944. After commissioning as *Shinyo* on 15 December 1943, she was employed on training duties until she was caught by the submarine USS *Spadefish* in the Yellow Sea on 17 November 1944, torpedoed and sunk.

Despite the priority being accorded rebuilding the carrier fleet, time was running out for the Japanese. The growing aerial supremacy of the Allies was more than matched by the activities of the US Navy's submariners once early problems with poor torpedo reliability had been rectified. As with *Kaiyo*, the passenger liner *Chichiba Maru* had been acquired in 1941 as a hospital ship and troop transport, but then in 1942 she was earmarked for conversion to an aircraft carrier but sunk by the submarine *Gudgeon* in April 1943 before work could start. When the conversion of the cruiser *Ibuki* was ordered in 1943, while she was still under construction, a growing shortage of materials meant that work was delayed and was finally abandoned in March 1945 when it was clear that it could not be completed. This was not really an auxiliary or escort carrier and would have been a more ambitious conversion than some of those already mentioned, with a starboard island and rocket launchers, although the complement of 1,015 seems to have been high for a ship of just 12,500 tons. Speed could have been a problem with half the boilers removed to accommodate extra fuel.

It is an indictment of the poor strategic vision of the Imperial Japanese Navy that the only two ships that could fairly be described as escort carriers were ordered by the Imperial Japanese Army. These were the two tankers *Yamishiro Maru* and *Chigusa Maru*, both of 10,100grt. These were in fact similar to MAC-ships in concept, having no hangar and therefore no lifts, and were intended to operate eight Kawanishi Ki-44 lightweight fighters of the Japanese Army Air Force to provide air cover, but once again nothing seemed to be in mind for protection against submarines other than an anti-submarine depth charge projector on the fore-castle. Despite the fighters, the first ship, *Yamishiro Maru*, was sunk in an American air raid on Yokohama on 17 February 1945, just three weeks after she had entered service on 27 January. Her sister ship was never completed.

The last aircraft carrying ship to be completed for the Imperial Japanese Army was the *Kumano Maru*, which took the concept of the *Akitsu Maru* a stage further by having a ramp at the stern down which landing craft could be launched, but unlike the earlier ship was based on a cargo vessel rather than a passenger cargo liner. Although commissioned on 30 March 1945, she is believed never to have seen active service – by this time the Japanese armed forces were going nowhere!

Finally, in late 1944, the Imperial Japanese Navy decided that escort carriers would be useful and ordered the conversion of two tankers, the *Shimane Maru* and *Otakisan Maru*. While the original hulls were not modified, these ships differed from the MAC-ships and the *Yamishiro Maru* in having a hangar built over the hull, and while there was no island, once again the starboard side down sloping smokestack was part of the design. The design provided a single lift and up to twelve aircraft could be carried on a ship of 11,800 tons. Commissioned on 28 February 1945, *Shimane Maru* was sunk by American aircraft off Takamatsu on the island of Shikoku on 24 July 1945 before she entered service.

Her sister ship was never completed and had the misfortune to drift onto a mine at Kobe on 25 August, later being scrapped. Had not the war ended, and had materials been available, another two ships would have been converted, although by this time the Japanese had no convoys to escort!

XI

AFTER THE WAR

As soon as hostilities were over, the first priority for the Royal Navy was the re-occupation of British territories lost in the rapid Japanese advance across Asia. The Dutch and the French had the same aim, but suffered from not having significant forces to dispatch to the area. This was not simply a case of the colonial power re-establishing its presence, another pressing consideration was the British and Empire prisoners of war held captive in the Japanese camps in appalling and inhumane conditions.

Operation Zipper was intended to re-occupy Singapore and Malaya, and in addition to the battleships *Queen Elizabeth*, *Renown* and the French *Richelieu*, there were no less than six escort carriers, *Ameer*, *Emperor*, *Empress*, *Hunter*, *Khedive* and *Stalker*. Unfortunately, the catapult on *Empress* broke down as the ship entered the Straits of Malacca and the ship was forced to return, reaching Trincomalee on 12 September. By this time, there were just a few pockets of resistance to be encountered when taking over from Japanese forces and even with a defective catapult, a carrier could have been useful. Certainly, even the light fleets found themselves pressed into service repatriating Allied ex-prisoners of war, with their hangar decks turned into one large dormitory or mess deck – hardly luxurious accommodation but no doubt a welcome improvement over the conditions endured in Japanese camps.

Serving with the Dutch and the French Navies

The war had created a wider awareness of the importance of naval aviation of the fleet taking its own air power to sea. Without the aircraft carrier, the Japanese could not have carried out a successful strike against the United States Pacific Fleet at Pearl Harbor, but with the aircraft carrier, the United States could not have driven back the Japanese across the wide reaches of the Pacific. The escort carrier played a role in this, providing additional flight decks so that at the landings in the Pacific, as in the Mediterranean, carrier-borne aircraft were able to provide close air support for troops on the ground. It was the escort carrier and the MAC-ship that first closed the Atlantic Gap, and turned the war against the U-boats. It took escort carriers to provide cover for Arctic convoys. Once longer-range shore-based maritime reconnaissance aircraft became available, the escort carriers were freed up for other tasks, including strikes against German convoys off the coast of Norway. In fact, the escort carriers proved to be more than just a stop-gap for it would have been a waste to have tied up fast aircraft carriers escorting convoys, or providing close air support, especially when, as in the Pacific, there was a large enemy fleet to attack.

Fresh from their experience aboard the MAC-ships, the Royal Netherlands Navy set up its own fleet air arm, the *Marine Luchtvaartdienst*, and in 1946 was loaned one of the few British-built escort carriers, HMS *Nairana*, which promptly became the *Karel Doorman*, named after the Dutch admiral who had commanded a mixed Allied force in the Battle of the Java Sea, losing the battle and his life for want of air cover.

By this time 860 Squadron, which had been manned by Free Dutch personnel during the war years, had replaced its Fairey Swordfish with the Fairey Barracuda, and was no doubt pleased to see these aircraft replaced in turn by the Fairey Firefly, with thirty of these aircraft introduced and a number operated from the *Karel Doorman*. When the ship was returned to the Royal Navy in 1948, she was replaced by one of the Royal Navy's new light fleet carriers, HMS *Venerable*, which subsequently was renamed and became the second *Karel Doorman*, remaining in service until eventually the *Marine Luchtvaartdienst* withdrew from carrier aviation and the ship was sold to the Argentine. The first *Karel Doorman*, on her return to the Royal Navy, was promptly 'demobbed' and converted to a merchantman.

The French had enjoyed the benefit of continuous naval

aviation from 1912, and between the wars had operated an aircraft carrier, the *Bearn*, converted from a battleship, while two ships of advanced design, the *Joffre* and the *Painleve*, were at the early stages of construction at the fall of France in 1940. In the first year of war, the *Bearn* operated as an aircraft transport, and was then laid up in the Caribbean at Martinique after French surrender. She returned to the transport role after a refit in the United States during 1943–44, and post-war continued serving in this role taking aircraft from France to the then French Indo-China, now Vietnam.

Even before the war in Europe was over, on 9 April 1945, one of the US-built escort carriers loaned to the Royal Navy under Lend-Lease, HMS *Biter*, was commissioned into the French *Marine Nationale* as the *Dixmude*. In French service the *Dixmude* joined the *Bearn* in the unglamorous duties of an aircraft transport. Her armament, which had been reduced prior to the transfer, was eliminated altogether by the early 1950s. Unlike the Dutch, the French retained the escort carrier in the transport role until 1960, after which *Dixmude* was hulked and used as an accommodation ship. She was returned to the US Navy in 1966 and scrapped – being rather too old for conversion to a merchantman. The French, meanwhile, had been loaned Independence-class light carriers from the United States, with the USS *Langley* becoming *La Fayette* in French service, and the *Belleau Wood* becoming *Bois Belleau*, and had purchased HMS *Colossus* as the *Arromanches*, giving France three operational carriers throughout the 1950s.

Searching for a Role Post-War

While it is tempting to think that the most demanding and interesting post-war careers were those of the escort carriers transferred to Dutch and French service, clearly this wasn't the case. The escorts were too slow to keep up with the fleet, and too slow to operate jet aircraft and, when steam catapults became available, it wasn't worthwhile to modify the ships to accommodate this option, which would, in any case, have been difficult on the diesel-powered ships. Many of the carriers were converted to the merchant role – it would be tempting to say 'converted back' – but, of course, most of them were built from scratch as carriers, simply using merchant hulls. For others, the role of an aircraft transport beckoned and, for the fortunate few, there was a continued and more active career due to that other wartime aviation innovation, the helicopter.

This was in complete contrast to the fate of the MAC-ships, which had quietly and without any undue fuss or drama been steadily converted back to their full civilian role starting at the end of 1944. By this time, not only had the submarine threat receded, but the numbers of escort carriers meant that the MAC-ships with their three or four aircraft were no longer necessary.

In fact, a review of the post-war lives of the surviving escort and auxiliary carriers shows that a certain pattern emerged, with ships either scrapped because they had been so badly damaged in wartime attacks, including, of course, kamikaze operations, converted into merchantmen, used as helicopter carriers or anti-submarine carriers post-war or as aircraft transports, sometimes returning to the latter role after being used as helicopter carriers or anti-submarine carriers. There were exceptions, of course, with one ship being used as the forerunner of the amphibious assault ships, while two ships, one British and one American, were present for the testing of atomic bombs and hydrogen bombs respectively. Given the development of naval weaponry post-war, perhaps it was not surprising that one vessel ended up as a target for guided missiles.

In the case of the Royal Navy, many of the ships had first to be returned to the Americans, and in a couple of cases, the 'return' was more in the imagination than the actuality as the vessels were stricken where they lay! Of the British Attacker-class of eleven vessels, eight were converted into merchantmen for a tonnage hungry world, and another three were scrapped. Of the earlier ships to serve under the White Ensign, *Archer* was not returned to the US Navy until January 1949, one of the last to get back, but she was converted for merchant service and served under a variety of names with no doubt a succession of owners, none of whom seemed to accept the old sea dogs' belief that to rename a ship was unlucky. In fact, she survived until she was scrapped in 1962, which was about the time when most of the ex-escorts seemed to have reached the end of their second careers, although a few lasted into the 1970s. After a spell ferrying replacement aircraft to British forces in the Far East, *Activity* was also converted to merchant service.

Of the Ameer-class, sometimes known as the Ruler-class, of twenty-three ships, no less than nineteen ended up as merchantmen, with *Nabob* surviving until 1977. Four were scrapped, with the badly battered *Thane* remaining resolutely in the UK. The Americans wouldn't have wanted her back anyway.

The same pattern seems to have applied to most of the British-built ships. *Pretoria Castle* was converted back to merchant service and returned to the South Africa run, while *Vindex* became *Port Vindex*, and was able to retain her ship's bell with 'HMS' inscribed on it to remind those aboard that she had indeed once been one of 'His Majesty's Ships'. *Nairana* returned but briefly to the Royal Navy, being converted to become the *Port Victor*, where she was no doubt occasionally to see her old sister ship.

Campania had a more interesting, if possibly shorter, life remaining with the Royal Navy after the war. Following a brief spell in reserve, she spent 1949–51 touring, promoting the Festival of Britain. That over, she went to the Pacific to be present as a support ship for the British nuclear test programme in 1952. A further spell in reserve followed before she was scrapped in 1955.

The period in which the former escort carriers were retired from their second careers is not too surprising. Newer and more economical ships were entering service, often faster and bigger. It was also the eve of containerization, with a typical first generation container ship able to replace at least six traditional break-bulk cargo ships. The supertanker was also on its way, its introduction eventually to be spurred on when first the Suez Campaign of 1956 and then the Arab-Israeli Wars of the 1960s and 1970s also closed the canal and ensured that even once re-opened, it could no longer be relied on as a shipping route for something as precious as oil, the lifeblood of civilized society in war and in peace.

The American Carriers

Despite having built up the largest carrier force the world has ever seen, the US Navy was less inclined to dispose of too many ships post-war. The hard fought battles with the Germans, Italians and Japanese had not been followed by peace, but by a succession of international crises as Soviet and Communist Chinese forces were maintained at high levels and Eastern Europe found that it had simply swapped one jackboot for another, while the Chinese supported North Korea and the Soviet Union North Vietnam in two Cold War 'hot spots'.

The first of the escorts, the USS *Long Island*, nevertheless soon found herself converted for merchant service, although her new name of *Nelly* seemed rather less dignified than one might have expected. *Charger*, who had trained so many pilots for the Royal Navy's Fleet Air Arm, also followed *Long Island* into merchant service. The two lakes steamers converted to train pilots for the US Navy, *Wolverine* and *Sable* were both sold and scrapped in 1947 and 1948 respectively.

One of the more notable achievements for the escort carriers post-war was when the USS *Wake Island* had the distinction of having the first landing of a jet-powered aircraft when a Ryan FR-1 Fireball flown by Ensign Jake West landed aboard on 6 November 1946. This event was not formally recognized as the first landing aboard a carrier by a jet aircraft, however, since the Fireball, with an auxiliary jet engine, was making an emergency landing after its piston main engine failed on the approach and the aircraft could not have sustained flight by jet power alone.

Ten of the eleven ships of the Bogue-class survived the war, and after a spell in reserve, all were re-classified as helicopter escort carriers, or CVHE, in 1955. Five of them, *Barnes, Breton, Card, Core* and *Croatan* were subsequently re-classified as CVU, or utility aircraft carriers, with some being later reclassified as AKV, aircraft ferries, for the US Maritime Sea Transportation Service, MSTS.

Out of the fifty ships of the Casablanca-class, forty-five survived the war, and of these eleven were scrapped after much hard pounding in the Pacific that had ships lost to shell fire, bombing and kamikaze attack, as well as Japanese torpedoes. Ten ships were placed in reserve to become CVHE in 1955, with some surviving to become aircraft ferries. The USS *Makassar Strait* had the unfortunate task of acting as a target for Tartar and Terrier missiles during 1961–62, and in the latter year finally sank after taking much damage from these weapons. Another twenty-three ships undertook a variety of duties, mainly as utility aircraft carriers. The one exception out of the twenty-three was the *Thetis Bay*, which in 1956 became CVHA, meaning that she became a helicopter amphibious carrier and paved the way for the later development of the Iwo Jima-class assault ships. The conversion involved fitting her out to take up to 1,000 US Marines. The potential of the helicopter in wartime had been brought home to the United States as early as 20 September 1951, when, during the Korean War, twelve of its Sikorsky S-55 helicopters had moved 228 fully-equipped US Marines to the top of a 3,000 feet high hilltop that was strategically important, following this by delivering nine tons of supplies for the marines, and then laying a field telephone cable back to headquarters. The entire operation took just four hours compared with the two days that it would have taken otherwise, with the potential for heavy losses under enemy fire. The slow speed of the escort carrier mattered not at all to the helicopter.

At one time, *Thetis Bay* was considered for loan to the Spanish Navy, but the Independence-class light carrier *Cabot* was provided instead.

The final expression of the escort or auxiliary carrier was the American Commencement Bay-class, some of which arrived too late for the war. This class of nineteen ships had far greater involvement by the US Navy in their design, and the ships themselves were amongst the larger escort carriers. Eight of the ships became CVHE in 1955, while another seven served as anti-submarine carriers, becoming CVS, leaving the business of providing strike capability to the larger fleet carriers. While anti-submarine warfare centred on fixed wing aircraft at first, here too the helicopter with its dunking sonar buoy came to play an increasingly important role. These ships played an important role in developing anti-submarine tactics for the nuclear age.

Two other Commencement Bay-class ships found other roles. *Bairoko* was present for the H-bomb tests at Eniwetok in 1954. *Gilbert Islands* became a major communications ship, and survived to see service during the Vietnam War.

This marked the end of the escort carriers' careers. Purpose-built ships had entered service for amphibious assault in all of the major navies, while frigates, destroyers and cruisers could carry helicopters for anti-submarine operations. The US Navy itself decided to concentrate on the large nuclear-powered aircraft carriers of the Nimitz-class, the largest warships in the world. The day of the escort carrier was over, but they had proved almost infinitely adaptable and useful. Yet, it is sad to think that not one example of these ships that had played such an important part in the Second World War survives today so that the present and future generations can see just what could be done.

XII

THE LIGHT CARRIERS

In addition to the programme of converting merchant vessels to provide escort carriers, the US Navy also turned over most of its Cleveland-class light cruisers to provide light carriers of the Independence-class. As mentioned earlier, this was done at the behest of President Franklin Roosevelt. In fact, US shipbuilding proceeded at such a pace that this expedient was to prove unnecessary, but the US Navy received the ships and had to use them. The large carriers of the Essex-class were also fast enough to compare with the light carriers, and had the advantage of being able to cope with bad weather or even an ocean swell without losing too much speed, unlike the smaller ships. At one stage it was suggested that the American light carriers should become fighter carriers, but this was not adopted until the closing stages of the war. The Independence-class suffered from being based on a cruiser design and the problems this gave, both to the flight deck and hangar deck, have already been mentioned.

The alternative to conversion of existing ships, whether merchant or naval or, as happened in most cases, of using a standardized merchantman design and completing this as an escort or auxiliary carrier rather than as a cargo ship or tanker, was to use shipyards that had no warship experience and had normally built merchantmen to build aircraft carriers designed to be built to merchant standards. This was the course taken by the Royal Navy, but the decision to press ahead with such a programme of construction was not taken until late 1941. The ships were not to be escort carriers, but 'utility' carriers, and intended to operate with the fleets, although somewhat slower than the fast armoured carriers and new battleships and cruisers at just 24 knots maximum.

Had such ships been conceived at the beginning of the war, or even better as an adjunct to the carrier construction programme initiated in the late 1930s, the outcome of the war at sea could have been much less costly, especially in the initial stages. The one and only advantage of the delay was that by early 1942, the Admiralty had a good idea of what was really essential in aircraft carrier design.

The specification for the new ships involved taking the radical decision for the Royal Navy of discarding armour protection in order that the available tonnage would result in the largest and most spacious vessels possible. Experience of losing carriers in action had shown that as soon as the ship began to list, flying was no longer possible, so the usual internal protection was also reduced to ensure that after taking heavy battle damage, the ships would settle in the water slowly whilst remaining upright. The hull up to the waterline was to be constructed using Lloyds' mercantile standards to both speed construction and increase the number of shipyards that could be involved, but naval pattern twin turbines with two shafts were to be used to increase survivability after an attack. While the maximum speed was to be 24 knots, the engines were to be capable of providing rapid acceleration. The intention was that the ships should be able to carry up to forty-eight aircraft, and just one catapult was provided.

In fact, no less than sixteen ships were launched by September 1945, fifteen of them by the end of the war. In the light of operational experience, two of the ships, *Perseus* and *Pioneer*, were designed to be maintenance carriers, something that also required a change of name for these two ships when the decision was taken in 1944, from *Edgar* and *Mars* respectively. Ten of the ships were to the original specification and known as the Colossus-class, despite their small size, while the remaining six were known as the Majestic-class, with similar dimensions to the original ships but with decks stressed to operate heavier aircraft, and in return fuel bunkerage was reduced, although even so there was a slight increase in tonnage.

That these ships were a compromise was later underscored by the fact that when the Royal Navy designed its next light fleet class, greater power and higher speed as well as a broader beam to provide improved underwater protection was specified, but these were to be true warships built in warship yards post-war.

HMS *Colossus* and her sisters have sometimes been described as converted merchant ship designs, but this would be wrong, and grossly unfair. They were designed as aircraft carriers from the keel upwards and it was the means of construction that relied on merchant ship practice. They even looked like aircraft carriers, and had none of the tell-tale signs of merchant hulls that so characterized all of the escort carriers, even the Commencement Bay-class which were the ultimate expression of these ships and had the greatest naval influence in their design. For the un-initiated, giving these ships a quick glance, they would have seemed like scaled down sisters of *Illustrious* although there were the features that showed this not to be quite right, such as the smaller smokestacks. In fact, while most of them were indeed built in yards more accustomed to merchant shipbuilding, such as Cammell Laird on Merseyside and Harland & Wolff in Belfast, some, such as *Pioneer* and *Majestic* were built in warship yards such as Vickers-Armstrong at Barrow.

The Colossus-class displaced 18,040 tons deep load, and were 695 feet overall, and were slightly unusual in that the beam was 80 feet both at the waterline and at the flight deck. Initially, arm-ament consisted of twenty-four 2-pounder guns and thirty-two 20-mm, which was far lighter than that of the Illustrious-class which included sixteen 4.5-in guns in eight turrets. Nevertheless, for close range air defence, the British 2-pounder has been described as one of the best AA weapons of the war. The com-plement was 1,300 and up to forty-eight aircraft could be carried. To make the best possible use of the space, the island, including the smokestack, was sponsored out to starboard so that there was little encroachment on the flight deck. The single catapult was offset to port.

Of the ten ships laid down, just four were commissioned before the war ended, *Colossus*, *Glory*, *Venerable* and *Vengeance*. These were deployed to the Far East to join the British Pacific Fleet in the final assault on Japan, but all arrived too late to see action. Whether or not their lightweight construction would have held up to heavy aerial attack, or a direct hit by a kamikaze, has to be something for speculation. Certainly, they would have suffered far heavier damage than the large fast armoured carriers, but on the other hand, they would also have been much easier to repair once damage was taken. As it was, they were only involved in mopping up operations, taking the Japanese surrender in British colonies, and bringing home British prisoners of war, with their hangar decks turned into large mess decks.

Post-war, these ships soon proved their worth. *Colossus* herself passed to the French Navy as the *Arromanches*, on loan in 1946 but eventually purchased outright in 1951. *Venerable* was sold to the Royal Netherlands Navy in 1948, replacing their escort carrier on loan from the Royal Navy, and took the same name as the interim ship, *Karel Doorman*, and after the Dutch opted out of carrier-borne naval aviation in 1968 following a fire aboard the ship, she was sold to Argentina to become the *Veinticinco de Mayo*. A heavy refit was provided in the Netherlands before the sale, including new boilers which came from the laid-up Majestic-class carrier *Leviathan*. In Argentine service, *Venerable* replaced a sister ship, *Independencia*, formerly HMS *Warrior*, which was scrapped in 1971. She was not available for operations during the Falklands campaign due to mechanical defects and was withdrawn from service some years later. *Vengeance* also saw service in three different navies, being transferred to the Royal Australian Navy early in the 1950s on loan, before returning in 1955 and being placed in reserve until she was sold to the Brazilian Navy as the *Minas Gerais*, serving there until replaced by a former French carrier, the *Foch*, in 2002. Today, she is the only surviving ship of this class but has been extensively rebuilt so that the island has changed almost beyond recognition.

One of the shortest-lived of the class was *Glory*, which saw service against Communist insurgents in Malaya during the early 1950s before being withdrawn later in the decade and broken up in 1961.

Of the post-war ships, several saw action during the Korean War, including *Triumph*, *Ocean* and *Theseus*. *Ocean* also had the distinction of being the first carrier to have a jet aircraft land on, when, on 3 December, 1945, Lieutenant Commander Eric 'Winkle' Brown, who had flown his Wildcat so effectively off the ill-fated HMS *Audacity*, landed a de Havilland Sea Vampire on board. Later, with her sister ship *Theseus*, *Ocean* saw service in the Suez Campaign of 1956, with both ships carrying Royal Marine commandos and helicopters that carried the commandos in the first heliborne amphibious assault.

Several more ships were exported. *Warrior* was loaned to the Royal Canadian Navy before being sold to Argentina. Of the later Majestic-class, *Majestic* herself was sold to the Royal Australian Navy where she joined her sister *Terrible*, the two ships being renamed *Melbourne* and *Sydney* respectively. *Magnificent* went to the Royal Canadian Navy, where she too was joined by a sister, *Powerful*, although the latter was renamed *Bonaventure* in Canadian service. *Hercules* was sold to India, becoming the *Vikrant*. In fact, the only ship not to be completed was *Leviathan*, and after donating her boilers to the *Karel Doorman*/*Veinticinco de Mayo*, the hull was scrapped. Of these ships, the only ones to see operational service were *Sydney*, which was operational during the Korean War and then acted as a fast troop transport during the Vietnam War; *Melbourne* which was operational while Australia was involved in the Vietnam War; and *Vikrant*, which took part in the last of the major Indo-Pakistani conflicts leading to the in- dependence of East Pakistan, now Bangladesh.

As so often happened, the growing size of carrier-borne aircraft meant that the number of aircraft these ships could accommodate fell during their operational lives. Rather than the forty-eight aircraft claimed at the time of their entry into service, a more typical figure was the twenty-seven aircraft carried by *Melbourne* during her later years. The use of aircraft as big as the Fairey Gannet and then the Grumman Tracker anti-submarine aircraft, as well as Sea King helicopters, took up a lot of space, and indeed it is doubtful whether even in 1945, with a squadron of Grumman Avengers embarked, anything like forty-eight aircraft could be carried.

More significant than size, nevertheless, since even a small number of aircraft with the fleet has to be better than none at all, was speed. This was the major weakness of the Colossus and Majestic-classes. Australian experience during the final years of operations with *Melbourne* was that getting contemporary aircraft off the deck took some considerable skill on the part of the pilots, who were flying Douglas A-4 Skyhawk fighter-bombers and Grumman Tracker anti-submarine aircraft by this time. This meant that while the US Navy and the Royal Navy were able to operate aircraft such as the McDonnell Douglas F-4 Phantom off their carriers, this ability was denied to the Royal Australian Navy.

Nor could it operate anything like the Grumman A-6 Intruder or the Hawker Siddeley Buccaneer bombers.

Nevertheless, these two closely-related classes of aircraft carrier served with seven navies other than the Royal Navy, a record that no other aircraft carrier or any warship of this size could match. Together with the escort carriers they have also led many to suggest that in future, navies might be better served with simpler carrier designs, cutting the tremendously high costs of naval aviation.

Appendix I

STANDARD CONVOY AIR PATROL CODENAMES

All suitable for a single aircraft.

ADDER: Patrol ahead of convoy at distance of eight to twelve miles, with the length of patrol thirty miles, that is, fifteen miles on either side of the centre line.

ALLIGATOR . . . port or starboard: Patrol on side indicated at distance of ten miles from the convoy along a line parallel to the convoy's course. The length of patrol would be twenty miles, that is ten miles ahead and astern of the aircraft's position on the convoy's beam.

COBRA 'Y': Patrol around convoy at a distance of Y miles, with Y being the distance from the convoy so that the instruction *Cobra* 12, would mean patrol at a distance of twelve miles.

CROCODILE 'Y': Patrol ahead of convoy from beam to beam at radius 'Y' miles, in effect a half *COBRA*. This was popular with fast convoys since they had little to fear from a U-boat sneaking up from astern.

FROG 'Y': Patrol astern of convoy at distance of 'Y' miles. Length of patrol would be two 'Y' miles, that is 'Y' miles on either side of the centre line. This was to stop U-boats trailing the convoy, often shortly before dusk. It was also essential prior to any change of course so that the U-boat commander would keep his craft submerged and not realize that the change had taken place until it was too late.

VIPER: Patrol around convoy at distance of visibility.

'X ' PYTHON 'Y': Given when a submarine had been spotted, so that the aircraft would patrol on bearing 'X' at a distance of 'Y' miles, and would carry out a square search around the indicated position for twenty minutes.

'X' LIZARD 'Y': Search sector bearing 'X' to a depth of 'Y' miles.

'X' MAMBA: Search along bearing 'X' to a depth of thirty miles and return.

Appendix II

MERCHANT AIRCRAFT CARRIERS – MAC-SHIPS

Two main types: Modified tankers with flight deck only, while grain carriers provided a limited small hangar with hoist rather than lift. Tanker-MAC ships carried 80 per cent of their original cargo, with the remainder AVGAS for the aircraft, usually three Swordfish. Ships retained their merchant designation of 'MV', motor ship.

Acavus – converted October, 1943. Anglo-Saxon Petroleum Co.
Similar: *Adula* – modified February, 1944, sister of above.

Amastra – modified September 1943.

Ancylus – modified October 1943.

Empire MacAlpine – modified grain ship, April 1943, and able to carry four Swordfish using small hangar below decks.
Similar: *Empire MacAndrew* – modified July 1943.

Empire MacCallum – modified December 1943.

Empire MacCabe – modified tanker, December 1943.

Empire MacColl – modified tanker, May 1943.

Empire MacDermott – modified grain ship, March 1944.

Empire MacKay – modified tanker, October 1943.

Empire MacKendrick – modified grain ship, December 1943.

Empire MacMahon – modified tanker December 1943.

Empire MacRae – modified grain ship, September 1943.

Gadila – modified tanker, March 1944.

Macoma – modified tanker, May 1944.

Miralda – modified tanker, January 1944.

Rapana – first modified tanker, July 1943.

Appendix III

ROYAL NAVY
ESCORT CARRIERS

Notes: All ships were prefixed HMS, His Majesty's Ship. Pennant numbers are shown in bold type. Unless otherwise stated, all references to beam apply to flight deck, but unlike purpose-designed aircraft carriers, the beam varied relatively little between hull and flight deck on these ships.

Activity, **D94:** Laid down at Caledon Shipyard, Dundee, Scotland as refrigerated cargo vessel *Telemachus* for Ocean Steamship, but converted on slipway. Commissioned 29 September 1942. Displacement: 11,800 tons standard, 14,529 tons deep load. LOA: 512 feet; beam: 66 feet. Armament: 1 × twin 4-in; 6 × twin 20-mm Oerlikon, 8 single 20-mm Oerlikon. Machinery: Twin diesel engines driving two shafts. Speed 18 knots. Complement: 700; aircraft: 10. Short hangar 100 feet long, single lift aft, arrester gear but no catapult.

Ameer, **D01:** lead ship of the class, although sometimes referred to as the Ruler-class. Similar in design, but larger, to the Avenger-class and US Bogue-class, these were built as carriers rather than converted, although still using merchantman hulls, and all were built by Seattle-Tacoma, although completion was sometimes by other yards. Originally laid down as USS *Baffins*, AVG-34, but transferred to the Royal Navy under Lend-Lease and commissioned on 20 July 1943. Intended as a strike and anti-submarine sweep carrier. Displacement, 11,400 tons standard, 15,400 tons deep load. LOA: 494.75 feet; beam: 88 feet. Armament varied according to role, but generally included: 2 × 5-in; 8 × twin 40-mm Bofors, 20 × 20-mm Oerlikon. Complement:646; Aircraft: 20; arrester gear aft and hangar with two lifts, with single accelerator on port side forward capable of handling heavier aircraft. Machinery: boilers and turbines driving a single shaft. Speed: 18 knots. Returned to US Navy on 17 January 1946 and converted to merchantman *Robin Kirk*.

Arbiter, **D31:** Ameer-class mainly used for aircraft trials and then as an aircraft transport in which role she could carry up to ninety aircraft. Originally intended to be *St Simon*, AVG-51, she was commissioned by the Royal Navy on 31 December 1943. Returned to the US Navy 3 March 1946 and converted to merchantman *Coracero*.

Archer, **D78:** Laid down as a US merchant vessel, *Mormcamacland*, using a standard C3 hull, converted at Newport News with a wooden planked flight deck and a small starboard side island for navigation and air control, but no smokestack as exhaust fumes discharged horizontally. Originally intended to enter US service as BAVG-1, but diverted to UK under Lend-Lease. Commissioned 17 November 1941, but suffered considerable technical problems that delayed entry into service. Displacement, 10,220 tons standard, 12,860 tons deep load. LOA: 492 feet; beam: 70 feet. Armament: 3 × 4-in; 6 × 20-mm twin Oerlikon; 7 × 20-mm single Oerlikon. Machinery: Diesel engine driving a single shaft. Speed: 16.5 knots. Complement: 550, aircraft 12–15. Quarter length hangar with single lift aft, arrester gear aft and a single hydraulic accelerator. Laid up as stores ship August 1943, decommissioned March 1945 and returned to US January 1946. Reconverted to merchant vessel as *Empire Lagan*.

Atheling, **D51:** Ameer-class escort carrier originally intended to be *Glacier*, AVG-33, but transferred to Royal Navy, commissioned on 1 August 1943. Returned to US Navy on 13 December 1946 and converted to merchantman *Roma*.

Attacker, **D02:** Known in the US Navy as the Bogue-class, but lead ship for Royal Navy class. Laid down as merchant vessel *Steel Artisan*, but renamed *Barnes* AVG-7 for the US Navy, then transferred under Lend-Lease to the Royal Navy. Built by Western Pipe

& Steel in San Francisco. Commissioned 10 October 1942. Displacement, 10,200 tons standard, 14,400 tons deep load. LOA: 465 feet; beam: 82 feet. Armament: 2 × 4-in; 4 × twin 40-mm Bofors; 4 × twin 20-mm Oerlikon; 4 × 20-mm Oerlikon. Machinery: boilers and geared turbines. Speed: 18.5 knots. Complement: 646; Aircraft: 20; Arrester wires aft; 2 lifts; single hydraulic accelerator forward. Returned to US Navy, January 1946 and re-converted as *Castel Forte*.

Audacity, **D10:** Originally built as Norddeutscher Line cargo vessel *Hannover*, and converted by Blyth Shipbuilding Company after capture. Commissioned 20 June 1941. Displacement, 10,200 tons standard, 11,000 tons deep load. LOA: 497.25 feet; beam: 56.25 feet. Armament: 1 × 4-in; 1 × 6-pounder; 4 × 2-pounder; 4 × single 20-mm Oerlikon. Aircraft: 8 fighters; arrester gear aft but no hangar, lifts or catapults. Machinery: Single diesel driving one shaft. Speed:15 knots. Torpedoed by *U-751* off Portugal, 20 December 1941.

Avenger, **D14:** Avenger-class lead ship built by Sun Shipyard as merchantman *Rio Hudson* and converted by Bethlehem Steel at Staten Island, New York, originally intended to be BAVG-2 but transferred to Royal Navy under Lend-Lease, commissioning on 2 March 1942 .Displacement, 12,150 tons standard, 15,700 tons deep load. LOA: 492 feet; beam: 70 feet. Armament: 3 × 4-in; 19 × single 20-mm Oerlikon. Complement: 555; Aircraft: 15; arrester gear aft and hangar with single lift, while flight decks were extended to 440 feet on arrival in UK. Machinery: Single diesel driving one shaft. Speed: 16.5 knots. Torpedoed by *U-155* off Gibraltar, 15 December 1942, exploded and sank.

Battler, **D18:** Attacker-class, built by Ingalls Shipbuilding, Pesagoula, originally laid down as *Mormactern* and intended to be *Altamaha*, AVG-6 before commissioning into Royal Navy on 15 November 1942. Returned to the US Navy on 12 February 1946. She was scrapped.

Begum, **D38:** Ameer-class originally intended to be *Bolinas*, AVG-36, but commissioning with the Royal Navy on 3 August

1943. Returned to the US Navy, 4 January 1946 and converted as merchantman *Raki*.

Biter, **D97**: Avenger-class converted by Atlantic Basin Iron Works from *Rio Parana* and intended as BAVG-3, but commissioned into Royal Navy on 1 May 1942. US-pattern 4-in replaced by UK 4-in autumn, 1942. Returned to US Navy 9 April 1945 and transferred to French *Marine Nationale* as *Dixmude*.

Campania, **R48**: Escort carrier with riveted construction similar to *Nairana* and *Vindex* but slightly longer and wider. Built by Harland & Wolff, Belfast, and commissioned into the Royal Navy on 7 March 1944. First British escort carrier to have an AIO, Action Information Organization. Displacement, 12, 450 tons standard, 15,970 tons deep load. LOA: 540 feet; beam: 70 feet. Armament: 2 × 4-in; 16 × 2-pounder; 8 twin 20-mm Oerlikon. Aircraft: 18; Complement: 700. Arrester gear aft but no catapults and just one lift. Machinery: Diesels driving two shafts. Speed:16 knots. Postwar acted as a troopship briefly and later took part in British nuclear tests in the Pacific in 1952, then placed in reserve before being sold for scrap in 1955.

Charger, Avenger-class ship retained by US Navy for carrier deck landing training for Royal Navy pilots trained in the US under the 'Towers Scheme' and not transferred to UK. See Appendix IV.

Chaser, **D32**: Attacker-class, but laid down as *Mormacgulf* and converted as *Breton*, AVG-10, before commissioning into Royal Navy on 9 April 1943. Built by Ingalls Shipbuilding, Pesagoula. Returned to US Navy on 12 May 1946, re-converted as *Aagteberk*.

Dasher, **D37**: Avenger-class converted by Tietjen & Lang from *Rio de Janeiro* and intended as BAVG-5, but commissioned into Royal Navy 1 July 1942. Sank as result of an aviation fuel explosion and sunk in Firth of Clyde, 27 March 1943.

Emperor, **D98 (E)**: Ameer-class intended for strike/CAP role, originally intended to be *Phybus*, AVG-34, commissioned into

Royal Navy on 6 August 1943. Returned to US Navy on 12 February 1946, and broken up shortly afterwards.

Empress, **D43:** Ameer-class intended for strike/CAP role, originally intended to be *Carnegie*, AVG-38, commissioned into Royal Navy on 13 August 1943. Returned to US Navy on 4 February 1946 and subsequently scrapped.

Fencer, **D64:** Attacker-class from Western Pipe, San Francisco, intended to be *Croatan*, AVG-14, before commissioning into Royal Navy on 20 February 1943. Returned to US Navy on 21 May 1946, and converted as *Sydney*.

Hunter, **D80:** Attacker-class from Ingalls Shipbuilding, Pesagoula, laid down as *Mormacpenn*, originally intended as USS *Block Island*, AVG-8, before commissioning into Royal Navy on 11 January 1943. Returned to the US Navy on 29 December 1945, she was converted as *Almdijk*.

Khedive, **D62 (K):** Ameer-class intended for strike/CAP role, originally intended to be *Cordova*, AVG-39, commissioned into Royal Navy on 23 August 1943. Returned to US Navy on 26 January 1946 and converted to merchantman *Rempang*.

Nabob, **D77:** Ameer-class escort carrier, originally intended to be *Edisto*, AVG-41, commissioned into Royal Navy on 7 September 1943. Crewed by Royal Canadian Navy. Torpedoed by *U-354* off North Cape on 22 August 1944, but saved by her crew. Paid off unrepaired 30 September 1944 and returned to US Navy 16 March 1945 while still on mud bank in Firth of Forth. Later salvaged and converted to merchantman whilst retaining her Royal Navy name.

Nairana, **D05:** Escort carrier built by John Brown on Clydebank using a refrigerated cargo ship hull design and lead ship of a small class of two ships with riveted construction (the other was *Vindex*, qv), commissioning on 12 December 1943. Displacement, 13,825 tons standard, 16,980 tons deep load. LOA: 528.5 feet; beam: 65 feet. Armament: 2 × 4-in; 16 × 2-pounder. Aircraft: 21;

Complement: 700. Arrester gear aft but no catapults and just one lift. Machinery: Diesels driving two shafts. Speed:16 knots. Transferred to the Royal Netherlands Navy 23 March 1946 as *Karel Doorman*.

Patroller, **D07:** Ameer-class intended aircraft transport, originally intended to be *Keeweemaw*, AVG-44, commissioned into Royal Navy on 25 October 1943. Returned to US Navy on 13 December 1946 and converted to merchantman *Almkerk*.

Premier, **D23:** Ameer-class intended for escort role, originally intended to be *Estero*, AVG-429, commissioned into Royal Navy on 3 November 1943. Returned to US Navy on 12 April 1946 and converted to merchantman *Rhodesia Star*.

Pretoria Castle, **F61:** A one-off conversion of the Union Castle passenger liner of the same name. While officially an escort carrier this ship – by far the largest auxiliary or escort carrier operated by the Royal Navy – was used solely for trials and training. Originally built by Harland & Wolff in Belfast, she was converted by Swan Hunter on the Tyne, commissioning on 9 April 1943. Displacement, 19,650 tons standard, 23,450 tons deep load. LOA: 594.5 feet; beam: 75 feet. Armament: 4 × 4-in; 16 × 2-pounder; 20 × single 20-mm Oerlikon. Complement: 580; Aircraft: 21; arrester gear aft, accelerator and hangar with one lift forward. Machinery: diesel engines powering two shafts. Speed: 18 knots. She was reconverted in 1947, and renamed *Warwick Castle*.

Puncher, **D79 (N):** Ameer-class intended for escort role but also used for carrier deck training, completed by Burrards of Vancouver and further modified in the UK, originally intended to be *Willapa*, AVG-53, commissioned into Royal Navy on 5 February 1944. Crewed by Royal Canadian Navy. Returned to US Navy on 16 January 1946 and converted to merchantman *Muncaster Castle*.

Pursuer, **D93:** Attacker-class from Ingalls Shipbuilding, Pesagoula, laid down as *Mormacland*, originally intended as USS *St George*, AVG-17, before commissioning into Royal Navy on 14 June 1943. Returned to the US Navy on 12 February 1946 and then scrapped.

Queen, **D19:** Ameer-class intended for strike role, originally intended to be *St Andrew*, AVG-49, commissioned into Royal Navy on 7 December 1943 and took part in the last Fleet Air Arm attack on German shipping in May 1945. Returned to US Navy on 31 October 1946 and converted to merchantman *Roebiah*.

Rajah, **D10:** Ameer-class intended for role of aircraft transport, originally intended to be *McClure*, then *Prince*, AVG-45, but commissioned into Royal Navy on 17 January 1944. Refitted as troopship 5 August 1945. Returned to US Navy on 13 December 1946 and converted to merchantman *Drente*.

Ranee, **D03:** Ameer-class intended for strike/CAP role, originally intended to be *Niantic*, AVG-46, commissioned into Royal Navy on 8 November 1943. Returned to US Navy on 21 November 1946 and converted to merchantman *Friesland*.

Ravager, **D90 (V):** Attacker-class, built by Seattle-Tacoma Shipbuilding intended to be AVG-24, but commissioned into Royal Navy on 26 April 1943. Returned to the US Navy on 27 February 1946, she was converted as *Robin Trent*.

Reaper, **D82:** Ameer-class intended for aircraft ferry role but also undertook fighter support, originally intended to be *Winjah*, AVG-54, commissioned into Royal Navy on 21 February 1944. Returned to US Navy on 20 May 1946 and converted to merchantman *South Africa Star*.

Ruler, **D72:** Ameer-class intended for strike/CAP role, originally intended to be *St Joseph*, AVG-50, commissioned into Royal Navy on 22 December 1943. Returned to US Navy on 20 May 1946 and scrapped.

Searcher, **D40:** Attacker-class, built by Seattle-Tacoma Shipbuilding intended as AVG-22, but commissioned into Royal Navy on 8 April 1943. Returned to the US Navy on 29 May 1945, she was converted as *Captain Theo*.

Shah, **D21:** Ameer-class intended for escort role, originally intended to be *Jamaica*, AVG-43, commissioned into Royal Navy on 27 February 1943. Returned to US Navy on 6 December 1945 and converted to merchantman *Salta*.

Slinger, **D26:** Ameer-class completed by Willamette Iron & Steel at Portland, Oregon, intended for aircraft ferry role but also undertook fighter support, originally intended to be *Chatham*, AVG-32, commissioned into Royal Navy on 11 August 1943. Disabled by a mine in February 1944, so non-operational for most of the rest of the year. Returned to US Navy on 27 February 1946 and converted to merchantman *Robin Mowbray*.

Smiter, **D55:** Ameer-class intended for escort role, originally intended to be *Vermillion*, AVG-52, commissioned into Royal Navy on 20 January 1944. Returned to US Navy on 6 April 1946 and converted to merchantman *Artillero*.

Speaker, **D90:** Ameer-class modified by Burrards of Vancouver before delivery and intended as an aircraft ferry but also used in the strike/CAP role, originally planned to be *Delgada*, AVG-40, commissioned into Royal Navy on 20 November 1943. Famed for carrying 500 ex-POWs from Tokyo to Sydney in September 1945. Returned to US Navy on 17 July 1946 and converted to merchantman *Lancero*.

Stalker, **D91:** Attacker-class from Western Pipe, San Francisco, intended to be *Hamlin*, AVG-15, before commissioning into Royal Navy on 30 December 1942. Returned to the US Navy on 29 December 1945, and converted as *Riouw*.

Striker, **D12:** Attacker-class from Western Pipe, San Francisco, originally intended as USS *Prince William*, AVG-19, before commissioning into Royal Navy on 29 April 1943. Returned to the US Navy on 12 February 1946, she was scrapped.

Thane, **D48:** Ameer-class completed for assault role, originally intended to be *Sunset*, AVG-48, commissioned into Royal Navy on 19 November 1943. Torpedoed by *U-482* in the Firth of Clyde on 15 January 1945 and later scrapped in the UK, although nominally returned to the US Navy 'as lies' 15 December 1945.

Tracker, **D24:** Attacker-class, built by Seattle-Tacoma Shipbuilding and designated BAVG-6 by the US Navy, before commissioning into Royal Navy on 31 January 1943. Returned to the US Navy on 29 November 1945, she was converted as *Corrientes*.

Trouncer, **D85:** Ameer-class for aircraft ferry role, originally intended to be *Perdito*, AVG-47, commissioned into Royal Navy on 31 January 1944. Returned to US Navy on 3 March 1946 and converted to merchantman *Greystoke Castle*.

Trumpeter, **D09:** Ameer-class for escort role although later used some of the last strikes against enemy shipping, as late as May 1945. Originally intended to be *Bastian*, AVG-37, commissioned into Royal Navy on 4 August 1943. Returned to US Navy on 6 April 1946 and converted to merchantman *Alblasserdijk*.

Vindex, **D15:** Escort carrier and a sister of *Nairana* (qv) with a riveted hull, but slightly smaller. Built from refrigerated cargo vessel at Swan Hunter, Tyneside, and commissioned into the Royal Navy on 3 December 1943. Operated as a troopship for a period post-war. Displacement, 13, 445 tons standard, 16,830 tons deep load. LOA: 528.5 feet; beam: 65 feet. Armament: 2 × 4-in; 16 × 2-pounder. Aircraft: 21; Complement: 700. Arrester gear aft but no catapults and just one lift. Machinery: Diesels driving two shafts. Speed:16 knots. Sold 2 October 1947 as merchantman *Port Vindex*.

Appendix IV

UNITED STATES NAVY ESCORT CARRIERS

Note: Initially, US-built escort carriers were designated AVG, aircraft escort vessel, or BAVG, British aircraft escort vessel for those being transferred under the 'Lend-Lease' programme, but this changed to ACV, auxiliary aircraft carrier, on 20 August 1942, and finally changed to the now generally-used designation of CVE, escort aircraft carrier, on 15 July 1943. In service, all ships were designated USS, United States Ship.

Admiralty Islands, **CVE-99:** Casablanca-class transport carrier originally to be called *Chapin Bay*, but her name was changed before launching. Commissioned into the US Navy on 13 June 1944, she moved to the air support role to cover the invasions of Iwo Jima and Okinawa. Post-war, she was decommissioned in April 1946 and almost immediately stricken and sold to the breakers.

Altamaha, **CVE-18:** Bogue-class ASW carrier and aircraft transport, commissioned into the US Navy on 15 September 1942. Decommissioned in September 1946, but re-designated CVHE-18 in 1955, being sold for scrap in 1961.

Anzio, **CVE-57:** Casablanca-class anti-submarine carrier originally named *Alikula Bay*, then *Coral Sea*, AVG-57, but designation changed to CVE-57 April 1943 and commissioned into the US Navy on 7 August 1943. She was renamed *Anzio* in September 1944 so that the name *Coral Sea* could be used for a fleet carrier. Decommissioned and placed in reserve in August 1946, but re-designated CVHE-57 in July 1958, but withdrawn in March 1959 and sold for scrap in 1960.

Attu, **CVE-102:** Casablanca-class transport carrier originally to be called *Elbour Bay*, but her name was changed before she co-mmissioned into the US Navy on 30 June 1944. She suffered extensive damage in a hurricane off Okinawa in June 1945. Post-war, she was decommissioned in June 1946 and within a month was stricken and scrapped by 1950.

Badoeng Strait, **CVE-116:** Commencement Bay-class training carrier originally named *San Alberto Bay* but re-named before launching. Commissioned into the US Navy on 9 April 1945, she was de-commissioned in June 1946, but returned to service in January 1947 to become an anti-submarine trials carrier before being engaged in ASW operations during the Korean War and was not decommissioned until May 1957. She was re-designated AKV-16 in May 1959, before being deleted in late 1970 and then scrapped.

Bairoko, **CVE-115:** Commencement Bay-class aircraft transport originally named *Portage Bay* but re-named before launching. Commissioned into the US Navy on 16 July 1945, she was de-commissioned in April 1950, but returned to service in September. Suffered an explosion aboard in May 1951, but was present for the H-bomb tests at Eniwetok in 1954 before being placed in reserve in 1955. Although re-designated AKV-15 in May 1959, she was sold to the breakers in 1960.

Barnes, **CVE-20:** Bogue-class aircraft transport, commissioned into the US Navy on 20 February 1943. Decommissioned in August 1946, but re-designated CVHE-20 in 1955 and AKV-38 in 1959, before being sold for scrap in June 1960.

Bismarck Sea, **CVE-95:** Casablanca-class transport carrier originally named *Alikula Bay*, but the name was changed between launching and commissioning into the US Navy on 20 May 1944. On 21 February 1945, she was hit by two kamikaze aircraft within minutes of one another and sank in two hours.

Block Island, **CVE-21:** Bogue-class ASW carrier and aircraft trans-port, commissioned into the US Navy on 8 March 1943. Torpedoed and sunk by *U-549* in May 1944 whilst in the Atlantic.

Block Island, **CVE-106:** Commencement Bay-class aircraft transport, anti-submarine and training carrier originally named *Sunset Bay* but re-named before launching. Commissioned into the US Navy on 30 December 1944, she was the first 'Marine carrier', supporting the invasion of Okinawa, she was decommissioned in May 1946 and used for harbour training at Annapolis until 1950. She returned to operational duties in April 1951, but entered reserve in late 1954. She received the designation LPH-1 in December 1957, but was never converted to the helicopter assault role and returned to her original designation briefly in 1959 before being re-designated AKV-38 and sold that year to the breakers.

Bogue, **CVE-9:** Lead ship of Bogue-class based on C3 merchant hulls built by Seattle-Tacoma, but with a number of improvements compared with *Long Island* and *Charger*, including a longer and higher hangar and two lifts, and a larger island with a lattice mast, while steam turbines provided a higher speed. Laid down as *Steel Advocate*, *Bogue* was commissioned into the US Navy on 26 September 1942 as an escort carrier but also acted as an air-craft transport. Displacement, 8,390 tons standard, 13,980 tons deep load. LOA: 496 feet; beam: 82 feet. Armament: 2 × 5-in; 10 × 20-mm. Complement: 890; Aircraft: 28 (more than 90 in the transport role); arrester gear aft and accelerator forward, hangar with two lifts. Machinery: Steam turbine driving single shaft. Speed: 18 knots. Withdrawn from service late 1946 and placed in reserve before being re-designated CVHE in 1955, but was sold for scrap in 1960.

Bougainville, **CVE-100:** Casablanca-class transport carrier originally to be called *Didrickson Bay*, but her name was changed before she was launched. Commissioned into the US Navy on 1 June 1944, she moved to the air support role for the invasions of Iwo Jima and Okinawa, suffering damage in a typhoon on 5 June 1945. Post-war, she was decommissioned in November 1946 and placed in reserve, but was re-designated CVU-100 in June 1955 and AKV-35 in May 1959, but without returning to service was stricken and sold to the breakers in 1960.

Breton, **CVE-23:** Bogue-class aircraft transport, commissioned into US Navy on 12 April 1943, decommissioned in August 1946, but re-designated CVHE-23 in 1955, and then as CVU-23 in 1958 and AKV-42 in 1959, but decommissioned in October 1970 and sold for scrap in 1972.

Cape Esperance, **CVE-88:** Casablanca-class transport carrier originally to be called *Tananek Bay*, but her name was changed before launching and she was commissioned into the US Navy on 9 April 1944. Post-war, she was decommissioned in August 1946 and placed in reserve, but was returned to service in 1950 as an aircraft transport for the Korean War. Re-designated CVU-88 in June 1955, she was decommissioned in January 1959 and was sold to the breakers in March.

Cape Gloucester, **CVE-109:** Commencement Bay-class aircraft transport, originally named *Willapa Bay* but re-named before launching. Commissioned into the US Navy on 5 March 1945, just in time for the closing stages of the Pacific campaign, and served as a 'Marine carrier' providing close air support for forces ashore. She was decommissioned in November 1946, being re-designated CVHE-109 in June 1955 and then AKV-9 for the MSTS in May 1959, but was stricken in April 1970 after an earlier decision to do this in 1960 had been revoked.

Card, **CVE-11:** Bogue-class anti-submarine carrier also used as aircraft transport, later becoming a training carrier, commissioned into the US Navy on 8 November 1942. Decommissioned in May 1946 and placed in reserve, she was re-designated CVHE-11 in 1955, and then again as CVU-11 on 1 July 1958, returning to service as an aircraft transport, before becoming AKV-40 in 1959. Sunk after striking a mine off Saigon in May 1964, but raised and repaired. Sold for scrap in 1971.

Casablanca, **CVE-55:** Lead ship of the Casablanca-class, slightly smaller than the Bogue-class and with all fifty ships built at the Kaiser Yard at Vancouver, Washington, intended mainly as aircraft transports. The design used the company's standard S4 hull which showed its naval intent through having a transom stern, even though it was also used for merchant vessels. Originally the class was intended to be split between the US Navy and Royal Navy, but it was decided to retain all ships and provide the Royal Navy with additional Bogue-class vessels. Displacement, 8,200 tons standard, 10,900 tons deep load. LOA: 475 feet; beam: 85 feet. Armament: 1 × 5-in; 8 × 40-mm Bofors; 12 × 20-mm Oerlikon. Complement: 860; Aircraft: 28 (more than 90 in the transport role); arrester gear aft, catapult forward, hangar with two lifts. Machinery: Steam triple expansion engines driving two shafts. Speed: 19 knots. *Casablanca* was originally intended to be the Royal Navy's *Ameer*, and originally designed AVG-55, the name was changed to *Alazon Bay* in January 1943, but changed again before commissioning into the US Navy on 8 July 1943. Decommissioned on 29 August 1946 but not scrapped until 1961.

Charger, **CVE-30:** Laid down as a US merchant vessel, *Rio de la Plata*, using a standard C3 hull, converted with a wooden planked flight deck and a small starboard side island sponsoned out from the flight deck for navigation and air control, but no smokestack as exhaust fumes discharged horizontally. Originally commissioned into US Navy as BAVG-4 (becoming AVG-30 in January 1942, ACV-30 in August 1942, and finally CVE-30 in July 1943), and although intended for the Royal Navy under Lend-Lease, retained to train British pilots. Commissioned 3 March 1942. An unusual feature was the provision of arrester gear forward as well as aft, similar to the arrangement in the USS *Wasp*. Displacement, 11,800 tons standard, 15,126 tons deep load. LOA: 492 feet; beam: 78 feet. Armament: 3 × 4-in; 10 × 20-mm Oerlikon. Machinery: Diesel engine driving a single shaft. Speed: 17 knots. Complement: 856, aircraft 36. Hangar 190 feet long with single lift aft, arrester gear aft and forward, but no accelerator. Withdrawn in March 1946 and later converted to merchantman *Fairsea*.

Chenango, **CVE-28:** Formerly *Esso New Orleans*, Sangamon-class converted by Bethlehem Steel at Staten Island and commissioned into US Navy 19 September 1942, initially designated AVG-28 but this changed to CVE-28 in July 1943. Operated as an attack carrier. Decommissioned in 1946 but retained in reserve and redesignated CVHE-28 in 1955 for helicopter operations, but withdrawn in 1959 and eventually scrapped.

Commencement Bay, **CVE-105:** Lead ship of the Commencement Bay-class, all of which were built at the Todd-Pacific Yard, the new name for Seattle-Tacoma Yard. Originally to comprise thirty-five ships, the arrival of peace meant that only nineteen were completed, although a number were laid down and scrapped on the slipway. Some of the cancelled vessels were to have been built by Kaiser at Vancouver, Washington. The largest of the CVE-classes, these also incorporated lessons learnt in action, including displaced machinery to improve survivability in an attack. Once again a merchant-style hull was chosen, in this case that of an oiler and like the smaller Sangamon-class these ships could act in this role if necessary. Displacement, 18,908 tons standard, 21,397 tons deep load. LOA: 557 feet; beam: 80 feet. Armament: 2 × 5-in; 36 × 40-mm Bofors; 20 × 20-mm Oerlikon. Complement: 1,066; Aircraft: 33 (more than 90 in the transport role); arrester gear aft, two catapults forward, hangar with two lifts. Machinery: steam turbines driving two shafts. Speed: 19 knots. *Commencement Bay* was originally intended to be *St Joseph Bay* but the name of this training carrier was changed before commissioning into the US Navy on 27 November 1944. Decommissioned in November 1946, she was re-designated CVHE-105 in June 1955 and then AKV-37 in May 1959, and was not deleted until 1 April 1971.

Copabee, **CVE-12:** Originally laid down as *Steel Architect*, Bogue-class carrier commissioned as an aircraft transport in the US Navy on 15 June 1942, although spent a short period on combat duties in late 1942. Decommissioned in July 1946 and re-designated CVHE-12 in June 1955, but sold for scrap in early 1960s.

Core, **CVE-13:** Bogue-class ASW carrier and aircraft transport, decommissioned in October 1946, but re-designated CVHE-13 in 1955, and then re-commissioned as CVU-13 on 1 July 1958 as a transport, becoming an aircraft ferry designated AKV-41 in May 1959. Sold for scrap in the early 1970s.

Corregidor, **CVE-58:** Casablanca-class aircraft transport, anti-submarine and training carrier originally designated ACV-58, *Anguilla Bay*, for the Royal Navy, but changed to CVE-58 April 1943 and commissioned into the US Navy on 31 August 1943. Put in reserve in July 1946, but returned to service as an aircraft transport in May 1951 and not decommissioned until September 1958. Sold for scrap in 1960.

Croatan, **CVE-25:** Bogue-class escort carrier and aircraft transport, commissioned into US Navy on 28 April 1943, and later became part of a 'hunter-killer' group. Decommissioned in May 1946, but re-designated CVHE-25 in 1955, and then as CVU-25 in May 1958 and AKV-43 in 1959. Used on experimental duties by NASA winter 1964–65, but decommissioned in October 1970 and sold for scrap in 1971.

Fanshaw Bay, **CVE-70:** Casablanca-class carrier originally designated ACV-70, she had been re-designated CVE-70 in July 1943, before commissioning into the US Navy on 9 December 1943. Badly damaged by Japanese shelling and bombs at Leyte Gulf, but returned to service in March 1945. Post-war, she was placed in reserve and re-designated CVHE in June 1955, before being deleted in March 1959 and sold to the breakers.

Gambier Bay, **CVE-73:** Casablanca-class carrier originally designated ACV-73, she was re-designated CVE-73 in July 1943, before commissioning into the US Navy on 28 December 1943. She was sunk by gunfire from three Japanese cruisers off Samar during the Battle of Leyte Gulf on 25 October 1944.

Gilbert Islands, **CVE-107:** Commencement Bay-class aircraft transport originally named *St Andrews Bay* but re-named before launching. Commissioned into the US Navy on 5 February 1945, and served as a 'Marine carrier' during the invasion of Okinawa, providing close air support for units ashore. At the end of the war she was decommissioned in May 1946, but returned to service in September 1951 as an aircraft transport during the Korean War and returned to reserve early in 1955. In late 1961 she was converted to a Major Communications Relay Ship and redesignated AGMR-1, renamed *Annapolis* when she re-commissioned in March 1964. She was finally withdrawn from service in late 1969, although remained in reserve until October 1976.

Guadalcanal, **CVE-60:** Casablanca-class anti-submarine and escort carrier originally designated ACV-60, *Astrolabe Bay*, but changed to CVE-60 April 1943 and commissioned into the US Navy on 25 September 1943. Operated in Atlantic 'hunter-killer' groups with destroyers and played a part in the capture of the German submarine, *U-505* in June 1944. Post-war, decommissioned in July 1946 and passed into reserve. Re-designated CVU-60 in June 1955, before being withdrawn in May 1958 and sold for scrap in April 1959.

Hoggatt Bay, **CVE-75:** Casablanca-class carrier commissioned into the US Navy on 11 January 1944. Damaged by an explosion while off Luzon in January 1945, but repaired in time to support the invasion of Okinawa. Post-war, she was decommissioned in July 1946 and re-designated CVU-75 in June 1955, and then AKV in May 1959, but was sold to the breakers in September of that year.

Hollandia, **CVE-97:** Casablanca-class training and transport carrier originally to be called *Astrolabe Bay*, but her name was changed before she commissioned into the US Navy on 1 June 1944. Post-war, she was decommissioned on 17 August 1947and placed in reserve, but was re-designated CVU-97 in June 1955 and AKV-33 in May 1959, but without returning to service was stricken and sold to the breakers in 1960.

Kadashan Bay, **CVE-76:** Casablanca-class aircraft transport and close air support carrier commissioned into the US Navy on 18 January 1944. Damaged by kamikaze attack while off Luzon in January 1945, but repaired, although relegated to transport duties. She was decommissioned in June 1946 and re-designated CVU-76 in June 1955, and then AKV in May 1959, but was sold to the breakers the following winter.

Kalinin Bay, **CVE-68:** Casablanca-class carrier that undertook close support operations, but was relegated to transport duties after suffering a kamikaze attack and being hit by gunfire during the Battle of Leyte Gulf on 25 October 1944. Originally designated ACV-68, she had been re-designated CVE-68 in July 1943, before commissioning into the US Navy on 27 November 1943. Post-war, she was decommissioned in May 1946 and sold to the breakers at the end of the year.

Kasaan Bay, **CVE-69:** Casablanca-class carrier initially deployed as a transport but soon moved to the Mediterranean providing close air support. Originally designated ACV-69, she had been re-designated CVE-69 in July 1943, before commissioning into the US Navy on 4 December 1943. Post-war, she was placed in reserve and re-designated CVHE in June 1955, before being deleted in March 1959 and sold to the breakers the following year.

Kitkun Bay, **CVE-71:** Casablanca-class carrier initially deployed as a transport and training carrier, but soon was providing close air support. Originally designated ACV-71, she had been redesignated CVE-71 in July 1943, before commissioning into the US Navy on 15 December 1943. Damaged off Samar in October 1944, she returned to transport duties. Post-war, she was deleted in May 1946 and scrapped in 1947.

Kula Gulf, **CVE-108:** Commencement Bay-class aircraft transport originally named *Vermillion Bay* but re-named before launching. Commissioned into the US Navy on 12 May 1945 and operated only briefly in the Pacific before the war ended, when she was put in reserve in early summer 1946. In 1950, she returned to service as an aircraft transport during the Korean War and then from mid-1953 operated on Atlantic ASW duties, before returning to reserve in December 1955. Becoming an MSTS ferry in June 1965 and re-designated AKV-8, she transported aircraft during the Vietnam War, until taken out of service in September 1970 and scrapped in 1971.

Kwajalein, **CVE-98:** Casablanca-class transport carrier originally to be called *Bucareli Bay*, but her name was changed before she was launched. Commissioned into the US Navy on 7 June 1944, operating in the Pacific where she was badly damaged in a hurricane off the Philippines. Post-war, she was decommissioned in August 1946 and placed in reserve, but was re-designated CVU-98 in June 1955 and AKV-34 in May 1959, but without returning to service was stricken and sold to the breakers in 1960.

Liscombe Bay, **CVE-56:** Casablanca-class aircraft transport originally designated AVG-56 but changed to CVE-56 April 1943 and commissioned into the US Navy on 7 August 1943. Torpedoed and sunk off the Gilbert Islands by *I-175* on 24 November 1943.

Long Island, **CVE-1:** The Moore-Macormick Line was home of many of the ships converted from cargo vessels, using the standardized C3 hull. The first of these was the *Mormacmail*, purchased in spring 1941 and converted in haste to conform to a Presidential stipulation that the work be completed within three months. *Long Island* commissioned into the US Navy on 2 June 1941, initially being designated an auxiliary aircraft carrier, AVG-1, although redesignated ACV-1 in 1942 and, finally, CVE-1 in July 1943. A genuine 'flat top' without superstructure and with the bridge below the flight deck with sponsons on either side. The original flight deck extended along 70 per cent of the hull length, but this was increased forward by a 100 feet to 420 feet after a few months' experience. The ship was used as a training carrier and aircraft transport. Displacement, 7,886 tons standard, 14,050 tons deep load. LOA: 492 feet; beam: 78 feet. Armament: 1 × 4-in; 2 × 3-in; 4 × 0.5-in. Complement: 970; Aircraft: 16; arrester gear aft and hangar with one lift. Machinery: Diesel engine driving single shaft. Speed: 16 knots. Withdrawn from service March 1946 and converted to merchantman *Nelly*.

Lunga Point, **CVE-94:** Casablanca-class transport carrier originally intended to be named *Alazon Bay*, but the name was changed at an early stage and she commissioned into the US Navy on 14 May 1944. Struck by a kamikaze off Iwo Jima in February 1945, she managed to remain operational and was present for the landings in Okinawa. Post-war, she was decommissioned in October 1946 and placed in reserve. Re-designated CVU-94 in June 1955 and AKV-32 in May 1959, she never returned to service and was sold to the breakers in 1960.

Makassar Strait, **CVE-91:** Casablanca-class transport carrier originally intended to be named *Ulitka Bay*, but the name was changed before construction started and she commissioned into the US Navy on 29 April 1944. Post-war, she was decommissioned in June 1946 and placed in reserve, before beginning an eventful career as a target to evaluate the anti-ship potential of Tartar and Terrier surface-to-air missiles, and sank in 1962 following the no doubt successful conclusion of the series of tests.

Makin Island, **CVE-93:** Casablanca-class transport carrier originally intended to be named *Woodcliff Bay*, but renamed at an early stage of construction and commissioned into the US Navy on 9 May 1944. Post-war, she was decommissioned in April 1946 and placed in reserve, before being sold to the breakers in 1947.

Manila Bay, **CVE-61:** Casablanca-class transport and attack carrier originally designated ACV-61, *Bucareli Bay*, but changed to CVE-61 July 1943 and commissioned into the US Navy on 5 October 1943. Post-war, decommissioned in August 1946 and passed into reserve. Later re-designated CVU-61, before being withdrawn in May 1958 and sold for scrapping in September 1959.

Marcus Island, **CVE-77:** Casablanca-class transport carrier originally named *Kanalku Bay*, but renamed in November 1943 and commissioned into the US Navy on 26 January 1944. Damaged by the hurricane that struck the Third Fleet in December 1944, but repaired and returned to transport duties. Post-war, she was decommissioned on 12 December 1946, re-designated CVHE-77 in June 1955, and then AKV-27 in May 1959, but was sold to the breakers during the winter of 1960-61.

Matanikau, **CVE-101:** Casablanca-class transport carrier originally to be called *Dolomi Bay*, but her name was changed before she was launched. Commissioned into the US Navy on 24 June 1944. Post-war, she was decommissioned in October 1946 and placed in reserve, but was re-designated CVU-101 in June 1955 and AKV-36 in May 1959, but without returning to service was stricken and sold to the breakers late the following year.

Mindoro, **CVE-120:** Commencement Bay-class training and ASW carrier commissioned into the US Navy on 4 December 1945, she operated mainly in the latter role before being decommissioned in

June 1955. Re-designated AKV-20, she was sold to the breakers in late 1959.

Mission Bay, **CVE-59:** Casablanca-class aircraft transport and escort carrier originally designated ACV-59, *Atheling*, for the Royal Navy, but changed to CVE-59 April 1943 and commissioned into the US Navy on 13 September 1943. Post-war, continued as an aircraft transport until February 1947 when placed in reserve and re-designated CVU-59 in June 1955, before being withdrawn in September 1958 and sold for scrapping in April 1959.

Munda, **CVE-104:** Casablanca-class support carrier originally to be called *Tonowek Bay*, but her name was changed before she commissioned into the US Navy on 8 July 1944. Post-war, she was decommissioned in September 1946 and placed in reserve, but was re-designated CVU-104 in June 1955, but without returning to service was stricken in September 1958 and sold to the breakers in 1960.

Nassau, **CVE-16:** Bogue-class aircraft transport, commissioned into the US Navy on 20 August 1942. Decommissioned in October 1946, but re-designated CVHE-13 in 1955 but never re-commissioned before being sold for scrap in 1961.

Natoma Bay, **CVE-62:** Casablanca-class transport and training carrier originally designated ACV-62, but changed to CVE-62 July 1943 and commissioned into the US Navy on 14 October 1943. A kamikaze strike in June 1945 brought her war service to a pre-mature end and she was decommissioned in May 1946 and passed into reserve. Re-designated CVU-62 in May 1958, but was sold to the breakers the following year.

Nebenta Bay, **CVE-74:** The first Casablanca-class carrier to be designated CVE from the outset and one of those originally intended for the Royal Navy, but retained by the US Navy and commissioned on 3 January 1944. Badly damaged by hurricanes during the winter of 1944-45. Post-war, she was decommissioned and re-designated CVU-74 in June 1955, and then AKV, but did not return to service and was sold to the breakers in 1960.

Ommaney Bay, **CVE-79:** Casablanca-class training and transport carrier originally named *Kanalku Bay*, but renamed in November 1943 and commissioned into the US Navy on 11 February 1944. Badly damaged by kamikaze attack in January 1945, she had to be sunk by torpedoes from the destroyer USS *Burns*.

Palau, **CVE-122:** Commencement Bay-class ASW carrier and transport commissioned into the US Navy on 15 January 1946, operated at intervals until decommissioned in mid-1954. Re-designated AKV-22 in May 1959, but was sold to the breakers in 1960.

Petrof Bay, **CVE-80:** Casablanca-class transport carrier commissioned into the US Navy on 18 February 1944. Damaged by the hurricane that struck the Third Fleet in December 1944, but repaired and returned to transport duties. Post-war, she was decommissioned in July 1946 and placed in reserve, re-designated CVU-80 in June 1955, but was sold to the breakers in 1958.

Point Cruz, **CVE-119:** Commencement Bay-class training carrier originally named *Trocadero Bay*, but changed before her keel was laid and commissioned into the US Navy on 16 October 1945, she remained in the training role until placed in the reserve fleet between June 1947 and July 1951, before re-commissioning as an anti-submarine carrier in which role she served until the mid-1950s, but operated again as an aircraft transport as AKV-19 between 1965 and 1970 during the Vietnam War. She was sold to the breakers in late 1970.

Prince William, **CVE-31:** Bogue-class aircraft transport, commissioned into US Navy on 9 April 1943, decommissioned in August 1946, re-designated CVHE-31 in 1955, but sold for scrap during the early 1960s.

Puget Sound, **CVE-113:** Commencement Bay-class aircraft transport originally named *Hobart Bay* but re-named before launching. Commissioned into the US Navy on 18 June 1945, almost too late for operational service, she decommissioned in October 1946. She remained in reserve, being re-designated CVHE-113 in July 1955 and again as AKV-13 in May 1959, before being sold to the breakers in 1962.

Rabaul, **CVE-121:** Commencement Bay-class carrier not commissioned into the US Navy although completed on 30 August 1946, passing straight into reserve where she was re-designated CVHE-121 in 1955 and then AKV-21 in May 1959, but was stricken in September 1971 and scrapped in 1971.

Rendova, **CVE-114:** Commencement Bay-class training carrier and aircraft transport originally named *Mosser Bay* but re-named before construction started. Commissioned into the US Navy on 22 October 1945, too late for the war. Operational for much of the post-war period with brief spells in reserve in 1950 and 1953, before passing into reserve in mid-1955, being re-designated CVHE-114 that summer and then again as AKV-14 in May 1959, before being scrapped in 1971.

Roi, **CVE-103:** Casablanca-class replenishment and supply carrier originally to be called *Alava Bay*, but her name was changed before she commissioned into the US Navy on 6 July 1944. Post-war, she was decommissioned in May 1946 and scrapped in 1947.

Rudyerd Bay, **CVE-81:** Casablanca-class transport carrier commissioned into the US Navy on 25 February 1944. Occasionally used on combat duties. Post-war, she was decommissioned in June 1946 and placed in reserve, re-designated CVU-81 in June 1955, and then in May 1959 as AKV-29, before being sold to the breakers the following winter.

Sable, **IX-81:** Differed from *Wolverine* (qv) in having a steel flight deck and a neater superstructure with homing beacons, but was another coal-burning Great Lakes excursion paddle-steamer, intended solely for deck landing training. Arrester wires were provided aft and there was a safety barrier forward as aircraft could be parked forward using outriggers, but there was no hangar, catapults or accelerators. No aircraft were kept aboard as the ship operated in conjunction with shore training stations. Known before conversion as *Greater Buffalo*, the ship was commissioned into the US Navy on 8 March 1943. Displacement, 8,000 tons standard. LOA: 519 feet; beam: 90 feet (hull 58 feet). No armament. Complement: 300; No aircraft. Machinery: Compound steam engines, coal-fired, driving two paddles. Speed: 18 knots. Withdrawn from service post-war and scrapped 1948.

Saginaw Bay, **CVE-82:** Casablanca-class transport carrier commissioned into the US Navy on 2 March 1944. Post-war, she was decommissioned in June 1946 and placed in reserve, re-designated CVHE-82 in June 1955, but was sold to the breakers during 1959-60.

Saidor, **CVE-117:** Commencement Bay-class carrier originally named *Saltery Bay* but re-named before her keel was laid. Commissioned into the US Navy on 4 September 1945, at the end of the war she became the headquarters ship for the A-bomb tests at Bikini in summer 1946, before being decommissioned in September 1947. She was re-designated CVHE-117 in June 1955 and AKV-10 in May 1959. She was sold to the breakers in late 1970.

St Lo, **CVE-63:** Casablanca-class transport and air support carrier originally designated ACV-63, *Chapin Bay*, but changed to *Midway*, CVE-63 April 1943 and commissioned into the US Navy on 23 October 1943. Her name was changed again in September 1944 to free the name *Midway* for a large fleet carrier, but on 25 October she had the unwanted distinction of becoming the first victim of a kamikaze attack when during the Battle of Leyte Gulf she was hit by a Zero which ruptured fuel lines setting off fires and explosions in the hangar, causing her to sink within thirty minutes.

Salamaua, **CVE-96:** Casablanca-class transport carrier originally to be named *Anguilla Bay* but renamed after the keel was laid and commissioned into the US Navy on 26 May 1944. She was the victim of a kamikaze attack in January 1945, and then of a hurricane on 5 June, and judged too badly damaged to return to service, she was stricken in late 1945 and scrapped in 1947.

Salerno Bay, **CVE-110:** Commencement Bay-class training carrier originally named *Winjah Bay* but re-named before launching. Commissioned into the US Navy on 19 May 1945, at the end of the war she continued in the training role before being decommissioned in October 1947. She returned to operational duties in 1951 as an anti-submarine carrier until early 1954. Re-designated AKV-10 in May 1959, but was sold to the breakers in late 1961.

Sangamon, **CVE-26:** Lead ship of a class of four carriers all converted from the US Navy's type T3 oilers, retaining this capability as a secondary function. Before purchase by US Navy had been *Esso Trenton*. Converted at Newport News and commissioned into US Navy service 25 August 1942, initially designated AVG-26 but this changed to CVE-26 in July 1943. Operated as an attack carrier and aircraft transport as well as in the deck training role. Displacement, 10,500 tons standard, 23,875 tons deep load. LOA: 525 feet; beam: 75.5 feet. Armament: 2 × 5-in; 8 × 40-mm Bofors; 12 × 20-mm Oerlikon. Complement: 1,080; Aircraft: 30; arrester gear aft, accelerator forward and hangar with two lifts. Machinery: Steam turbines driving two shafts. Speed: 18 knots. Seriously damaged by Japanese bombs and two kamikaze strikes, so withdrawn in autumn 1945 and sold for scrap in 1948.

Santee, **CVE-29:** Formerly *Esso Seakay*, Sangamon-class converted at Norfolk Navy Yard and commissioned into US Navy service 24 August 1942, initially designated AVG-29 but this changed to CVE-27 in July 1943. Operated as an attack carrier and then an anti-submarine carrier before becoming aircraft transport. Torpedoed at Samar in October 1944, but repaired. Placed in reserve post-war and later re-designated CVHE-29 in 1955 for helicopter operations, but withdrawn in 1959 and eventually scrapped.

Sargent Bay, **CVE-83:** Casablanca-class air support and transport carrier commissioned into the US Navy on 9 March 1944. Post-war, she was decommissioned in June 1946 and placed in reserve, re-designated CVU-83 in June 1955, but was sold to the breakers in 1959.

Savo Island, **CVE-78:** Casablanca-class transport carrier originally named *Kaita Bay*, but renamed in November 1943 and commissioned into the US Navy on 3 February 1944. Damaged by a kamikaze early in 1945. Post-war, she was decommissioned in December 1946, re-designated CVHE-78 in June 1955, and then AKV-28 in May 1959, but was sold to the breakers the following winter.

Shamrock Bay, **CVE-84:** Casablanca-class transport carrier commissioned into the US Navy on 15 March 1944. Post-war, she was decommissioned in July 1946 and placed in reserve, re-designated CVHE-84 in June 1955, but was sold to the breakers late in 1959.

Shipley Bay, **CVE-85:** Casablanca-class transport carrier commissioned into the US Navy on 21 March 1944. Post-war, she was decommissioned in June 1946 and placed in reserve, re-designated CVHE-85 in June 1955, but was sold to the breakers in 1959.

Siboney, **CVE-112:** Commencement Bay-class aircraft transport originally named *Frosty Bay* but re-named before launching. Commissioned into the US Navy on 14 May 1945, at the end of the war she remained in service until late 1947, but remained in reserve only briefly as she returned to service for 1948-49, before returning to the reserve only to be re-activated again in 1951 for ASW duties. Returning to reserve she was re-designated AKV-12, but was sold to the breakers in 1971.

Sicily, **CVE-118:** Commencement Bay-class ASW carrier originally named *Sandy Bay* but re-named before launching. Commissioned into the US Navy on 27 February 1946, she remained operational until July 1954 and was later re-designated AKV-18. She was sold to the breakers in June 1960.

Sitkoh Bay, **CVE-86:** Casablanca-class re-supply and replenishment carrier commissioned into the US Navy on 28 March 1944. Post-war, she was decommissioned in late 1946 and placed in reserve, but returned to service as an aircraft transport in 1950 for the Korean War. Returned to reserve in July 1954, but survived to be re-designated AKV-30 before being sold to the breakers in 1960.

Solomons, **CVE-67:** Casablanca-class carrier that undertook anti-submarine and transport roles, originally intended for the Royal Navy as HMS *Emperor*, she was designated ACV-67, *Nassuk Bay*, but she was re-designated CVE-67 in July 1943, and the name was changed shortly before commissioning into the US Navy on 21 November 1943. Post-war, she was decommissioned in June 1946 and scrapped the following year.

Steamer Bay, **CVE-87:** Casablanca-class transport carrier commissioned into the US Navy on 4 April 1944, although she became involved in combat operations in the final year of the war. In April 1945 she was damaged in a collision with a destroyer, and then damage from an aircraft landing accident resulted in a short withdrawal for repairs. Post-war, she was decommissioned during 1947 and placed in reserve, re-designated CVHE-87 in June 1955, but was never re-commissioned before being sold to the breakers in 1959.

Suwannee, **CVE-27:** Sangamon-class converted at Newport News and commissioned into US Navy service 24 September 1942, initially designated AVG-27 but this changed to CVE-27 in July 1943. Operated as an attack carrier. Badly damaged by bombs and by an internal explosion so decommissioned in 1946 but retained in reserve and re-designated CVHE-27 in 1955 for helicopter operations, but withdrawn in 1959 and eventually scrapped.

Takanis Bay, **CVE-89:** Casablanca-class aircraft transport and training carrier commissioned into the US Navy on 15 April 1944. Post-war, she was decommissioned in May 1946 and placed in reserve, re-designated CVU-89 in June 1955, and then AKV-31 in May 1959, but was sold to the breakers during 1959-60.

Tinian, **CVE-123:** Commencement Bay-class carrier completed on 30 July 1946, and placed immediately in reserve. Re-designated CVHE-123 in June 1955 and then AKV-23 in May 1959, she was never operated and was eventually broken up in 1971.

Tripoli, **CVE-64:** Casablanca-class anti-submarine and escort carrier originally designated ACV-64, *Didrickson Bay*, but changed to CVE-64 April 1943 and re-named in November shortly after being commissioned into the US Navy on 31 October 1943. Towards the end of the war she operated on transport and training duties. Post-war was put in reserve in May 1946, but re-commissioned in January 1952 as an aircraft transport. Re-designated CVU-64 in June 1955, before being withdrawn in November 1958 and sold to the breakers in 1959.

Tulagi, **CVE-72:** Casablanca-class transport and anti-submarine carrier originally named *Fortezela Bay*, ACV-72, but re-designated CVE-72 in July 1943, and re-named in November 1944, after commissioning into the US Navy on 21 December 1943. Operated in the Mediterranean and in the Pacific off Okinawa. Post-war she was decommissioned in April 1946 and scrapped in 1947.

Vella Gulf, **CVE-111:** Commencement Bay-class training carrier originally named *Totem Bay* but re-named before launching. Commissioned into the US Navy on 9 April 1945, and served as a 'Marine carrier' providing close support for ground forces ashore during the final months of the war. At the end of the war she was decommissioned in August 1946. She was re-designated CVHE-111 in May 1955 and again as AKV-11 in May 1959, before being deleted in December 1970.

Wake Island, **CVE-65:** Casablanca-class carrier that undertook anti-submarine and transport roles as well as training duties, originally designated ACV-65, *Dolomi Bay*, but the name was changed before launching and she was re-designated to CVE-65 July 1943 and commissioned into the US Navy on 7 November 1943. Struck by two kamikazes off Okinawa in April 1945, she was withdrawn for repairs and did not see further service before decommissioning in April 1946. Was in such poor condition that she was scrapped in 1947.

White Plains, **CVE-66:** Casablanca-class carrier that undertook combat, training and transport roles as well as training duties, originally designated ACV-66, *Elbour Bay*, but the name and designation were both changed before commissioning into the US Navy on 15 November 1943. Struck by a kamikaze at Leyte Gulf on 25 October 1944, she was withdrawn for repairs. Placed in reserve in July 1946, she was re-designated CVU-66 on 12 June 1955, but was decommissioned in June 1958 and scrapped the following year.

Windham Bay, **CVE-92:** Casablanca-class training and transport carrier commissioned into the US Navy on 3 May 1944. Damaged in a hurricane in June 1945 but post-war, she was not decommissioned until early 1947 and placed in reserve. She returned to service in late 1951 as an aircraft transport, and was re-designated CVU-92 in June 1955. She was withdrawn from service in 1959 and was sold to the breakers in 1961.

Wolverine, **IX-64:** A coal-burning Great Lakes excursion paddle-steamer, *Seeandbee*, intended solely for deck landing training, the superstructure was completely removed and a wooden flight deck built onto the hull overhanging it fore and aft and at the sides. No hangar deck was necessary, but an island with four smokestacks was built out over the starboard paddle box. Arrester wires were provided aft but there were no catapults or accelerators. No aircraft were kept aboard as the ship operated in conjunction with shore training stations. Commissioned into the US Navy on 12 August 1942. Displacement, 7,200 tons standard. LOA: 500 feet; beam: 98 feet (hull 58.25 feet). No armament. Complement: 270; No aircraft. Machinery: Compound steam engines, coal-fired, driving two paddles. Speed: 16 knots. Withdrawn from service post-war and scrapped 1947.

Appendix V

UNITED STATES NAVY ESCORT CARRIERS BY PENNANT NUMBER

CVE-1: *Long Island;*

Bogue-class (Note: Gaps in numbering usually indicate ships transferred immediately to the Royal Navy.)

CVE-9:	*Bogue;*	**CVE-11:**	*Card;*
CVE-12:	*Copabee;*	**CVE-13:**	*Core;*
CVE-16:	*Nassau;*	**CVE-18:**	*Altamaha;*
CVE-20:	*Barnes;*	**CVE-21:**	*Block Island;*
CVE-23:	*Breton;*	**CVE-25:**	*Croatan;*
CVE-31:	*Prince William;*		

Sangamon-class

CVE-26:	*Sangamon*	**CVE-27:**	*Suwannee*
CVE-28:	*Chenango*	**CVE-29:**	*Santee*
CVE-30:	*Charger*		

Casablanca-class

CVE-55:	*Casablanca*	**CVE-56:**	*Liscombe Bay*
CVE-57:	*Anzio*	**CVE-58:**	*Corregidor*
CVE-59:	*Mission Bay*	**CVE-60:**	*Guadalcanal*
CVE-61:	*Manila Bay*	**CVE-62:**	*Natoma Bay*
CVE-63:	*St Lo*	**CVE-64:**	*Tripoli*
CVE-65:	*Wake Island*	**CVE-66:**	*White Plains*
CVE-67:	*Solomons*	**CVE-68:**	*Kalinin Bay*
CVE-69:	*Kasaan Bay*	**CVE-70:**	*Fanshaw Bay*

CVE-71:	Kitkun Bay	**CVE-72:**	Tulagi
CVE-73:	Gambier Bay	**CVE-74:**	Nebenta Bay
CVE-75:	Hoggatt Bay	**CVE-76:**	Kadashan Bay
CVE-77:	Marcus Island	**CVE-78:**	Savo Island
CVE-79:	Ommaney Bay	**CVE-80:**	Petrof Bay
CVE-81:	Rudyerd Bay	**CVE-82:**	Saginaw Bay
CVE-83:	Sargent Bay	**CVE-84:**	Shamrock Bay
CVE-85:	Shipley Bay	**CVE-86:**	Sitkoh Bay
CVE-87:	Steamer Bay	**CVE-88:**	Cape Esperance
CVE-89:	Takanis Bay	**CVE-90:**	Thetis Bay
CVE-91:	Makassar Strait	**CVE-92:**	Windham Bay
CVE-93:	Makin Island	**CVE-94:**	Lunga Point
CVE-95:	Bismarck Sea	**CVE-96:**	Salamaua
CVE-97:	Hollandia	**CVE-98:**	Kwajalein
CVE-99:	Admiralty Islands	**CVE-100:**	Bougainville
CVE-101:	Matanikau	**CVE-102:**	Attu,
CVE-103:	Roi	**CVE-104:**	Munda

Commencement Bay-class

CVE-105:	Commencement Bay	**CVE-106:**	Block Island
CVE-107:	Gilbert Islands	**CVE-108:**	Kula Gulf
CVE-109:	Cape Gloucester	**CVE-110:**	Salerno Bay
CVE-111:	Vella Gulf	**CVE-112:**	Siboney
CVE-113:	Puget Sound	**CVE-114:**	Rendova
CVE-115:	Bairoko	**CVE-116:**	Badoeng Strait
CVE-117:	Saidor	**CVE-118:**	Sicily
CVE-119:	Point Cruz	**CVE-120:**	Mindoro
CVE-121:	Rabaul	**CVE-122:**	Palau
CVE-123:	Tinian		

IX-64:	Wolverine	**IX-81:**	Sable

Appendix VI

JAPANESE AUXILIARY CARRIERS

Akitsu Maru: Akitsu Maru-class lead ship transport carrier, all built by Harima, commissioned into the Imperial Japanese Army on 30 January 1942. Displacement, 11,800 tons standard. Length: 498.6 feet; beam: 74 feet (hull 64 feet). Armament: 12 × 3-in, Complement: not known; 20 aircraft; One lift. Machinery: Geared steam turbines driving two shafts. Speed: 20 knots. Sunk by submarine USS *Queenfish*, 15 November 1944, off Kyushu.

Chigusa Maru: Yamishiro Maru-class escort carrier for air defence, never completed conversion and entered service as tanker post-war.

Chuyo: Taiyo-class transport and training carrier commissioned into the Imperial Japanese Navy on 25 November 1942. Later, AA armament increased to 14 × 25-mm and 5 × 13.2-mm. Sunk by submarine USS *Sailfish* off Yokosuka, 4 December 1943.

Ibuki: Strike carrier built at Kure and converted from heavy cruiser that had been commissioned into the Imperial Japanese Navy on 21 May 1943. Displacement, 12,500 tons standard. LOA: 650.75 feet; beam: 75.5 feet (hull 69.5 feet). Armament: 4 × 76-mm; 48 × 25-mm; plus rocket launcher. Complement: 1,015; 27 aircraft; Two lifts. Machinery: Geared steam turbines driving two shafts. Speed: 24 knots. Never fully completed and broken up post-war.

Kumano Maru: Transport and training carrier with secondary assault role built by Hitachi, converted from cargo ship and commissioned into the Imperial Japanese Army on 30 March

1945. Displacement, 8,000 tons standard. LOA: 501 feet; beam: 70.5 feet (hull 64.25 feet). Armament: 8 × 75-mm; 6 × 25-mm. Complement not known; 37 aircraft; One lift. Machinery: Geared steam turbines driving two shafts. Speed: 19 knots. Believed never to have entered service, but instead used as repatriation transport post-war and later converted back for merchant service.

Nigitsu Maru: Akitsu Maru-class transport carrier, commissioned into the Imperial Japanese Army in March 1943. Sunk by submarine USS *Hake* while south of Okinawa, 12 January 1944.

Otakisan Maru: Shimane Maru-class escort carrier, never completed and scrapped after drifting on to a mine at Kobe, 25 August 1945.

Shimane Maru: Lead ship of Shimane Maru-class escort carrier, all built by Kawasaki, converted from tankers and commissioned into the Imperial Japanese Navy on 28 February 1945. Displacement, 11,800 tons standard. LOA: 526.5 feet; beam: 75.5 feet (hull 65.5 feet). Armament: 2 × 4.7-in; 52 × 25-mm. Complement not known; 12 aircraft; One lift. Machinery: Geared steam turbines driving single shaft. Speed: 18.5 knots. Sunk by US aircraft off Takamatsu, Shikoku Island, 24 July 1945.

Shinyo: Training and transport carrier converted from Norddeutscher liner *Scharnhorst* and commissioned into the Imperial Japanese Navy on 15 December 1943. Displacement, 17,500 tons standard. LOA: 621.25 feet; beam: 80 feet (hull 84 feet). Armament: 8 × 5-in; 30 (later increased to 50) × 25-mm. Complement: 942; 33 aircraft; Two lifts. Machinery: Geared steam turbines driving two shafts. Speed: 22 knots. Sunk by submarine USS *Spadefish* in the Yellow Sea, 17 November 1944.

Taiyo: Taiyo-class lead ship training and transport carrier, all built by Mitsubishi, commissioned into the Imperial Japanese Navy on 15 September 1941. Displacement, 17,830 tons standard. LOA: 591.25 feet; beam: 75.5 feet (hull 74 feet). Armament: 6 × 4.7-in; 8 (later increased to 16) × 25-mm. Complement: 747; 27 aircraft; Two lifts. Machinery: Geared steam turbines driving two shafts.

Speed: 21 knots. Supported *Yamato* in Eastern Solomons. Sunk by submarine USS *Rasher* 18 August 1944, off Luzon, Philippines.

Unyo: Taiyo-class transport and training carrier commissioned into the Imperial Japanese Navy on 31 May 1942 and like *Taiyo* had her AA armament augmented later. Sunk by submarine USS *Barb* in East China Sea near Hong Kong, 16 September 1944.

Yamishiro Maru: Yamishiro Maru-class lead ship escort carrier for air defence, all built by Mitsubishi on tanker hulls, commissioned into the Imperial Japanese Army on 17 January 1945. Displacement, around 11,000 tons standard. Length: 516.75 feet; beam: 75.5 feet (hull 67 feet). Armament: 16 × 25-mm. Complement: 221. 8 aircraft; One lift. Machinery: Geared steam turbines driving two shafts. Speed: 20 knots. Sunk by US aircraft at Yokohama, 17 February 1945.

BIBLIOGRAPHY

Chesnau, Roger, *Aircraft Carriers of the World, 1914 to the Present*, Arms & Armour Press, London, 1992

Gallery, Rear Admiral Daniel V., USN, *Clear the Decks!*, George G. Harrap, London, 1952

Gelb, Norman, *Desperate Venture*, Hodder & Stoughton, London, 1992

German, Commander Tony, RCN, *The Sea Is At Our Gates: The History of the Canadian Navy*, McClelland & Stewart, Toronto, 1990

Hickey, Des and Smith, Gus, *Operation Avalanche: Salerno Landings 1943*, Heinemann, London

Hobbs, Commander David, *Aircraft Carriers of the Royal & Commonwealth Navies*, Greenhill Books, 1996

Kennedy, Ludovic, *Menace: The Life and Death of the Tirpitz*, Sidgwick & Jackson, London, 1979

Kilbracken, Lord, *Bring Back My Stringbag: A Stringbag Pilot at War*, Pan Books, London, 1980

Moore, Captain John, RN, *Escort Carrier*, London, 1944

Poolman, Kenneth, *Escort Carrier: HMS Vindex at War*, Secker & Warburg, London, 1983

— *The Sea Hunters: Escort Carriers v U-boats 1941–1945*, Arms & Armour Press, London, 1982

Roskill, Captain, S. W., *The Navy at War, 1939–45*, HMSO, London, 1960

— *The War at Sea, 1939-45, Vols I-III*, HMSO, London, 1976

Sturtevant, Ray and Balance, Theo, *The Squadrons of the Fleet Air Arm*, Air Britain, Tonbridge, 1994

Sweetman, Jack, *American Naval History: An Illustrated Chronology of the US Navy and Marine Corps 1775–1978*, Naval Institute Press, Annapolis, 1978

Terzibaschitsch, Stefan, *Escort Carriers and Aviation Support Ships of the US Navy*, Conway Maritime Press, Greenwich, 1981

Thompson, Julian, *Imperial War Museum Book of the War at Sea, 1939–45: The Royal Navy in the Second World War*, IWM/Sigwick & Jackson, London, 1996

Vian, Admiral Sir Philip, *Action This Day*, Muller, London, 1960

Winton, John, *The Forgotten Fleet*, Michael Joseph, London, 1960

— *Air Power at Sea, 1939–45*, Sidgwick & Jackson, London, 1976

Woodman, Richard, *Artic Convoys*, John Murray, London, 1974

Woods, Gerard A., *Wings at Sea: A Fleet Air Arm Observer's War, 1940–45*, Conway Maritime, London, 1985

Wragg, David, *Stringbag: The Fairey Swordfish at War*, Pen & Sword, Barnsley, 2004

— *Second World War Carrier Campaigns*, Pen & Sword, Barnsley, 2004

— *The Fleet Air Arm Handbook 1939–1945*, Sutton, Stroud, 2001 and 2003

— *Carrier Combat*, Sutton, Stroud, 1997

— *Wings Over The Sea: A History of Naval Aviation*, David & Charles, Newton Abbot and London, 1979.

INDEX

228